HISTORICAL FIGURES

MEMOIRS OF THE REIGN OF KING GEORGE THE SECOND

VOLUME 1

HISTORICAL FIGURES

Additional books and e-books in this series can be found on Nova's website under the Series tab.

HISTORICAL FIGURES

MEMOIRS OF THE REIGN OF KING GEORGE THE SECOND

VOLUME 1

HORACE WALPOLE
AUTHOR
AND
HENRY RICHARD VASSALL HOLLAND
EDITOR

Copyright © 2019 by Nova Science Publishers, Inc.

All rights reserved. No part of this book may be reproduced, stored in a retrieval system or transmitted in any form or by any means: electronic, electrostatic, magnetic, tape, mechanical photocopying, recording or otherwise without the written permission of the Publisher.

We have partnered with Copyright Clearance Center to make it easy for you to obtain permissions to reuse content from this publication. Simply navigate to this publication's page on Nova's website and locate the "Get Permission" button below the title description. This button is linked directly to the title's permission page on copyright.com. Alternatively, you can visit copyright.com and search by title, ISBN, or ISSN.

For further questions about using the service on copyright.com, please contact:
Copyright Clearance Center
Phone: +1-(978) 750-8400   Fax: +1-(978) 750-4470   E-mail: info@copyright.com.

NOTICE TO THE READER

The Publisher has taken reasonable care in the preparation of this book, but makes no expressed or implied warranty of any kind and assumes no responsibility for any errors or omissions. No liability is assumed for incidental or consequential damages in connection with or arising out of information contained in this book. The Publisher shall not be liable for any special, consequential, or **exemplary damages resulting, in whole or in part, from the readers'** use of, or reliance upon, this material. Any parts of this book based on government reports are so indicated and copyright is claimed for those parts to the extent applicable to compilations of such works.

Independent verification should be sought for any data, advice or recommendations contained in this book. In addition, no responsibility is assumed by the Publisher for any injury and/or damage to persons or property arising from any methods, products, instructions, ideas or otherwise contained in this publication.

This publication is designed to provide accurate and authoritative information with regard to the subject matter covered herein. It is sold with the clear understanding that the Publisher is not engaged in rendering legal or any other professional services. If legal or any other expert assistance is required, the services of a competent person should be sought. FROM A DECLARATION OF PARTICIPANTS JOINTLY ADOPTED BY A COMMITTEE OF THE AMERICAN BAR ASSOCIATION AND A COMMITTEE OF PUBLISHERS.

Additional color graphics may be available in the e-book version of this book.

Library of Congress Cataloging-in-Publication Data

ISBN: 978-1-53615-822-9

Published by Nova Science Publishers, Inc. † New York

Contents

Editor's Preface	ix
The Author's Postscript to These Memoirs	xxiii
Chapter 1	1
Chapter 2	15
Chapter 3	35
Chapter 4	53
Chapter 5	71
Chapter 6	99
Chapter 7	119
Chapter 8	149
Chapter 9	165
Chapter 10	185
Chapter 11	209
Chapter 12	233

Appendix	**265**
Index	**291**
Related Nova Publications	**299**

Figure 1. George II. London. Henry Colburn, 1846.

Editor's Preface[*]

The work now submitted to the public is printed from a Manuscript of the late Horace Walpole, Earl of Orford.

Among the papers found at Strawberry Hill, after the death of Lord Orford, was the following Memorandum, wrapped in an envelope, on which was written, "Not to be opened till after my Will."

"In my Library at Strawberry Hill are two wainscot chests or boxes, the larger marked with an A, the lesser with a B. I desire, that as soon as I am dead, my Executor and Executrix will cord up strongly and seal the larger box, marked A, and deliver it to the Honourable Hugh Conway Seymour, to be kept by him unopened and unsealed till the eldest son of Lady Waldegrave, or whichever of her sons, being Earl of Waldegrave, shall attain the age of twenty-five years; when the said chest, with whatever it contains, shall be delivered to him for his own. And I beg that the Honourable Hugh Conway Seymour, when he shall receive the said chest, will give a promise in writing, signed by him, to Lady Waldegrave, that he or his Representatives will deliver the said chest unopened and unsealed, by my Executor and Executrix, to the first son of Lady Waldegrave who shall attain the age of twenty-five years. The key of the said chest is in one of the cupboards of the Green Closet, within the Blue

---

[*] This is an edited, augmented and reformatted version of "Memoirs of the Reign of King George the Second, Volume 1" by Horace Wallace, edited by Henry Richard Vassall Holland, originally published by London: Henry Colburn, dated 1847.

Breakfast Room, at Strawberry Hill, and that key, I desire, may be delivered to Laura, Lady Waldegrave, to be kept by her till her son shall receive the chest.

(Signed) "Hor. Walpole, Earl of Orford.

"August 19, 1796."

In obedience to these directions, the box described in the preceding Memorandum was corded and sealed with the seals of the Honourable Mrs. Damer and the late Lord Frederick Campbell, the Executrix and Executor of Lord Orford, and by them delivered to the late Lord Hugh Seymour, by whose Representatives it was given up, unopened and unsealed, to the present Earl of Waldegrave, when he attained the age of twenty-five. On examining the box, it was found to contain a number of manuscript volumes and other papers, among which were the Memoirs now published.

Though no directions were left by Lord Orford for the publication of these Memoirs, there can be little doubt of his intention that they should one day or other be communicated to the world. Innumerable passages in the Memoirs show they were written for the public. The precautions of the Author to preserve them for a certain number of years from inspection, are a proof, not of his intention that they should remain always in the private hands of his family, but of his fears lest, if divulged, they might be published prematurely; and the term fixed for opening the chest seems to mark the distance of time when he thought they might be made public without impropriety. Ten years have elapsed since that period, and more than sixty years since the last of the historical events he commemorates in this work.[1] No man is now alive whose character or conduct is the subject of praise or censure in these Memoirs.

The printed correspondence of Lord Orford contains allusions to this work. In a letter written in 1752,[2] he informs Mr. Montagu, that "his Memoirs of last year are quite finished," but that he means to "add some pages of notes that will not want anecdotes;" and in answer to that

---

[1] The reader will bear in mind, that some years have elapsed since this was written.
[2] June 6th, 1752.

gentleman,[3] who had threatened him in jest with a Messenger from the Secretary's Office to seize his papers, after a ludicrous account of the alarm into which he had been thrown by the actual arrival of a King's Messenger at his door, he adds, "however, I have buried the Memoirs under the oak in my garden, where they are to be found a thousand years hence, and taken, perhaps, for a Runic history in rhyme."

The Postscript, printed in this edition at the end of the Preface, but annexed by the Author to his Memoirs of the year 1751, evidently implies, that what he had then written was destined for publication. It is addressed in the usual style of an author to his reader, and contains an answer to objections that might be made to him. In this answer or apology for his work he justifies the freedom of his strictures on public men, vindicates the impartiality of his characters and narrative, claims the merit of care and fidelity in his reports of parliamentary proceedings, and explains the sources of information from which he derived his knowledge of the many private anecdotes and transactions he relates.

In the beginning of his Memoirs of 1752, he again speaks of his work as one ultimately destined for the public. "I sit down," he says, "to resume a task, for which I fear Posterity will condemn the Author, at the same time that they feel their curiosity gratified."

Many other passages might be quoted that imply he wrote for Posterity, with an intention that at some future time his work should be given to the public. "These sheets," he remarks, "were less intended for a history of war than for civil annals. Whatever tends to a knowledge of the characters of remarkable persons, of the manners of the age, and of its political intrigues, comes properly within my plan. I am more attentive to deserve the thanks of Posterity than their admiration."—"I am no historian," he observes in another place; "I write casual memoirs, I draw characters, I preserve anecdotes, which my superiors, the historians of Britain, may enchase into their mighty annals, or pass over at pleasure."—"To be read for a few years is immortality enough for such a writer as me."—"Posterity, this is an impartial picture."

---

[3] July 20th, 1752.

At the conclusion of his Memoirs of 1758, where the Author makes a pause in his work, and seems uncertain whether he should ever resume it or not, he again addresses himself to his readers in the style of an author looking forward to publication. If he should ever continue his work, he warns his readers "not to expect so much intelligence and information in any of the subsequent pages as may have appeared in the preceding."— "During the former period," he goes on to observe, "I lived in the centre of business, was intimately acquainted with many of the chief actors, was eager in politics, indefatigable in heaping up knowledge and materials for my work. Now, detached from these busy scenes, with many political connections dropped or dissolved, indifferent to events, and indolent, I shall have fewer opportunities of informing myself or others."

He then proceeds to give a character of himself, and to "lay open to his readers his nearest sentiments." He acknowledges some enmities and resentments, confesses that he has been injured by some, and treated by others with ingratitude, but assures his readers, as he probably thought himself, that he has written without bias or partiality, "that affection and veneration for truth and justice have preponderated above all other considerations," and that when he has expressed himself of particular men with a severity that may appear objectionable, it was "the unamiableness of the characters he blames that imprinted the dislikes," to which he pleads guilty. Can it be supposed, he asks, that "he would sacrifice the integrity of these Memoirs, *his favourite labour*, to a little revenge that he shall never taste?" Whatever may be thought of the soundness of this reasoning, and whatever opinion may be formed of the impartiality of his work, it seems impossible that anything short of a positive injunction to commit his Memoirs to the Press could have conveyed a stronger indication of the intention and desire of the Author, that, at some future period after his decease, this *his favourite labour* should be communicated to the public.

The extraordinary pains taken by Lord Orford to correct and improve his Memoirs, and prepare them for publication, afford no less convincing proof of his intentions in the legacy of his work. The whole of the Memoirs now published have been written over twice, and the early part three times. The first sketches or foul copies of the work are in his own hand-writing;

then follows what he calls the corrected and transcribed copy, which is also written by himself; and this third or last copy, extending to the end of 1755, is written by his secretary or amanuensis, Mr. Kirkgate, with some corrections by himself, and the notes on the blank pages, opposite to the fair copy, entirely in his own hand. This last copy was bound into two regular volumes, with etchings from designs furnished by Bentley and Muntz, to serve as a frontispiece to the whole work, and as head-pieces for each chapter, explanations of which were subjoined at the end.

So much for the authenticity of the present work, and obvious intention of the Author that after a sufficient lapse of years it should be published. Of the Author himself, so well known by his numerous publications, little need be said, except to give the dates of his entrance into Parliament, and of his retirement from public life, with some few observations on his political character and connections.

Horace Walpole, afterwards Earl of Orford, was third son of the celebrated Sir Robert Walpole. He was born on the 5th of October, 1717, and brought into Parliament in 1741, for the borough of Callington. At the general election in 1747, he was returned a second time for the same borough; and in 1754 he came into Parliament for Castle Rising. On the death of his uncle, Lord Walpole, of Wolterton, in 1757, he accepted the Chiltern Hundreds, in order to succeed his cousin, become Lord Walpole, in the representation of Lynn Regis, "the Corporation of which had such reverence for his father's memory, that they would not bear distant relations while he had sons living."[4] At the general election for 1761, he was again returned for Lynn without opposition; but being threatened with a contested election, and heartily tired of politics, from which he had in a great measure withdrawn after the accession of his friends to office in 1765, he voluntarily retired from Parliament in 1768. In 1791 he succeeded his nephew as Earl of Orford, and died on the 2nd of March, 1797, in the eightieth year of his age.

The House of Commons, in which Mr. Walpole first sat, was the one that overturned his father's Administration. In the very first week of the

---

[4] Correspondence, Feb. 13th, 1757.

session, the Minister was left in a minority. He still, however, kept his place, and so nearly were parties balanced, that for two months he maintained, with alternate victories and reverses, a contest with his adversaries. At length, secretly betrayed by some of his colleagues, who had entered into private engagements with his enemies, and defeated in an election question, which had been made a trial of strength between Ministry and Opposition, he retired from office, and became Earl of Orford.

His son Horace, though exempt from ambition, was roused by his father's danger, and, while the struggle lasted, took a lively interest in all that passed. In his letters, he gives an entertaining and not uncandid account of the Debates that took place, and communicates freely to his Correspondent the hopes and fears, the good and bad success of his party; his anticipations of their strength in the different questions as they arose, are followed by his explanations of their failures, as far as he could account for them at the time; the desertion and falling off of their friends are stigmatized as they occurred, with the severity such conduct deserved; and when Sir Robert was compelled to resign, his son records with satisfaction the successful efforts used to secure him from the vengeance of his enemies, by disuniting the parties coalesced against him, and rendering them odious to the public, and hostile to one another.

But, though assiduous in his attendance on Parliament during this period, and sincerely anxious for his father, Mr. Walpole, who had no turn for public speaking, once and once only addressed the House. It was on a motion of Lord Limerick, seconded by Sir John St. Aubin, to appoint a Committee of Inquiry into the conduct of Robert, Earl of Orford, during the last ten years of his Administration.[5] A similar motion to inquire generally into the conduct of affairs at home and abroad for the last twenty, had been made and rejected a fortnight before.[6] The selection of this occasion for his maiden speech, did credit to the judgment and feelings of Mr. Walpole; and, though there is little force in his arguments against the motion, there is modesty, right feeling, and some happiness, both of

---

[5] March 23rd, 1742.
[6] March 9th, 1742.

thought and expression, in what he said. The speech, as he delivered it, is preserved in his Correspondence; and as it has no sort of resemblance to the speech published in his name by the London Magazine, and since reprinted in the Parliamentary History, we subjoin it for the satisfaction of our readers. The report of it, given by Mr. Walpole himself the day after it was made, is as follows:—

"Mr. Speaker,

"I have always thought, Sir, that incapacity and inexperience must prejudice the cause they undertake to defend; and it has been diffidence of myself, not distrust of the cause, that has hitherto made me so silent upon a point on which I ought to have appeared so zealous.

"While the attempts for this inquiry were made in general terms, I should have thought it presumption in me to stand up and defend measures in which so many abler men have been engaged, and which, consequently, they could so much better support: but when the attack grows more personal, it grows my duty to oppose it more particularly; lest I be suspected of an ingratitude, which my heart disdains. But I think, Sir, I cannot be suspected of that, unless my not having abilities to defend my father can be construed into a desire not to defend him.

"My experience, Sir, is very small; I have never been conversant in business and politics, and have sat a very short time in this House. With so slight a fund, I must mistrust my power to serve him, especially as in the short time I have sat here, I have seen that not his own knowledge, innocence, and eloquence, have been able to protect him against a powerful and determined party. I have seen, since his retirement, that he has many great and noble friends, who have been able to protect him from farther violence. But, Sir, when no repulses can calm the clamour against him, no motives should sway his friends from openly undertaking his defence. When the King has conferred rewards on his services; when the Parliament has refused its assent to any inquiries of complaint against him, it is but maintaining the King's and our own honour to reject this Motion, for the repeating which, however, I cannot think the authors to blame, as I suppose, now they have turned him out, they are willing to inquire whether they had any reason to do so.

"I shall say no more, Sir, but leave the material part of this defence to the impartiality, candour, and credit of men who are no ways dependent on him. He has already found that defence, Sir, and I hope he always will. It is to their authority I trust; and to me it is the strongest proof of innocence, that for twenty years together no crime could be solemnly alleged against him; and, since his dismission, he has seen a majority rise up to defend his character, in that very House of Commons in which a majority had overturned his power. As, therefore, Sir, I must think him innocent, I must stand up to protect him from injustice—had he been accused, I should not have given the House this trouble; but I think, Sir, that the precedent of what was done upon this question a few days ago, sufficient reason, if I had no other, for me to give my negative now."

This speech of a son, in defence of his father, appears to have been well received by the House. Mr. Pitt, who was at that time one of the most violent against Lord Orford, said in reply, "How very commendable it was in Mr. Walpole to have made the above speech, which must have made an impression on the House; but, if it was becoming in him to remember that he was the child of the accused, the House ought to remember, too, that they are the children of their country." "It was a great compliment from him," adds Mr. Walpole, "and very artful, too." The Motion was carried by a majority of 252 to 245. Nothing was made of the inquiry.

For many years after the fall of Lord Orford, Mr. Walpole took an active part in all the political intrigues and dissensions of the times. Though he had not been treated, as he frequently hints, with any great kindness or indulgence by his father, he was indignant at the persecution against him, and appears to have been warmly and affectionately attached to his memory. In his private correspondence, he continually alludes to the mild and prudent policy of Sir Robert, and contrasts it with the violence and rashness of succeeding Ministers; and, as he advanced in life, these impressions became stronger, and recur more frequently in his writings. His political connections were originally with his father's friends; and for many years he appears to have indulged in sentiments of bitter hostility towards his enemies. When any of them were guilty of tergiversations, either in their public conduct or political friendships, he never fails in his correspondence to mark their perfidy and inconsistencies, and seems to enjoy with delight their apostasy and disgrace. But after a certain time he became less inimical to their persons, though to the end of his life he never ceased to blame their persecution of his father, which, indeed, many of them subsequently acknowledged to have been unmerited and unjust.

At the time when these Memoirs commence, the resentments he retained on his father's account were directed less against the enemies who had openly opposed, than against the friends who had secretly betrayed and deserted him. He appears, for instance, to have been reconciled very speedily to Lord Granville, and ultimately to have become a warm admirer of Mr. Pitt. But against the Pelhams and Lord Hardwicke, whom he repeatedly and unequivocally charges with treachery to his father, his resentment was implacable.[7] In the early part of his public life, his chief political friends appear to have been Mr. Winnington and Mr. Fox. For the former, who died in 1746, his admiration was unbounded.

In his Memoirs, indeed, where in no instance but one he ever confers praise unmixed with censure, he bestows on Mr. Winnington the character of being one "whom it was impossible to hate or to trust;" and, in a subsequent passage, he describes him "as perniciously witty, affecting an honesty in avowing whatever was dishonourable." But, in his private correspondence, written immediately after the sudden and melancholy death of Mr. Winnington,[8] he calls him one of the first men in England, and adds, "I was familiarly acquainted with him, loved and admired him, for he had great good-nature, and a quickness of wit most peculiar to himself; and for his public talents he has left nobody equal to him, as before nobody was superior to him but my father."

With Mr. Fox he appears to have lived on the most confidential terms, till that gentleman accepted the Seals in 1755 under the Duke of Newcastle. Mr. Walpole, whose inveteracy to the Pelhams was unabated,

---

[7] A story of the private intrigues of the Duke of Newcastle with Lord Carteret, during Sir Robert Walpole's Administration, is told by Lord Orford in his Common Place Book. When Lord Hervey was to be made Privy Seal (in 1740), the Duke of Newcastle, to prevent the appointment, obtained Lord Carteret's consent to accept the office, and moved at Council, that it should be offered to him. Sir Robert said he did not know whether Lord Carteret (who was then in Opposition) would take the place. The Duke said he would answer for him. Sir Robert replied, "I always suspected you had been dabbling there, now I know it; but if you make such bargains, I don't think myself obliged to keep them." Lord Hervey had the office.

[8] Correspondence, April 25, 1746.

could not pardon in his father's friend, a connection with the man whom he regarded as the chief traitor in the accomplishment of his father's ruin. The step too was taken without consulting him. This added to his indignation; and from that time, though he continued in habits of intimacy with Mr. Fox, he became cold to his interests, and, by his own account, was, on one important occasion, active and successful in traversing his designs.

He was, in truth, during the whole of his public life, too much under the guidance of personal feelings and resentments, and too apt to sacrifice his friendships to his aversions; and as the latter were often excited by trivial and accidental causes, his political conduct, though unexceptionable on the score of interest or ambition, was fluctuating and uncertain, and his judgment of men variable and capricious. The affair of Admiral Byng, in which he took a part that does credit to his feelings and humanity, completed his estrangement from Mr. Fox. He animadverts with great severity on the cruelty of obstructing an irregular application for mercy with the view of embarrassing an Administration. The questionable conduct of Mr. Fox on that occasion seems to have deserved some such censure; but Mr. Walpole betrays his own partiality by the comparative tenderness with which he treats the Ministers themselves. They had it in their power to save Admiral Byng, and justice as well as humanity required them to exert it if they thought him either injured or innocent. Yet they chose to sign the warrant for his execution rather than incur the odium with the King or the public of insisting on his pardon.

About the time of his separation from Mr. Fox, Mr. Walpole appears to have lost the influence he had acquired over the Duke of Bedford through the intervention of Mr. Rigby; and during the latter part of these Memoirs, detached from all political intimacies, he seems to have had no better means of information than might have been possessed by any other industrious and attentive member of the House of Commons.

On the merits of the present work it would be improper to enlarge in this place. That it contains much curious and original information will not be disputed. The intimacy which the Author enjoyed with many of the chief personages of the times, and what he calls, "his propensity to faction," made him acquainted with the most secret intrigues and negotiations of parties; and where his resentments did not cloud his judgment, his indifference to the common objects of ambition rendered him an impartial spectator of their quarrels and accommodations. The period of which he treats was not distinguished by splendid virtues or great vices, by extraordinary events or great revolutions; but it is a part of our history little known to us, and not undeserving our curiosity, as it forms the transition from the expiring struggles of Jacobitism to the more important contests that have since engaged, and still occupy our attention.

The account of Parliamentary Debates in these Memoirs would alone be a valuable addition to our history. No one is ignorant, that from the fall of Sir Robert Walpole to the American war, our reports of the proceedings in Parliament are more barren and unsatisfactory than at any period since the reign of James the First. For the last ten years of George the Second, Mr. Walpole has supplied that deficiency in a manner equally entertaining and instructive. His method was to make notes of each speaker's argument during the Debate, and frequently to take down his expressions. He afterwards wrote out the speeches at greater length, and described the impression they made on the House. The anecdotes interspersed in the work are numerous, and, from the veracity of the Author, when they are founded on his personal knowledge, they may always be received as authentic. When derived from others, or from the common rumour of the day, he gives his authority for them, and enables his readers to judge of the credibility they deserve.

To his portraits it will be objected, that in general they incline to severity, and though he professed, and probably intended the strictest impartiality in his delineations of character, it cannot be denied that they are sometimes heightened by friendship, and more frequently discoloured by resentment; and on many occasions it is evident, that they are dictated by the conduct of the persons he describes in the last occurrence that brought them before his eyes, rather than by a steady and comprehensive view of their merits and defects. His observations on the Cavendishes may be taken as an illustration of this remark. He seldom mentions the two Dukes of Devonshire, who flourished in his time, without some sneer or malignant reflection. The truth was, that notwithstanding his Whiggism, he held all the members of that family in detestation, on account of the part they had taken against him on his breach with his uncle Lord Walpole. Yet, within a few years after the conclusion of these Memoirs, when William, fourth Duke of Devonshire, had bequeathed five thousand pounds to his friend Mr. Conway, in approbation of his public conduct, he uses the following exaggerated expressions in speaking of the legacy.

"You might despise," he writes to Mr. Conway,[9] "the acquisition of five thousand pounds simply; but when that sum is a public testimonial to your virtue, and bequeathed *by a man so virtuous*, it is worth a million. Who says virtue is not rewarded in this world? It is rewarded by virtue, and persecuted by the bad: can greater honour be paid to it?"

There are, indeed, few persons in his Memoirs, of whom he does not vary his opinion in the course of his work. Marshal Conway, the Pelhams, and Lord Hardwicke, are almost the only exceptions. He always speaks of Marshal Conway with affection and respect; of Mr. Pelham with dislike; of Lord Hardwicke with hatred; and of the Duke of Newcastle with contempt and aversion. Of other persons mentioned in his book, there is scarcely any strong expression of commendation or censure, which in some subsequent passage he does not qualify, soften, or contradict. It is a proof, however, of his fairness, at least of his desire to give his readers the impression he formed at the time of the personages and transactions he describes, that even when he changed his opinion, he allowed his original account to remain, leaving it to be effaced in the minds of others, as it was not unfrequently in his own, by subsequent reflections and events. In some instances, but rarely, he subjoins a note correcting his first impression: more frequently he only intimates to his readers his change of sentiment by the difference of his language with respect to the person he had before described. In his Memoirs of 1752, for example, he characterizes Lord George Sackville as a man "of distinguished bravery," and that passage he has left as originally written, though after the battle of Minden he appears to have had more than doubts of Lord George's courage. He was, in truth,

---

[9] Letter to Mr. Conway, October 13, 1764.

as he says of himself, a bitter, but placable enemy, a warm, but (one instance only excepted) an inconstant friend.

It remains only to say a few words of the labours of the Editor. He has added some notes marked (E), and in some very few instances added or altered a word for the sake of delicacy or perspicuity. On such occasions the word added, or substituted, is printed between brackets of this shape [ ].

The spelling of the manuscript is peculiar, and different from that in ordinary use. It was the intention of the editor to have followed this orthography in the printed book, knowing it was the result of system and affectation, and not of accident or carelessness. He has accordingly retained it in the title of the book, and in words of unfrequent recurrence; but, finding such vicious and affected orthography disfigured the text, and fearing it might perplex on perusal, he determined in common words to revert to the usual and approved mode of spelling. The word *to-morrow*, for instance, which Lord Orford always writes *to-morow*, he has printed in the usual manner.

With respect to omissions, it is right to inform the reader, that one gross, indelicate, and ill-authenticated story had been cut out by Lord Waldegrave before the manuscript was delivered to the Editor; but he is assured the Author himself acknowledged that the facts related in it rested on no authority but mere rumour. Some, though very few, coarse expressions, have been suppressed by the Editor, and the vacant spaces filled up by asterisks; and two or three passages, affecting the private characters of private persons, and nowise connected with any political event, or illustrative of any great public character, have been omitted. Sarcasms on mere bodily infirmity, in which the Author was too apt to indulge, have in some instances been expunged; and where private amours were mentioned in the notes or appendix, the name of the lady has been seldom printed at length, unless the story was already known, or intimately connected with some event of importance, to the elucidation of which it was indispensable. Such liberties would be still more necessary if the remaining historical works of Lord Orford were ever to see the light. They have been very sparingly used on the present occasion, and appeared to be warranted by the consideration, that, though the work had been obviously written for publication, it was left without directions how to dispose of it, and entirely at the discretion of those by whose authority it is now given to the public. Greater freedom might perhaps have been taken, without prejudice to the Author, or to his Memoirs. But the Editor was unwilling to omit any fact or anecdote, that had a direct or indirect tendency to illustrate the causes, or trace the progress of any political change or public event. The few omissions made are entirely of a private nature, and, in general, regard persons comparatively insignificant.

The Author had himself affixed an Appendix to the work. Some of his notes, which were of an inconvenient length, have been transferred to that part of the book, and some articles have been added by the Editor. The latter are marked with asterisks, and are for the most part taken from notes and compilations of Lord Orford himself, or of some contemporary pen.

THE AUTHOR'S POSTSCRIPT[10]
TO THESE MEMOIRS

The reader has now seen these Memoirs; and though some who know mankind, and the various follies, faults and virtues, that are blended in our imperfect natures, may smile with me at this free relation of what I have seen and known, yet I am aware that more will be offended at the liberty I have taken in painting men as they are; and that many, from private connections of party and family, will dislike meeting such unflattered portraits of their heroes or their relations. Yet this, I fear, must always be the case in any history written impartially by an eye witness: and eye witnesses have been generally allowed the properest historians. Indeed, the editor of Chalon's History of France was of a different opinion, and lamented that Thuanus, who has obliged the world with so complete and so ample a history of his own times, should have *confined* himself to write nothing but what passed in his own time, and *comme sous ses propres yeux*.[11]

Thus much I shall premise: if I had intended a romance, I would not have chosen real personages for the actors in it; few men can sit for patterns of perfect virtue. If I had intended a satire, I would not have amassed so many facts, which, if not true, would only tend to discredit the

---
[10] Vide Preface.
[11] See the Preface to the first volume of L'Histoire de France. Paris, 1720.

Author, not those he may censure. Yet councils and transactions, not persons, are what I anywhere mean[12] to blame. The celebrated Bayle has indeed offered a notable excuse for all who may offend on the severer side. "The perfection of a history," says he,[13] "is, when it displeases all sects and all nations, this being a proof that the author neither flatters nor spares any of them, and tells the truth to all parties." A latitude this, in which I am not at all desirous of being comprehended; nor very reconcileable with a notion of history which he has laid down in another place.[14] There he says, "As the sacred history was not the work of a particular person, but of a set of men, who had received from God a special commission to write; in like manner, civil history ought to be drawn up by none but persons appointed by the State for that purpose."

Unless State writers could be inspired, too, I fear history would become the most useless of all studies. One knows pretty well what sort of directions, what sort of information would be given from a Secretary's office; how much veracity would be found, even if the highest in the historical commission were a Bishop Sprat. It is not easy to conceive how Bayle, who thought it his duty to collect and publish every scandalous anecdote from the most obsolete libels, should at last have prescribed a method of writing history, which reduces it to the very essence of a gazette; a kind of authorized composition which the most partial bigots to a Court have piqued themselves upon exposing. Roger North, the voluminous squabbler in defence of the most unjustifiable excesses of Charles the Second's Administration, has drawn[15] the following picture of State Historians. "It was hard to varnish over the unaccountable advancement of this noble Lord without aid of the Gazetteer—but the historian has made sure of a lofty character of his Lordship, by taking it from the Court. We may observe in his book in most years a catalogue of preferments, with dates and remarks, which latter, by the secretarian

---

[12] As personal enmity undoubtedly operates on every man's mind more or less, I have, in a subsequent part of these Memoirs, specified the persons whom I did not love, that so much may be abated in the characters I have given of them, as are not corroborated by facts.
[13] Vide Gen. Dict. vol. 10, p. 426.
[14] Vide Gen. Dict. vol. 10, p. 336.
[15] Vide his Examen, part i. chap. 2, p. 33.

touches, show out of what shop he had them; and certainly the most unfit for history of any, because they are for the most part not intended for truth but flourish; and what have Court compliments to do with history?" Here I beg leave to rest this part of my apology; and proceed to answer other objections, which I foresee will be made to me.

For the facts, such as were not public, I received chiefly from my father and Mr. Fox, both men of veracity; and some from communication with the Duke of Bedford at the very time they were in agitation. I am content to rest their authenticity on the sincerity of such men; at the same time I beg it may be remembered, that I never assert anything positively unless from very good authority; and it may be observed, that where I am not certain, I always say, *it was said, it was believed, it was supposed*, or use some such phrase. The speeches, I can affirm, nay, of every one of them, to be still more authentic, as I took notes at the time, and have delivered the arguments just as I heard them; never conceiving how it can be proper in a real history to compose orations, as very probably counsels were not taken in consequence of those arguments which the Author supplies; and by that means his reasoning is not only fictitious, but misleads the reader. I do not pretend by this to assert, that parliamentary determinations are taken in consequence of any arguments the Parliament hears; I only pretend to deliver the arguments that were thought proper to be given, and thought proper to be taken.

It will perhaps be thought that some of the characters are drawn in too unfavourable a light. It has been the mode to make this objection to an honest Author, Bishop Burnet, though he only did what Tacitus, the Cardinal de Retz, and other most approved historians taught him to do, that is, speak the truth. If I have thought such authorities sufficient, I have at least acted with this farther caution, that I have endeavoured to illustrate, as far as I could, my assertions by facts, and given instances of effects naturally flowing from the qualities I ascribe to my actors. If, after all, many of the characters are bad, let it be remembered, that the scenes I describe passed in the highest life, *the soil the Vices like*:[16] and whoever

---

[16] The soil the Virtues like.—Pope.

expects to read a detail of such revolutions as these brought about by heroes and philosophers, would expect—what? why, transactions that never would have happened if the actors had been virtuous.

But to appease such scrupulous readers—here are no assassins, no poisoners, no Neros, Borgias, Catilines, Richards of York! Here are the foibles of an age, no very bad one; treacherous Ministers, mock Patriots, complaisant Parliaments, fallible Princes. So far from being desirous of writing up to the severe dignity of Roman historians, I am glad I have an opportunity of saying no worse—yet if I had, I should have used it.

Another objection which I foresee will be made to me, is, that I may have prejudices on my father's account. I can answer this honestly in a word: all who know me, know, that I had no such prejudice to him himself, as blinded me to his failings, which I have faithfully mentioned in my character of him. If more is necessary, let me add, his friends are spared no more than his enemies; and all the good I know of the latter I have faithfully told. Still more; have I concealed my father's own failings? I can extend this defence still farther. Some of my nearest friends are often mentioned in these Memoirs, and their failings I think as little concealed as those of any other persons. Some whom I have little reason to love, are the fairest characters in the book. Indeed, if I can call myself to any account for heightening characters, it is on the favourable side; I was so apprehensive of being thought partial, that I was almost willing to invent a Lord Falkland.

With more reason I can avow myself guilty of the last objection, I apprehend, and that is, having inserted too many trifling circumstances. Yet, as this is but the annal of a single year, events which would die away to nothing in a large body of history, are here material; and what was a stronger reason with me, the least important tend to illustrate either the character of the persons or the times. The objection will particularly have weight against the notes; I do not doubt but some anecdotes in them will be thought very trifling; it is plain, I thought them so myself, by not inserting them in the body of the work. I have nothing to say for them, but that they are trifles relating to considerable people; and such all curious persons have ever loved to read. Are not such trifles valued, if relating to any reign of 150 years ago? If this book should live so long, these too may become acceptable; if it does not, they will want no excuse. If I might, without being thought to censure so inimitable an author, I would remark that Voltaire, who in his *Siècle de Louis XIV* prescribes the drawing only the great outlines of history, is as circumstantial as any chronicler, when he feels himself among facts and seasons that passed under his own knowledge.

If it is any satisfaction to my readers to assist them in censuring the Author, I may say that I have spared the most inconsiderable person in the book as little as the demigods: obliquely it is true, for my own character could have very little to do directly in this Work: but I have censured very freely some measures, for which I voted, particularly the transactions about Mr. Murray, which I must confess were carried on with an intemperate rashness very ill-becoming Parliament or justice. Among these measures I must not have involved the rigorous clauses in the Mutiny Bill, or the *præmunire* clause in the Regency Bill, for none of which, I thank God, I ever voted!

When I said I foresaw no other objections, let me be understood to mean objections to faults that I might have avoided, such as want of sincerity, partiality, &c.: I hope I have cleared myself from them. As to the composition, I fear faults enough will appear in it: I would excuse them too if I could: but if imputations must lie upon my memory, let my character as a writer be the scape-goat to bear my offences!

Chapter 1

1751.
An nescis, Mî Filî, quantillâ Prudentiâ regitur Orbis?
Chancellor Oxenstiern to his Son.

It had been much expected that on the King's return from Hanover several changes would be made in the Ministry. The Duke of Newcastle had, for some time before his attending the King thither, disagreed with the other Secretary of State, the Duke of Bedford, not only because he had brought the latter into the Ministry (his incessant motive of jealousy,) nor from the impetuosity of the Duke of Bedford's temper, but from the intimate connections that Lord Sandwich had contracted with the Duke.[17] Lord Sandwich had been hoisted to the head of the Admiralty by the weight of the Duke of Bedford, into whose affection he had worked himself by intrigues, cricket-matches, and acting plays, and whom he had almost persuaded to resign the Seals in his favour. There had been a time when he had almost obtained the Duke of Newcastle's concurrence; and if he could have balanced himself between the Duke and the Duke of Newcastle, one may, without wronging the delicacy of his political character, suspect that he would have dropped the Duke of Bedford's confidence. But a blind devotion to the Duke's inclinations, which he

---

[17] William, second son of George the Second, Commander of the army in Flanders, and Duke of Cumberland. He was, by an affectation of adopting French usages, called emphatically "The Duke," during the latter years of George the Second and the beginning of the reign of George the Third.—E.

studied in all the negotiations[18] of the war and the peace, protracting the one to flatter his command, and hurrying on the other when no part of Flanders was left for the Duke's army, and himself was impatient to come over to advance his interest in the Cabinet, this had embroiled him with the Duke of Newcastle, and consequently cemented his old attachments.

Mr. Pelham had, according to his manner, tried to soothe where his brother provoked, been convinced by trifles that his brother's jealousy was solidly grounded, adopted his resentments, and promoted them. While the Court was at Hanover, Lord Sandwich had drawn a great concourse of the young men of fashion to Huntingdon races, and then carried them to Woburn to cricket-matches made there for the entertainment of the Duke. These *dangerous* practices opened Mr. Pelham's eyes; and a love affair between one of his [relations] and a younger brother[19] of the Duchess of Bedford fixed his aversion to that family. At this period the Duke of Richmond[20] died, who besides the Duchess and his own dignity, loved the Duke of Newcastle—the only man who ever did. The Pelhams immediately offered the Mastership of the Horse to the Duke of Bedford, which he would have accepted, had they left him the nomination of Lord Sandwich for his successor.

The King came over: but though the brothers were resolved to disagree with their associates in the Ministry, they could not resolve to remove them; none of the great offices were filled up but the Lieutenancy of Ireland, from which Lord Harrington[21] was removed in the most unworthy

---

[18] Lord Sandwich had been Plenipotentiary at the Conference at Breda in 1747, and concluded the Peace at Aix-la-Chapelle in 1749.

[19] Richard Levison Gower.

[20] The second son of that name, Knight of the Garter and Master of the Horse, died Aug. 8, 1750, aged 49.

[21] Yesterday morning (Dec. 8, 1756), died at his house in the Stable-yard, St. James's, the Right Hon. William Stanhope, Earl of Harrington, a General of his Majesty's Forces, a Governor of the Charter-house, a Fellow of the Royal Society, and one of the Lords of his Majesty's Most Honourable Privy Council.
His Lordship served in the reign of Queen Anne in Spain, being Captain of a Company, with the rank of Lieutenant-Colonel, in the third regiment of Guards; and in the end of the year 1710 was constituted Colonel of a regiment of Foot.
On the accession of his late Majesty he was appointed Colonel of a regiment of Dragoons, and returned to Parliament for the town of Derby; and in 1715 was made Colonel of a regiment of Horse. On the 19th of August, 1717, he was appointed Envoy Extraordinary and Plenipotentiary to the King of Spain.

Chapter 1 3

manner. He had raised himself from a younger brother's fortune to the first posts in the Government, without either the talent of speaking in

---

November 17, 1718, he was appointed Envoy and Plenipotentiary to the Court of Turin; from whence he returned to Paris; and, May 31, 1719, set out for the Duke of Berwick's camp before Fontarabia. After Admiral Byng had destroyed the greatest part of the Spanish fleet, Colonel Stanhope procured an English squadron to fall upon the port of St. Anthony in the Bay of Biscay, in which were one Spanish man-of-war of seventy guns, and two of sixty, newly built, with an incredible quantity of timber, pitch, and tar, and other naval stores, for building more; all which were destroyed by the English squadron, assisted by a detachment which the Duke of Berwick spared from his army, at the solicitation of Colonel Stanhope, who contrived the design, and, serving as a volunteer in the enterprise, principally contributed to the execution of it; where, finding it necessary to encourage and animate troops which had not been used to enterprises by sea, he was the first that leaped into the water when the boats approached the shore.

At the end of that war he was declared a Brigadier-General, and returned with the same character as before to Spain. But the Spaniards having laid siege to Gibraltar, he left Madrid on the 11th of March, 1726, and his late Majesty was pleased, in May, 1727, following, to appoint him Vice-Chamberlain of his Household, and to command him to be sworn of his Privy Council.

After his present Majesty's accession, he was nominated first Ambassador and Plenipotentiary to the Congress at Soissons; and September 9, 1729, declared Ambassador to the King of Spain. On the 20th of November following, he was advanced to the degree of a Peer of Great Britain, by the title of Lord Harrington; and on the 13th of June, 1730, was constituted principal Secretary of State. December 18, 1735, he was declared Major-General of the Horse; and Lieutenant-General, July 17, 1739. His Lordship resigned the Seals, February 12, 1741-2, and the next day was declared Lord President of the Council. February 9, 1741-2, he was raised to the dignity of a Viscount and Earl of Great Britain, by the title of Viscount Petersham, Earl of Harrington.

On the resignation of Earl Granville, October 18, 1744, his Lordship was again appointed principal Secretary of State; and in 1745 attended on his Majesty to Hanover. February 10, 1745-6, his Lordship resigned the Seals; but his Majesty was pleased to re-deliver them to him four days after.

November 22, 1746, his Lordship was declared Lord-Lieutenant of Ireland, in the room of the Earl of Chesterfield, in which post he continued until 1771. March 22, 1746-7, he was constituted General of his Majesty's Foot forces.

His Lordship's rare accomplishments were such, that it is difficult with justice to determine whether he deserved most our admiration for his political integrity in the Cabinet, or for his military conduct in the field; whether he excelled most as a perfectly fine gentleman, or as a man of letters. But, without flattery, he deserved to have it said of him—

His life was gentle, and the elements
So mix'd in him, that Nature might stand up,
And say to all the world, "This was a man!"

His Lordship married Anne, daughter and heir of Colonel Edward Griffith, one of the Clerks Comptrollers of the Green Cloth, by Elizabeth his wife, daughter of Dr. Thomas Laurence, first Physician to Queen Anne; and by her had two sons, twins, born December 18, 1719; but their mother died in child-bed. Thomas, the younger, was in August, 1741, appointed Captain in Honeywood's Dragoons, and going over sea, died February, 1742-3.

William, Viscount Petersham, the eldest son, succeeds his Lordship in honour and estate; and thereby makes a vacancy in the House of Commons for Bury St. Edmunds. [Extracted from some printed paper of 1756, and annexed to the MS. as a note by the author of the Memoirs.]

Parliament, or any interest there. He had steered through all the difficulties of the Court and changes of Ministry, with great dexterity, till, in the year 1746, notwithstanding all his personal obligations to the King, he was the first man who broke into his closet at the head of those insulting and disloyal resignations that were calculated and set on foot by the Pelhams, in the very heat of the rebellion, to force their master, by a general desertion of his servants, to abandon Lord Granville, whom he was recalling into the Ministry. The King had brooded over this ingratitude, not with much hope of revenging it, but as he sometimes resented such indignities enough to mention them, the Pelhams sacrificed Lord Harrington to their master, astonished at their complaisance, in order to bargain for other victims on his part, which they would have forced, not purchased, if there had been any price necessary but their own ingratitude. Lord Harrington was removed, and the Lieutenancy of Ireland again heaped on the Duke of Dorset, then President of the Council.

January 10.—The South Sea Company having consented to receive the hundred thousand pounds on the new treaty with Spain in lieu of all their demands, thought they had a title to some favour with the King, and accordingly came to a resolution to address him, to be pleased to continue their Governor, and to take into his consideration the state of the Company. To this message they received an answer in general terms. They addressed again for one more particular: they were told in very harsh phrase, that the King had obtained for them from the Crown of Spain all that was possible to be obtained.

This was the conclusion of the Spanish war; fomented (to overturn Sir Robert Walpole) by Lord Granville, who had neglected it for a French war; by Lord Sandwich, who made a peace that stipulated for no one of the conditions for which it was undertaken; by Pitt, who ridiculed and condemned his own orations for it, and who declared for a peace on any terms; and by the Duke of Newcastle, who betrayed all the claims of the merchants and the South Sea Company, when he had got power, to get more power by sacrificing them to the interests of Germany and the Electorate. As there never was a greater bloom of virtue and patriotism than at that period, if posterity should again see as fair a show, it will be taught to expect as little fruit.

17th.—The Parliament met. The King acquainted the Houses with the new treaties concluded with Spain for terminating our differences, and with Bavaria for securing the peace of the Empire (by the meditated election of the Archduke Joseph for King of the Romans, was understood). The Address was moved in the House of Lords by the Earl of Northumberland[22] and the Lord Archer; and in the Commons by Horace Walpole[23] (son of the late Earl of Orford) and Mr. Probyn. Lord Egmont opposed the Address, on the approbation it gave to the treaties, and the subsidies it promised to pay, and proposed leaving out many of the paragraphs. The House sat till near eight; the speakers against the Address were Mr. Henley, Mr. Bathurst, Sir John Cotton, Mr. Vyner, Mr. Martin, Mr. Doddington, Mr. Potter, and Dr. Lee; for it, Mr. W. Pitt, Mr. Pelham, Sir J. Barnard, General Oglethorpe, Horace Walpole senior, and Mr. Fox. Mr. William Pitt recanted his having seconded the famous question for the *no search* in the last Parliament; said it was a mad and foolish motion, and that he was since grown ten years older and wiser: made a great panegyric on the Duke of Newcastle's German Negotiations of this summer, and said he was himself so far from wishing to lessen the House of Commons, that whatever little existence he had in this country, it was owing to the House of Commons. These recantations of his former conduct were almost all he had left to make. On his first promotion he had declared against secret committees, and offered profuse incense to the manes and friends of Sir Robert Walpole. He now exploded his own conduct in contributing to kindle the Spanish war, and hymned that Hanoverian adulation in the Duke of Newcastle, which he had so stigmatized in Lord Granville. Indeed, the Duke of Newcastle had no sooner conquered his apprehensions of crossing the sea, than he adopted all Lord Granville's intrepidity in negotiation. The Address was carried by 203 to 74.

---

[22] Sir Hugh Smithson had married the Lady Elizabeth Seymour, only surviving child of Algernon, Duke of Somerset, and heiress of the house of Percy, on which account they were created Earl and Countess of Northumberland.

[23] The author of these Memoirs.

The morning the Parliament met, great numbers of treasonable papers were dispersed by the Penny Post, and by being dropped into the areas of houses, called "Constitutional Queries,"[24] levelled chiefly at the Duke, whom they compared to Richard III. As it was the great measure of the Prince's Opposition to attack his brother, the Jacobites bore but half the suspicion of being authors of this libel.

On the 22nd the Duke of Marlborough[25] moved in the House of Lords to have the Queries burnt by the hangman, which was agreed to, and they communicated their resolution to the Commons at a conference in the Painted Chamber. Sir John Strange, Master of the Rolls, in a lamentable discussion, seconded by the Attorney-General, Rider, moved to concur with the Lords. Sir Francis Dashwood, after much disclaiming of Jacobitism, objected to the word *false* in the resolution, as he thought some of the charges in the Queries not ungrounded, particularly in the complaint against alarm-posts, and the dismission of old officers, an instance of which he quoted in the person of his uncle, the Earl of Westmoreland, who had been removed seventeen years before, and under the administration of Sir Robert Walpole. General Handasyde, a blundering commander on the Prince's side, spoke strongly against the Queries; and Colonel Richard Lyttelton, with a greater command of absurdity, spoke to the same points as Sir Francis Dashwood; like him, disclaimed Jacobitism, and wished that "even a worse punishment than burning could be found out for the paper;" told a long story of Colonel George Townshend's having been refused leave to stay in Norfolk, "though he was cultivating the Whig interest;" and an alarming history of the Duke's having placed two Sentinels to guard the ruins of Haddock's Bagnio and the Rummer Tavern at Charing-cross, which had been burnt down; and then ran into a detail of the abuse on the King about the Hanover troops in the year 1744, when his own relations and friends had been at the head of the Opposition.

Mr. Pelham answered in a very fine speech, and said, he had a new reason for condemning this paper, as he saw it already had had part of its

---

[24] Vide the Appendix, B. [A.] The author of these Memoirs, in a MS. note on Doddington's Diary, asserts, that the Constitutional Queries were generally ascribed to Lord Egmont.—E.

[25] Charles Spencer, Duke of Marlborough and Earl of Sunderland, Knight of the Garter and Lord Steward.

intended effects, in catching honest minds. Lord Egmont made an extremely fine and artful speech, "That in general he disliked such methods of proceeding against libels, for two reasons; that he did not approve of Parliament taking the business of the law upon them, and because such notice only tended to spread the libel more; but that the present was of so evil a nature, that no censure could be too severe, especially as it was calculated to sow division between two brothers of the Blood Royal, where he was persuaded and hoped there was no such thing: that if there were any grounds for the accusations in the paper, he should choose a more proper day to inquire into them, and would; that as to the case of the Hanover troops,[26] he did not know why, as the same Ministry continued, *that* satire was left so unpunished, this so condemned; or why the author of this was so sought after, the authors of the other so promoted." The resolution was agreed to, *nemine contradicente*, and an Address presented to the King, to desire him to take effectual means to discover the author, printers, and publishers of the Queries, which were burnt on the 22nd.

The same day, Lord Barrington[27] moved that the number of seamen should be but eight thousand for the present year. Nugent, Lord Egmont, Potter, and the Opposition, declared for the old number of ten thousand, on a supposition that the view of the Ministry was to erect the land army into our principal force. W. Pitt, who, with his faction, was renewing his connections with the Prince of Wales, as it was afterwards discovered, and impatient to be Secretary of State, which he expected to carry, as he had his other preferments, by storm; and the competition between him and Fox, the principal favourite of the Duke, breaking out more and more, said (without previously acquainting Mr. Pelham with his intention) that if the motion had been made for ten thousand, he should have preferred the greater number. Potter immediately moved for them, and Pitt agreed with him. Mr. Pelham seemed to acquiesce; but when the question was put,

---

[26] In the year 1744, besides several other libels and ballads, had been published two pamphlets that made much noise, called "The Case of the Hanover Troops," and the Vindication of that Case, supposed to be written by or under the direction of Pitt, Lyttelton, Doddington, &c. The first was answered by old Horace Walpole, in a pamphlet called "The Interest of Great Britain steadily pursued."

[27] William Barrington Shute, Viscount Barrington, one of the Lords of the Admiralty.

Lord Hartington, a favourite by descent of the old Whigs, to show Pitt that he would not be followed by them if he deserted Mr. Pelham, divided the House, and the eight thousand were voted by 167 to 107; only Pitt, Lyttelton, the three Grenvilles, Colonel Conway, and eight more, going over to the minority.

On the 28th, Mr. Cooke, a pompous Jacobite, and Member for Middlesex, presented a long petition from several of the Electors of Westminster against Lord Trentham. This election and scrutiny had taken up above five months of the last year. The resentment of the Jacobites against Lord Gower for deserting their principles had appeared in the strongest colours, on the necessity of his son being rechosen, after being nominated into the Admiralty. They had fomented a strong spirit against Lord Trentham, on his declining to present a petition to the King in favour of a young fellow[28] hanged for a riot; and on his countenancing a troop of French players[29] in the little theatre in the Haymarket. Lord Egmont, who was intriguing to recover his interest in Westminster, had set up a puppet, one Sir George Vandeput; and the Pelhams were suspected of not discouraging the opposition. On Lord Trentham's success, a petition had been framed in such treasonable terms, that Mr. Cooke himself waved undertaking it, and this new one was drawn up: Sir John Cotton opposed the party's petitioning at all, but did not prevail. Both Mr. Cooke and the petition severely abused the High Bailiff (whose practice, as a lawyer, the

---

[28] Bosavern Penlez, condemned for stealing linen, and demolishing a bagnio in the Strand. Fielding wrote a pamphlet to justify the condemnation of him.

[29] During Sir Robert Walpole's administration, a troop of French Players had been brought over, but the audience and populace would not suffer them to perform. Another company came over in 1750, but with no better success. Several young men of quality had drawn their swords in the riot, endeavouring to support them: Lord Trentham's being present had been exaggerated into his being their chief protector. French Players had been no uncommon spectacle in England. The foundation of the late animosity against them was this. The opposition to the Court had proceeded so far, as to be on the point of ridiculing the King publicly on the stage of the little theatre in the Haymarket, in a dramatic satire, called the "Golden Rump," written by Fielding. Sir R. Walpole, having intelligence of this design, got the piece into his hands—[I have in my possession the imperfect copy of this piece, as I found it among my father's papers after his death]—and then procured the act to be passed for regulating the stage, by which all theatres were suppressed but such as should be licensed by the Lord Chamberlain. This provoked the people so much, that the French company having a licence granted soon after, when several English companies were cashiered, it was made a party point to silence foreign performers.

Jacobites totally destroyed), and who, as Mr. Cooke said, had attempted to violate the maiden and uncorrupted city of Westminster.

Lord Trentham,[30] who had never spoken in Parliament before, replied with great manliness and sense, and spirit, reflecting on the rancour shown to him and his family, and asserting that the opposition to him had been supported by perjury and by subscriptions, so much condemned and discountenanced by the Opposition, when raised to maintain the King on the Throne during the last Rebellion. In answer to the censure on the High Bailiff, he produced and read a letter from Mr. Cooke to the High Bailiff, while he was believed in their interest, couched in the strongest terms of approbation of his conduct and integrity. This was received with a loud and continued shout. It was long before Mr. Cooke could get an opportunity of replying, and longer before he had anything to reply. He reflected on Lord Trentham's not telling him of this letter, and justified it. Lord Egmont talked of his own obligations to Westminster, called Mr. Cooke's letter honest flattery, to encourage a man to do his duty; and said that the opposition to Lord Trentham was the sense of the nation, expressed against the Administration.

Mr. Fox replied with great wit and abilities, and proved that of all men in England Lord Egmont had least obligation to Westminster, which had rejected him at the last general election, and exposed the doctrine of honest flattery, which was only given, when the person it was given to was thought honest, by acting as his flatterer desired. Mr. Fox was apt to take occasion of attacking Lord Egmont, the champion against the Duke, and because, after Mr. Fox had managed and carried through his contested election, Lord Egmont had not given one vote with the Court. Mr. Cooke moved to hear the petition that day fortnight; Lord Trentham for the morrow se'nnight, which was agreed to. Lord Duplin then moved to call in the High Bailiff to give the House an account how he had executed the orders which he received last February of expediting the scrutiny as much as possible. He came, pleaded many obstructions, and being asked why he

---

[30] Granville Leveson Gower, eldest son of John, Earl Gower.—A. Created Marquis of Stafford in 1786. Died, 1803.—E.

had not complained, said, he had feared being taxed with putting an end to the scrutiny.

Lord Trentham then desired he might be asked, if he remembered any threats used to him. Lord Egmont objected to the question, and the High Bailiff was ordered to withdraw. A long debate ensued, though Mr. Fox proposed to put the question in these less definite words, "how he had been obstructed." At last it was proposed that the Speaker should decide, whether, supposing the High Bailiff accused any person, they could be heard to their defence, consistently with the orders of the House, before hearing the merits of the petition. The oracle was dumb—at last being pressed, it said, "I wish, without using many words, I could persuade gentlemen to go upon some other matter." Lord Trentham finding the Speaker against him, and the Ministry and one or two of the old Whigs inclined to give it up, gave it up with grace and propriety. But the young Whigs, headed by Lord Coke, grew very riotous, and though the Speaker declared still more fully against them, they divided the House, and carried it by 204 to 106 to call in the High Bailiff, who, returning to the bar, charged Crowle, Sir George Vandeput's Counsel, with triumphing in having protracted the scrutiny, and with calling the orders of the House *brutum fulmen*. Being further questioned, he said he had been scandalously abused; had received papers threatening his life; had been charged with running away to Holland; had been pursued into the vestry after declaring the majority for Lord Trentham; had been stoned there, and that one gentleman at the head of the mob had asked them, if nobody had courage enough to knock the dog down, and that he ought to be killed. Being asked who this was, he named Mr. Alexander Murray, brother of Lord Elibank; both such active Jacobites, that if the Pretender had succeeded, they could have produced many witnesses to testify their zeal for him; both so cautious, that no witnesses of actual treason could be produced by the Government against them: the very sort of Jacobitism that has kept the cause alive, and kept it from succeeding. Mr. Murray, with Crowle and one Gibson, an upholsterer, were ordered to attend on the Thursday following with the High Bailiff, to have his charge made out.

29th.—The report for the eight thousand seamen was made from the committee, and debated again till past eight at night, when it was agreed to by 189 to 106. Mr. W. Pitt spoke with great affectation of concern for differing with Mr. Pelham, protested he had not known it was his measure (which Mr. Pelham made many signs of not allowing), and that it was his fear of Jacobitism which had made him differ on this only point with those with whom he was determined to lead his life. He called the fleet our standing army, the army a little body of military spirit, so improved by discipline, that that discipline alone was worth five thousand men; made great panegyrics on Mr. Pelham (so did Lyttleton and George Grenville), and concluded with saying, "I do not believe the majority of this House like eight thousand better than ten."

The times were changed! Men who remembered how Sir Robert Walpole's fears of the Pretender and his Spithead expeditions were ridiculed by his opponents, admired Mr. Pitt's humility and conviction, who was erecting a new opposition on those arguments.

He was attacked by Hampden, who had every attribute of a buffoon but cowardice, and none of the qualifications of his renowned ancestor but courage. He drew a burlesque picture of Pitt and Lyttleton under the titles of *Oratory* and *Solemnity*, and painted in the most comic colours what mischiefs rhetoric had brought upon the nation, and what emoluments to Pitt. Pitt flamed into a rage, and nodded menaces of highest import to Hampden, who retorted them, undaunted, with a droll voice that was naturally hoarse and inarticulate. Mr. Pelham interposed, and, according to his custom, defended Pitt, who had deserted him; gave up Hampden, who had supported him. It was not unusual for Pitt to mix the hero with the orator; he had once blended those characters very successfully, when, having been engaged to make up a quarrel between his friend Hume Campbell[31] and Lord Home, in which the former had kissed the rod, Pitt within very few days treated the House with bullying the Scotch declaimer.

---

[31] Alexander Hume Campbell, brother to the Earl of Marchmont, a very masterly speaker and able lawyer, had been Attorney-General to the Prince of Wales, which post he resigned when his Royal Highness erected his last Opposition, and was supposed to have a considerable pension, on which he neglected the House of Commons, giving himself up entirely to his profession.

On the present occasion, the Speaker insisted on the two champions promising to proceed no farther, with which Punch first, and then Alexander the Great, complied.

31st.—Mr. Crowle appeared with the High Bailiff at the bar of the House, and owned the words charged on him, but endeavoured to prove that the protraction was meant for the benefit of his client; and that the *brutum fulmen* was applied to those who urged him with the orders of the House impertinently. He showed great deference and submission to the House. It was then debated till six o'clock, whether any witnesses should be called in against him, and carried by 204 to 138, that there should. Three were called, who proved the words. Lord Hartington, (whose head being filled with the important behaviour of the Cavendishes and Russels at the Revolution, was determined that it should be the fault of the times, not his, if his conduct did not always figure equally with theirs in solemnity), moved, with a pomp of tragic tenderness, and was seconded by Lord Coke, who abused the independent electors, "that Mr. Crowle had wilfully protracted the scrutiny, and showed contempt of the House."

This was opposed;[32] the lawyers pleaded *in earnest* for their brother, and the Ministry were inclined to give it up, till Lord Egmont made a furious speech for Crowle, and called the Whigs the Rump of their old party. Mr. Fox took this up warmly in an exceedingly fine speech of spirit and ridicule, and concluded with telling Lord Egmont, that though he intended to have interceded for Crowle (who had interest at Windsor, where Fox was chosen), he must now be for this resolution; but yet should show compassion for Mr. Crowle, if it were only on his having such a friend. The House divided at eleven at night, and the resolution passed by 181 to 129. Lord Hartington then offered to the House to take Mr. Crowle into custody, or to reprimand him immediately; the latter of which was

---

[32] Nugent very absurdly told the House, "that he could not help recollecting the epitaph on Lord Brooke, *Here lies the friend of Sir Philip Sidney*, which he begged leave to apply, by acquainting them that Mr. Crowle was the friend of that excellent man, Lord Lonsdale, who then lay dying, and that he hoped they would not disturb his death-bed by any harsh treatment of his friend." Henry, the last Lord Viscount Lonsdale, died soon after this. He had been Constable of the Tower and Lord Privy Seal, which he resigned with outgoing into Opposition. He was a man of very conscientious and disinterested honour, a great disputant, a great refiner—no great genius. Nugent published two or three poems on his virtues.

chosen for him by Mr. Fox, and he was reprimanded on his knees by the Speaker. As he rose from the ground,[33] he wiped his knees, and said, "it was the dirtiest house he had ever been in."

The Whigs took pleasure in copying the precedents,[34] that had been set them at the famous Westminster Election, in 1742; and the Speaker had the satisfaction both times of executing the vengeance of either party, and indulging his own dignity. On the former occasion, his speech to the kneeling Justices was so long and severe, that the morning it was printed, Sir Charles Hanbury Williams complained to him of the printer's having made a grievous mistake—"Where?—how? I examined the proof sheet myself!" Sir Charles replied, "in the conclusion he makes you say, *more* might have been said; to be sure you wrote it, *less* might have been said."

The King on these votes commended the young men, and said to the Duke of Newcastle before the Duke of Bedford, "they are not like those puppies who are always changing their minds. Those are your Pitts and your Grenvilles, whom you have cried up to me so much! You know I never liked them."

February 1.—Mr. Murray appeared at the bar of the House of Commons, and heard the High Bailiff's charge. He asserted his innocence; said he should deny nothing that was true; that much was false; smiled when he was taxed of having called Lord Trentham and the High Bailiff rascals, and desired Counsel, which, after a debate of two hours, was granted to him, and a respite till the Wednesday following, upon condition of his being taken into custody, and giving bail for his appearance. Gibson, the upholsterer, was then brought to the bar, witnesses for and against him heard, and the words proved, though some members[35] of the House, who had been present at the conclusion of the scrutiny, did not hear him speak them. Sir William Yonge moved a resolution of his guilt, which was carried by 214 to 63, and he was committed to Newgate.

---

[33] Crowle was a noted punster. Once, on a circuit with Page, a person asked him if the Judge was not just behind? He replied, "I don't know; but I am sure he never was *just* before."

[34] When Sir Charles Wager and Lord Sundon were declared illegally chosen by military influence, on the prevailing of the opposition against Sir Robert Walpole; and the Justices of Peace who had called in the soldiers were committed at five o'clock in the morning, the Speaker having been seventeen hours in the chair.

[35] Sir John Cotton and Sir Charles Fynte.

Sir William Yonge[36] was still employed in any government causes where the Ministry wanted to inflict punishments and avoid odium—their method of acquiring merit! His vivacity and parts, whatever the cause was, made him shine, and he was always content with the lustre that accompanied fame, without thinking of what was reflected from rewarded fame—a convenient ambition to Ministers, who had few such disinterested combatants! Sir Robert Walpole always said of him, "that nothing but Yonge's character[37] could keep down his parts, and nothing but his parts support his character."

---

[36] August 10, 1755.—Sunday died at his seat at Escott, near Honiton in Devonshire, the Right Hon. Sir William Yonge, Bart., LL.D., F.R.S., Knight of the Most Honourable Order of the Bath, one of his Majesty's Most Honourable Privy Council, and Lord Lieutenant and Custos Rotulorum of Carnarvonshire. He was chosen to represent the borough of Honiton in the sixth Parliament of Great Britain, which was summoned to meet on the 10th of May, 1722, and served for that borough in the five succeeding Parliaments; for though chosen for Ashburton in the eighth, and Tiverton in the seventh and tenth, he each time made his election for Honiton, and was five times re-elected on his accepting places. In the present Parliament he represented Tiverton. He was appointed to be one of the Lords of the Treasury in March, 1724; a Lord of the Admiralty in May, 1728; again a Lord of the Treasury in May, 1730; Secretary at War in May, 1735; and in May, 1746, joint Vice-Treasurer of Ireland. He is succeeded in his estates and title of Baronet by his only son, now Sir George Yonge, member for Honiton.—[From a printed paper of 1755, annexed as a note to MS. text by the author of the Memoirs.]

[37] He was vain, extravagant, and trifling: simple out of the House, and too ready at assertions in it. His eloquence, which was astonishing, was the more extraordinary, as it seemed to come upon him by inspiration, for he could scarce talk common sense in private on political subjects, on which in public he would be the most animated speaker. Sir Robert Walpole has often, when he did not care to enter early into the debate himself, given Yonge his notes, as the latter has come late into the House, from which he could speak admirably and fluently, though he had missed all the preceding discussion. He had been kept down for some time by the prevailing interest of General Churchill with Sir Robert Walpole, on the following occasion. Yonge, in a poetic epistle (to which he had great proneness, though scanty talents) addressed to Hedges, who was supposed to be well with Mrs. Oldfield, said, speaking of that actress in the character of Cleopatra,
"But thou who know'st the dead and living well."
[The dead and living Cleopatra.]—This coming to the fair one's knowledge, she never ceased, till she had made such a rupture between her fond General and Yonge, as had like to have ended in the total ruin of the latter.

Chapter 2

February 4th.—An army of 18,850 men was proposed. Lord Limerick[38] moved for 15,000. Ever since the defeat of Lord Bath, he had been listed under the Prince, but for the last three or four years had lived retired in Ireland. He had preserved a sort of character from the impossibility of his being dismissed with the rest of his friends, as he had secured the reversion of a large sinecure for life, and, consequently, had less occasion to be intriguing after new preferment. His speeches were reckoned severe, and it was not his fault if they did not answer the character; he meant to wound, but his genius did not carry equal edge with his temper. Martin, a West Indian lawyer, attached to the Prince, made a speech of great wit against standing armies, with very new arguments. The eighteen thousand men were voted in the committee by 240 to 117, and carried next day on the report, after a long debate, by 175 to 75.

6th.—The High Bailiff produced eight witnesses against Mr. Murray, who gave the strongest evidence of his menaces and seditious behaviour. He was then heard by his Counsel, who brought the High Constable, Carne, Mr. Gascoyne, Lord Carpenter, and Sir John Tyrrel, to invalidate the charge. The first only proved that the words might have been said without his hearing them; the second confirmed the accuser's charge in some particulars. Lord Carpenter, with the greatest decency, gave the most unconscientious evidence; but though he confined it to negatives, he at last

---

[38] James Hamilton, Lord Viscount Limerick, a great friend of Lord Bath, who had obtained the reversion of King's Remembrancer for him and his son on the change of the Ministry in 1742. He was created Earl of Clanbrazil in 1756.

contradicted himself, and was materially contradicted by Sir John Tyrrel, a foolish young Knight, who did not know how to reconcile his awe of the House with the little regard he had for what he was ready to depose. Lord Carpenter was undertaking Westminster, and having lately succeeded to a large estate, seemed to think elections the most equal way of restoring the sums which his father had amassed by excessive usury. The Counsel made small defence; one of them even made an excuse for engaging in that cause. Mr. Murray then advanced to the bar, and said he was ashamed of nothing he was accused of having said, but calling Lord Trentham a rogue to the chimney-sweeper, which was below him to have done.

The High Bailiff made short, clear, and fair observations on the evidence. Colonel Richard Lyttleton then moved a long resolution of the proofs being full, and was seconded by Colonel George Townshend. Sir Francis Dashwood opposed it, and would have reduced all the proofs to immaterial words, and the probability of one of the witnesses having mistaken the sound of a voice when he did not see the face of the person who spoke them, though he turned immediately and saw Mr. Murray, whose voice he had recollected. Lord Duplin replied. Sir John Cotton reflected on the length of the motion brought ready drawn, and complained of the House not having paid due regard to his evidence for Gibson; and both he and Sir Francis laid great stress on the dignity and character of Lord Carpenter. Mr. Fox answered in one of the finest, most spirited, and artful speeches that he ever made; set Lord Duplin's evidence against Cotton's; summed up the whole charge and proofs, and instead of ridiculing Sir John Tyrrel's ridiculous evidence, as less able speakers would have done, he enforced it, commented it, and then produced it against Lord Carpenter's. Lord Egmont made an artful speech, W. Pitt a florid one, T. Pitt a dull one.

During the debate, the strangers in the gallery were called to, to withdraw; the Speaker said that was his business, unless any gentleman would move it, and then he would be obliged to him. Lord Coke rose, moved it, and said, "Sir, I am that gentleman, and grant your request." The Speaker immediately ordered them to withdraw, and said with a smile, "and, my Lord, I have obeyed your commands." But as soon as they were gone, he fell into a pompous passion, and complained of Lord Coke's repeating his words; having mistaken a disposition to pomp in another for burlesque, which he did not perceive was the result of the thing, and not of the intention. The episode concluded with Lord Coke's begging his pardon, and with his being content to have thought himself affronted, as at all events it had procured him submission.

Of the Prince's people only thirteen stayed to vote; and towards midnight, the resolution was carried by 210 to 74. It was then moved to send Mr. Murray close prisoner to Newgate. Sir John Cotton and others divided on the word *close*, but were only 52 to 169: Lord Egmont and his faction had retired. The young Whigs, angry at this second division, determined to bring Murray on his knees; and it was proposed to Mr. Pelham in the lobby: he consented, and it was moved by Colonel Lyttleton and Lord Coke. The Tories were enraged, and divided again, after Mr. Dowdeswell had moved for the Tower; but a precedent having been quoted of Middleton, the Sheriff of Denbigh, being sent to Newgate (in times[39] that the Whigs loved now to imitate, from the aversion they had felt to the first example), while they were disputing on the word *close*, and Mr. Harding had made the Clerk read the journal till it came to the resolution of addressing the King even to take away an office from Middleton, Mr. Fox recurred to that precedent, and said, "If the gentlemen of North Wales, where the Middletons of Chirk Castle are one of the most ancient families, would yield the precedence to the Murrays, he would consent that the latter should go to the Tower."

It being carried by 163 to 40, that he should be brought on his knees, he was called in. He entered with an air of confidence, composed of something between a martyr and a coxcomb. The Speaker called out, "Your obeisances! Sir, your obeisances!"—and then—"Sir, you must kneel." He replied, "Sir, I beg to be excused; I never kneel but to God." The Speaker repeated the command with great warmth. Murray answered, "Sir, I am sorry I cannot comply with your request, I would in anything else." The Speaker cried, "Sir, I call upon you again to consider of it."

---

[39] In 1742.

Murray answered, "Sir, when I have committed a crime, I kneel to God for pardon; but I know my own innocence, and cannot kneel to anybody else." The Speaker ordered the Serjeant to take him away, and secure him. He was going to reply; the Speaker would not suffer him. The Speaker then made a representation to the House of his contemptuous behaviour, and said, "However you may have differed in the debate, I hope you will be unanimous in his punishment! Pray consider on it; if he may with impunity behave thus, there is an end of the dignity and power of this House!"

Sir George Oxenden said he had foreseen this refusal, and had not voted for bringing him on his knees, and was not answerable for the consequences—a fine consolation in their dilemma! Mr. Harding quoted three precedents where persons, and some of them members, had received their sentence on their knees. Mr. Pelham proposed a committee to search for precedents how to treat him, and that they should give their opinion upon it. Mr. Cooke went out, and tried to persuade him to submit; but he said he would sooner cut his throat. Mr. Fox went so far as to mention a place of confinement in the Tower, called Little Ease; but Mr. Pelham declared against such severe corporal punishment. Sir William Yonge proposed the closest confinement in Newgate without being visited, (a triumph which the Tories meditated for him,) and without pen, ink, and paper. This opinion was afterwards taken up by Lord George Sackville, and agreed to, though Vyner urged that he would be punished twice if they adhered to the former sentence after his submission. Alderman Jansen moved in vain to adjourn. W. Pitt hinted at a bill to be passed against him if he would not comply. Admiral Vernon made such an outrageous speech against these proceedings, desiring to have Magna Charta referred to the committee, that he was several times taken to order by the Speaker, Sir John Mordaunt, and Mr. Pelham, and was on the brink of falling under the sentence of the House. The Speaker himself proposed the question on Murray's contempt, which Sir John Cotton tried to prevent being inserted in the votes, but it passed, with the order for his closer confinement; and then, after naming the committee, the House, at near two o'clock in the morning, adjourned over the next day.

At five in the morning, Mr. Murray was carried in a hackney-coach strictly guarded to Newgate. He sung ballads all the way; but on entering the gaol burst into tears, kissed the Serjeant, said he was very ill, and must have a physician. In two days the House was mollified, permitted him to be ill, and gave leave for his brother to visit him with a physician and an apothecary; and in five days more, their compassion grew so tender as to indulge him with the company of his sister, a nurse, and his own servant.

11th.—The staff was opposed by Lord Egmont, Dr. Lee, Nugent, Potter, and Bathurst; defended by Mr. Fox, Mr. Pelham, Sir William Yonge, Lord George Sackville, Lord Barrington, and General Mordaunt, and carried by 205 to 88. In the night, new Queries[40] abusing the House of Commons for their proceedings on the Westminster affair were dispersed at several doors, but no notice was taken of them. The Commons were not eager to have more prisoners to nurse!

12th.—Sir George Vandeput's and the Westminster petitions were withdrawn. Some of the independents had tried to prevent it; and, at a meeting on the 9th, thirty-seven divided for going on with them against thirty-one: but Sir George declaring he would withdraw his, and he, Lord Carpenter, and Sir Thomas Clarges leaving the meeting, it was agreed to drop both petitions.

13th.—Sir William Yonge acquainted the House, that the committee of which he was chairman was ready with their report on Mr. Murray's case; but as the prisoner was ill, they desired to postpone it to the following Monday. Mr. Cooke presented a petition from Gibson the upholsterer, who had not caught the infection of heroism from his fellow captive, but begged for enlargement, which was granted, and he was ordered to attend on the morrow, when he was reprimanded on his knees, and discharged.

The same day Mr. Pelham opened the Ways and Means, in which he generally shined, and did not disgrace his master, Sir Robert Walpole, though the latter had gathered his chief laurels from his knowledge and perspicuity in that service. Sir John Cotton piddled with a little opposition to the land-tax of three shillings, but it was carried by 106 to 43, and on the

---

[40] Vide the Appendix, C.

report by 229 to 28. They could not conjure up a spirited division now on the most popular points: if they were not new, they would scarce furnish a debate.

Sir John Cotton had wit, and the faithful attendant on wit, ill-nature, and was the greatest master of the arts of the House, where he seldom made but short speeches, having a stammering in his elocution, which, however, he knew how to manage with humour.[41] In the end of Queen Anne's reign he was in place;[42] during Sir Robert Walpole's administration constantly and warmly in opposition, and was so determined a Jacobite, that though on the late coalition he accepted a place in the Household, and held it two years, he never gave a vote with the Court, which argued nice distinction, not only in taking the oaths to the King (for that all the Jacobites in Parliament do), but in taking his pay, and yet obstructing his service: and as nice in the King's Ministers, who could discover the use of making a man accept a salary without changing his party. When the Duke of Bedford, with all my Lord Russel's integrity of Whiggism, was involved in a Jacobite opposition, he had been so suspicious, as to mistrust Sir John's principles, till my Lord Gower quieted his uneasiness by assuring him, "Cotton is no more a Jacobite than I am."

18th.—Sir William Yonge read the report of the committee appointed to search for precedents on Murray's case. It concluded with proposing to send for him again to the bar of the House: but as gentler counsels, and a

---

[41] Soon after Mr. Winnington deserted the Tories, and had made a strong speech on the other side, Sir John Cotton was abusing him to Sir Robert Walpole, and said, "That young dog promised that he would always stand by us." Sir Robert replied, "I advise my young men never to use *always*." "Yet," said Cotton, stammering, "you yourself are very apt to make use of *all—ways*."

[42] Feb. 1752.—On Tuesday night last, died at his house in Park-place, Sir John Hinde Cotton, Bart. He was a Commissioner of Trade and Plantations in the reign of Queen Anne; also member in several Parliaments in that reign for the town of Cambridge; and in the last Parliament of his late Majesty was one of the Knights of the Shire for the county of Cambridge; and in the two first Parliaments called by his present Majesty served again for the town of Cambridge; in the last and present Parliaments for Marlborough. He was also Treasurer of the Chamber to his Majesty in 1742. He married first a daughter of Sir Ambrose Crawley, Knt., and has issue one son, now Sir John Hinde Cotton, and one daughter, married to Jacob Houblon, of Hallingbury, in Essex, Esq. He married to his second lady, the daughter of the late James Craggs, Esq., one of the Commissioners of the Post-office, and relict of Samuel Trefusis, Esq., who died August 23, 1724, by whom he had only one daughter, who died young.
[From a printed paper annexed as a note by the author of the Memoirs.]

candour that might have been equitable before his contempt, though absurd now, prevailed, Sir William only moved to have the report lie on the table, saying, that if Murray should not submit this session, he should move in the next to resume the sentence. Mr. Pelham spoke much for moderate proceedings—more moderate indeed it would have been difficult to pursue after the lengths themselves and Murray had gone; but they who wanted to extort a submission from him for offences which he had not acknowledged, were ready to release him after an outrage which he gloried in, and had no ways atoned. Mr. Fox read a paragraph from the Whitehall Evening Post, by which it appeared that Murray had had the use of pen, ink, and paper, and had been writing an apology for some part of his private conduct;[43] the greatest part of which his future historian may be glad to colour over with the varnish of martyrdom. Mr. Fox, on this apparent recovery of the prisoner's nerves, moved to order the physician and apothecary to attend that day se'nnight with an account of Mr. Murray's state of health, which was agreed to.

On the 19th, 20th, and 21st, the Mutiny Bill was debated each day for several hours. This Bill, which formerly had passed as quietly as the Malt Act, had, for the two or three last years, constantly afforded the longest contests. Lord Egmont[44] had gained his greatest reputation by opposing it; and he was not a man to forget, or to let anybody else forget where his strength lay. His great talent was indefatigable application, which he loved rather than wanted, for his parts were strong, and manly, and quick: his heart rather wanted improvement than his head; though when his ambition and lust of Parliament were out of the question, he was humane, friendly, and as good-humoured as it was possible for a man to be who was never known to laugh; he was once indeed seen to smile, and that was at chess. He did not dislike mirth in others, but he seemed to adjourn his attention till he could bring back the company to seriousness. He was personally very brave, as brave as if he were always in the right.

---

[43] Mr. Murray's very first step to preferment was by presenting himself and being received into a commission in the Army, which had been made out for another Alexander Murray.

[44] John Perceval, the second Earl of Egmont of that name. He was scarce a man before he had a scheme of assembling the Jews, and making himself their King.

His father had trained him to history and antiquities; and he early suckled his own political genius with scribbling journals and pamphlets. Towards the decline of Sir Robert Walpole's power, he had created himself a leader of the Independents, a contemptible knot of desperate tradesmen,[45] many of them converted to Jacobitism by being detected and fined at the Custom-house for contraband practices. By those people he was shoved into Parliament on the expulsion of Lord Sundon and Sir Charles Wager; but having written that masterly pamphlet called "Faction Detected," in defence of Lord Bath's political apostasy, the patron and champion mutually lost their popularity, and nothing was openly remembered of Lord Percival's works, but a ridiculous history[46] of his own family, which he had collected and printed at an immense expense. Thus exploded, he was very willing to take sanctuary with his leader in the House of Lords; but the Ministry did not think his sting formidable enough to extract it by so dear an operation: how often since has Mr. Pelham wished him laid up in ermine!

At the beginning of this Parliament, rejected by Westminster, and countenanced nowhere, he bought the loss of an election at Weobley, for which place, however, on a petition, Mr. Fox procured him to be returned by Parliament, and had immediately the satisfaction of finding him declare against the Court, declared a Lord of the Bedchamber to the Prince, and, on the first occasion, the warmest antagonist of the Duke and the Mutiny Bill. On Lord Trentham's being opposed at Westminster last year, Lord Egmont tried, by every art and industry, to expiate his offences in the eyes of his old electors, and was the great engine of the contest there. All the morning he passed at the hustings; then came to the House, where he was a principal actor; and all the evening he passed at hazard; not to mention the hours he spent in collecting materials for his speeches, or in furnishing

---

[45] One of the principal Independents was Blakiston, a grocer in the Strand, detected in smuggling, and forgiven by Sir R. Walpole; detected again and fined largely, on which he turned patriot, and has since risen to be an alderman of London, on the merit of that succedaneum to money—Jacobitism.

[46] It was called the "History of the House of Yvory," in two large volumes. The collecting and consulting records and genealogies, and engraving and publishing, cost him (as the Heralds affirm) near £3000. He endeavoured afterwards to recall it, and did suppress a great many copies.

them to his weekly mercenaries. With this variety of life, he was as ignorant of the world as a child, and knew nothing of mankind though he had acted every part in it. But it is time to continue the history of the Mutiny Bill, and to conclude with the conclusion of his Lordship's memoirs of his family and himself—"let us here leave this young nobleman struggling for the dying liberties of his country!"

When the Duke had set himself to restore the discipline of the army, and bring it nearer to the standard of German severity, he found it necessary to reform the military code, that whatever despotism he had a mind to establish might be grounded in an appearance of law. The Secretary at War, with a few General Officers, was ordered to revise the Mutiny Bill, and (if one may judge by their execution of this commission) to double the rigour of it. The penalty of death came over as often as the curses in the Commination on Ash-Wednesday. Oaths of secrecy were imposed on Courts Martial; and even officers on half-pay were for the future to be subject to all the jurisdiction of military law. My Lord Anson, who governed at the Admiralty Board, was struck with so amiable a pattern, and would have chained down his tars to a like oar; but it raised such a ferment in that boisterous profession, that the Ministry were forced to drop several of the strongest articles, to quiet the tempest that this innovation had caused.

The Mutiny Bill was likely to pass with less noise; when Colonel Richard Lyttleton, intending mischief, though without seeing half way into the storm he was raising, took notice of the extraordinary novelties and severity of these modern regulations. He was a younger brother of the pious George Lyttelton, with less appearance of, but with not much more real integrity. He was grown a favourite of the Prince of Wales by a forwardness of flattery that had revolted even the Duke, at whose expense on some disobligations he was now paying court to the elder brother.

He was seconded by Colonel George Townshend, eldest son of my Lord Townshend, a very particular young man, who, with much oddness, some humour, no knowledge, great fickleness, greater want of judgment, and with still more disposition to ridicule, had once or twice promised to make a good speaker. He was governed by his mother, the famous Lady

Townshend,[47] who having been neglected by the Duke, after some overtures of civility to him, had dipped into all the excess of Scotch Jacobitism, and employed all her wit and malice, the latter of which, without any derogation to the former, had vastly the ascendant, to propagate the Duke's unpopularity. The Pelhams, who were very near as ill with her, had placed their nephew, Mr. Townshend, in the Duke's family, to remove him from her influence; and the Duke had softened his haughtiness as much as possible to second their views. But my Lady Townshend's resentments were not at all disappointed by this notable scheme, nor by the opportunities it gave her son of learning more of his commander's temper, nor by the credit it gave to any reflections on him when authorized by, or coming directly from one of his own servants and a supposed favourite. The Duke has often said since, that he was never hurt but by the ingratitude[48] of Mr. Townshend and Lord Robert Sutton, whom he had made the greatest efforts to oblige.

This attack from two officers was artfully relieved by Lord Egmont, who had stickled so vehemently against the innovations, that one after another they were given up, or much softened one year after another, though not till many disagreeable instances had been publicly produced of his Royal Highness's arbitrary control, and though they had been defended in a masterly manner by Mr. Fox, Lord George Sackville, and Colonel Henry "Seymour" Conway;[49] the latter a young officer, who having set out upon a plan of fashionable[50] virtue, had provoked the King and Duke by

---

[47] Ethelreda Harrison, wife of Charles, Lord Viscount Townshend.
[48] Mr. Townshend had quitted the Army at the end of the last year, had connected himself with the Prince, and took all opportunities of opposing any of the Duke's measures, and ridiculing him, and drawing caricatures of him and his Court, which he did with much humour. A *bon mot* of his was much repeated. Soon after he had quitted the Army, he was met at a review on the parade by Colonel Fitzwilliam, one of the Duke's military spies, who said to him, "How came you, Mr. Townshend, to do us this honour?—but I suppose you only come as a spectator!" Mr. Townshend replied, "And why may not one come hither as a *Spectator*, Sir, as well as a *Tatler*?" Lord Robert Sutton was second son to the Duke of Rutland, and had been preferred to the command of a favourite regiment which the Duke had nearly instituted, before Lord Robert was of any rank in the Army; yet he deserted him, and accepted the place of Lord of the Bedchamber to the Prince.
[49] Honourable Henry Seymour Conway, second son of Lord Conway, and brother of the first Earl of Hertford. Commander-in-Chief in 1782; Field-Marshal in 1793.—E.
[50] This is surely a slip of the pen; should we not read *un*fashionable virtue?—E.

voting against the Army at the beginning of the war. He was soon after, by the interest of a near relation of his, placed in the Duke's family, where he grew a chief favourite, not only by a steady defence of military measures on all occasions, but by most distinguished bravery in the battles of Fontenoy and Laffelt (in the latter of which he was taken prisoner), by a very superior understanding, and by being one of the most agreeable and solid speakers in Parliament, to which the beauty of his person, and the harmony of his voice, did remarkably contribute.

This year a new field was opened, during the discussion of the Mutiny Bill, by Sir Henry Erskine, another young officer, lately brought into Parliament by the Duke of Argyle. This man, with a face as sanguine as the disposition of the Commander-in-Chief, had a gentle plausibility in his manner, that was not entirely surprising in a Scotchman, and an inclination to poetry, which he had cultivated with little success either in his odes, or from the patrons to whom they were dedicated; one had been addressed to the Duke, and another to an old gentlewoman at Hanover, mother of my Lady Yarmouth. Of late he had turned his talent to rhetoric, and studied public speaking under the baker at the Oratorical Club[51] in Essex-street, from whence he brought so fluent, so theatrical, so specious, so declamatory a style and manner, as might have transported an age and audience not accustomed to the real eloquence and graces of Mr. Pitt.

It was on the second debate on the Mutiny Bill this year, that Sir Harry Erskine, complaining of the exorbitant power of General Officers on Courts Martial, instanced in his own case, and severely abused General Anstruther, who had treated him very rigorously some years before at Minorca. The charge was so strong, that Mr. Nugent said, if the General (who was not present) did not appear next day and justify himself, he would move for an inquiry into his conduct. This was so well received, that the Secretary at War thought proper to write to General Anstruther to acquaint him with the accusation. He appeared the next day, and spoke some time, but with so low a voice, and so strong a Scotch accent, that

---

[51] This went by the name of the Robin Hood Society, and met every Monday. Questions were proposed, and any persons might speak on them for seven minutes; after which, the baker, who presided with a hammer in his hand, summed up the arguments.

scarce ten people heard or understood him. He said "he had undergone a long persecution from his countrymen, who all hated him for having been the only Scot that, on Porteous's affair, had voted for demolishing the Nether Bow at Edinburgh." He produced and read an anonymous and bitter letter wrote against him to the late Duke of Argyle, with two letters to himself, one from the author to own the former, and to beg his pardon for it; the other from the council of war at Minorca to vindicate him to the General. He said he suspected Sir Harry Erskine of having been in the conspiracy against him, which he had not punished near so rigorously as it deserved: and he concluded with justifying his government, where, he affirmed, he had eased the people of all taxes imposed by former Governors.

Sir Harry Erskine, with all the false lustre of oratory, and all the falsehood of an orator, replied in an affected gesture of supplication; besought the House to proceed no further in this affair; said he had forgiven all the ill-usage, had mentioned nothing out of revenge, and now pardoned the General's suspicions. This justification ill-heard, and this deprecation as ill-founded, concluded the affair for the present as awkwardly as it had been begun. The General's charge against his countrymen was undoubtedly well-grounded, and that of tyranny against him, no less. Indeed, the Scotch would have overlooked his tyranny to the Minorchese, if they could have forgot his supporting the Government, when it was necessary to chastise the mutinous disposition of Scotland, where Captain Porteous had been murdered insolently and illegally by the mob.

Anstruther had been tried before the Council for his unwarrantable behaviour in his government a few years ago, and a heavy number of articles proved against him; but Lord Granville defeated the charge by calling in a Minorchese, and talking to him for an hour in Spanish, and then assuring the Council that the witness had fully justified the General. The secret of Erskine's being willing to drop his accusation was on receiving intimation that Anstruther, if pushed, would recriminate on General St. Clair, Sir Henry's uncle, who, on the expedition to Port L'Orient, had used the most violent methods to bring a Court Martial over to his opinion, and had abused Lord John Murray, the President of it, in the grossest terms, who, on this occasion, begged Mr. Fox to tell the King and Duke from him, that his only reason for having taken no steps to complain of that usage, was for fear of increasing the heats already raised on the Mutiny Bill; but that at a proper time he would seek some redress.

A committee had been appointed to consider on amending the laws enacted against the vices of the lower people, which were increased to a degree of robbery and murder beyond example. Fielding, a favourite author of the age, had published an admirable treatise on the laws in question, and agreed with what was observed on this occasion, that these outrages proceeded from gin. The depopulation of the city was ascribed to the same cause, which gave Nugent occasion very properly to offer again his Bill of general Naturalization, a favourite Whig point, overthrown in the Queen's time by the narrow ignorance of the Tories, and defeated in the first session of this Parliament by Mr. Pelham's complaisance for Sir John Barnard. It was now received, and the second reading ordered for the 20th, the day before which a petition was presented against it from the city of London. The next day they presented another against gin, on which old Horace Walpole attacked Sir John Barnard on the absurdity of their remonstrating on the decrease of people, and their making interest against replacing them by foreigners. Nugent ridiculed him on the same topic, and made a distinction of humour between the good citizen in his fur gown and corporate capacity, and really wishing well in his mercantile capacity to trade and populousness: and he observed, that even in this enlightened age, the city of London had not got beyond the prejudices of the reign of Harry the Third, the laws of that age against aliens, and the reasoning of the present petition against naturalizing foreigners being exactly the same.

Sir John Barnard was as little ready to reply to banter, as Nugent was inferior to him in reasoning. The citizen, with the most acute head for figures, made that sort of speaking still more unpleasant by the paltriness of his language, as the arrogance of his honesty clouded the merit of it. The Irishman's style was floridly bombast; his impudence as great as if he had been honest. Sir John's moroseness looked like ill-nature, and may be was so. Nugent affected unbounded good-humour, and it was unbounded but by much secret malice, which sometimes broke out in boisterous railing, oftener vented itself in still-born satires. Sir John Barnard had been attached to Lord Granville, but had been flattered from him by Mr. Pelham. Nugent's attachments were to Lord Granville; but all his flattery addressed to Mr. Pelham, whom he mimicked in candour, as he often resembled Lord Granville in ranting. Sir John Barnard meant honestly, and preserved his disinterestedness: he would probably have sunk in his character of a great genius, if he had come into business with Sandys and others—as they did. Nugent[52] * * * * had lost the reputation of a great poet, by writing works of his own, after he had acquired fame by an ode[53] that was the joint production[54] of several others. One would have thought his speeches had as different an origin; sometimes nothing finer, generally nothing more crowded with absurdities.

At this time all was faction, and splitting into little factions. The Pelhams were ill with one another, and ill with the Bedfords. The latter Duke would have set up Fox against Mr. Pelham; and the former Duke[55] was countenancing Pitt against all. Mr. Pelham supported Pitt and his clan against the Duke of Cumberland, who was united with the Bedfords. The Prince's Court, composed of the refuse of every party, was divided into twenty small ones. Lord Egmont at the head of one, Nugent of another, consisting of himself and two more, Lady Middlesex and Doddington of a third, the chief ornament of which was the Earl of Bute, a Scotchman, who, having no estate, had passed his youth in studying mathematics and mechanics in his own little island, then simples in the hedges about Twickenham, and at five and thirty had fallen in love with his own figure, which he produced at masquerades in becoming dresses, and in plays which he acted in private companies with a set of his own relations. He

---

[52] Robert Nugent, bred a Roman Catholic, had turned Protestant, and not long after married Mrs. Knight, sister and daughter to the two Craggs's.

[53] It was addressed to Lord Bath upon the author's change of his religion; but was universally believed to be written by Mallet, who was tutor to Newsham, Mrs. Nugent's son, and improved by Mr. Pulteney himself and Lord Chesterfield.

[54] Had this ode been really his own, he would resemble the poet Tynnichus in Plato's Io, "who never composed any other poem worth the mention or remembrance, besides that poem which everybody sings."—See Sydenham's Translat. p. 49.

[55] The Duke of Newcastle included in the word "Pelhams."—E.

became a personal favourite of the Prince, and was so lucky just now as to give up a pension to be one of the Lords of his Bedchamber. The Jacobites had quarrelled at Oxford on the choice of a member, and would not join with the Prince, who courted them. Lord Granville, Lord Chesterfield, and Lord Winchelsea, were each separately courted by the Duke of Newcastle, and Lord Oxford by Mr. Pelham, who at the same time was making new connections, trying to preserve the old ones, adopting his brother's jealousies, and yet threatening to resign on account of them. He had once solemnly declared in the House of Commons, that he would retire from business as soon as the rebellion should be extinguished. When the Duke of Grafton was told of this vow, he said, "God, I hope my friend will see the rebellion twinkle a good while yet in the Highlands!"

22d.—Sir Hugh Dalrymple moved for Mr. Golding (apothecary to the Prince of Wales) to have leave to attend Murray, being used to bleed him, which, as his veins laid low, was difficult for any other person to do. Mr. Pelham observed on the impropriety of this, as the doctor and apothecary were to appear on Monday. Mr. Fox said, he had heard that they would report he was very well, and proposed that the House should name a surgeon. It was at last agreed that Golding should go to bleed him, but should not be called for any account of his health.

Mr. Pelham, in the committee, opened the subsidy of forty thousand pounds a year to be paid to Bavaria for six years, twenty by England, and ten each by the Empress-queen and Holland. Martin made a speech of great wit against it, Lyttleton a learned one, and Murray, Solicitor-General, a very masterly one for it. It was obvious that the latter, not Mr. Pelham, had been instructed in the true secret of this negotiation by his friend Stone, secretary to the Duke of Newcastle. They had been bred at Christ Church together, and had tasted of the politics of Oxford as well as of its erudition. Sir Robert Walpole, on quitting the Ministry, had cautioned Mr. Pelham against Stone, having touched upon the scent of some of his intrigues, as he was hunting after Jacobite cabals. Mr. Pelham neglected the advice, as he had before rejected the offer of having Sir Robert's clue of secret intelligence put into his hands. He would scarce have found either Stone's or Murray's name there from this time; they were converted by their own interest,[56] a conviction preferable to all detection. Lord Egmont spoke ill, and owned it was rather a right than a wrong measure; and was answered by Pitt in a good but too general a speech. Between seven and eight the House divided, but the majority for the subsidy appearing very great, it was given up without telling. This treaty with some others was calculated to purchase a majority of votes to choose the Archduke King of the Romans, but France and Prussia defeated the scheme: our Ministry could not buy off their opposition, as they bought off opponents at home, and they knew no other art of baffling an enemy.

25th.—The Bavarian Subsidy was debated on the report, and carried by 194 to 77. Then Dr. Lamont was called in and asked several questions about Murray's health. He said he had found him with a cold and a fever, of which he was so well recovered this day se'nnight, that he had since visited him only every other day; but that going to Newgate on Saturday, he had found him with the cramp in his stomach, to which he had been subject these seven years, and of which his sister expected he would have died the day before: that he thought close confinement, without riding, dangerous for him: that he had advised him to petition the House for his liberty, though he had heard nobody else give him the same advice; but that Mr. Murray had replied in a passion, "he would take his prescriptions, but not his counsel." Sir William Yonge then moved to restrain everybody but the Physician, Apothecary, and Nurse from visiting him, which being opposed, particularly by Lord Egmont, who reflected on the want of precedents, the Speaker made a warm and solemn speech for the honour of the House, instanced in the Earl of Shaftesbury and others, who had knelt to receive the reprimand of the House of Lords, and said that the want of a precedent of such behaviour as Murray's did but conclude more strongly against him. Sydenham, a mad High-Church zealot, taking notice of some epithets the Speaker had used on Murray, was interrupted by him, saying, "I called him high-spirited too; if he had been only wrong-headed, I should have forgiven him." The restriction was voted by 166 to 81.

---

[56] Yet it was remarkable that Dr. Gally, the Minister of his parish, could never get admitted to Murray, when he was collecting subscriptions against the Rebellion, though he went several times to his house at all hours.

Chapter 2

The same day, Lord Chesterfield brought a Bill into the House of Lords for reforming our Style according to the Gregorean account, which had not yet been admitted in England, as if it were matter of heresy to receive a Kalendar amended by a Pope. He was seconded by Lord Macclesfield, a mathematical Lord, in a speech soon after printed, and the Bill passed easily through both Houses. Lord Chesterfield had made no noise since he gave up the Seals in 1748, when he published his Apology for that resignation. It was supposed to be drawn up by Lord Marchmont, under his direction, and was very well written; but to my Lord Chesterfield's great surprise, neither his book nor his retirement produced the least consequence. From that time he had lived at White's, gaming, and pronouncing witticisms among the boys of quality.

He had early in his life announced his claim to wit, and the women believed in it. He had besides given himself out for a man of great intrigue, with as slender pretensions; yet the women believed in that too—one should have thought they had been more competent judges of merit in that particular! It was not his fault if he had not wit; nothing exceeded his efforts in that point; and though they were far from producing the wit, they at least amply yielded the applause he aimed at. He was so accustomed to see people laugh at the most trifling things he said, that he would be disappointed at finding nobody smile before they knew what he was going to say. His speeches were fine, but as much laboured as his extempore sayings. His writings were—everybody's: that is, whatever came out good was given to him, and he was too humble ever to refuse the gift. But, besides the passive enjoyment of all good productions in the present age, he had another art of reputation, which was, either to disapprove the greatest authors of other times, or to patronize and commend whatever was too bad to be ascribed to himself. He did his admirers the justice to believe that they would applaud upon his authority every simple book that was published, and every bad actor that appeared upon the stage.

His first public character was Embassador to Holland, where he courted the good opinion of that economical people by losing immense sums at play. On his return he attached himself to Lord Townshend, who was then breaking with Sir Robert Walpole, and did himself no good by that connection: but what pinned down his disgrace, was the Queen's seeing him one Twelfth Night, after winning a large sum of money at hazard, cross St. James's Court, to deposit it with my Lady Suffolk till next morning:—the Queen never pardoned an intimacy there. He continued in Opposition for the remainder of Sir Robert Walpole's Ministry, and after the ineffectual motion in 1740 for removing that Minister, Lord Chesterfield was dispatched to Avignon by the party to solicit, by the Duke of Ormond's means, an order from the Pretender to the Jacobites, to concur roundly in any measure for Sir Robert's destruction: they had retired without voting on the question abovementioned. Lord Chesterfield had accepted no employment till the removal of Lord Granville, when he was sent again to Holland, and then made Lord Lieutenant of Ireland, and became the most popular Governor they ever had. Nothing was cried up but his integrity, though he would have laughed at any man who really had any confidence in his morality: and how little he repented his negotiations at Avignon would appear, if a story told of him is authentic (which I do not vouch), that being at Dublin in the height of the Rebellion, a zealous Bishop came to him one morning before he was out of bed, and told him he had great grounds to believe the Jacobites were going to rise. The Lord Lieutenant coolly looked at his watch, and replied, "I fancy they are, my Lord, for it is nine o'clock."

He had married the Duchess of Kendal's niece,[57] designing to become heir to her aunt, but had not the address to succeed; yet, miscarrying with the late King's mistress, he was rewarded by old Marlborough among the rest of the legatees,[58] whom she had selected for the prejudice they had done to the Royal Family. She was scarce cold before he returned to the King's service. In short, my Lord Chesterfield's being the instrument to introduce this new era into our computation of time will probably preserve his name in almanacs and chronologies, when the wit that he had but laboured too much, and the gallantry that he could scarce ever execute, will be no more remembered.

---

[57] Melusina Schulemburgh, Countess of Walsingham.
[58] She left £20,000 to Lord Chesterfield, and £10,000 to William Pitt.

Chapter 2

26th, 27th.—The Mutiny Bill was finished. Sir Henry Erskine declared he should postpone till next year the offer of several more clauses and amendments.

28th.—The Naturalization Bill was read a second time. Petitions for it had been presented from Bristol and Liverpool; and this day Mr. Nugent presented another from one hundred and forty-two very considerable Merchants of London. Mr. Sydenham desired to have the names read, that it might appear many of them were Foreigners. Nugent observed, that it was evident from thence that men of all denominations were for it; and Sir William Yonge, that Foreigners already composed a very serviceable and considerable part of our Merchants. Sir John Barnard spoke an hour and a half against the commitment, and then stalked away to dinner, according to his custom, without deigning to wait for any reply. To every body's surprise, Mr. Pelham declared for the Bill, said he had always approved the principle of it, but had formerly feared its raising disturbances; but that finding no reason to apprehend that consequence now, since our trading cities concurred in petitioning for it; that we were daily in want of recruits for Nova Scotia, and to repair our losses by the war; and having last year received applications from Spitalfields for encouragement of Foreign hands and materials, and having actually encouraged the importation of the latter, he hoped we should, and he would now vote for encouraging the former. On Mr. Pelham's having formerly offended the Whigs by opposing this scheme, the Duke of Bedford, trusting to his adhering to the same style, had eagerly taken up the protection of this Bill, and privately made great interest to carry it through. Mr. Pelham discovered this, and turned short, and carried it for the commitment. The Duke of Bedford's faction being thus baffled, made a shorter turn, kept away, and the Bill was lost at last. Mr. Fox, who had formerly at Mr. Pelham's desire spoken against the Bill, stuck to his former vote, at the same time showing that he approved the Bill, though he said he doubted if it would have any effect. Pitt spoke immediately after Fox for the Bill; and it was committed by a majority of 146 to 81, three only of the Whigs adhering with Mr. Fox to their former vote. The House sat till past nine.

Chapter 3

March 4.—George Townshend moved to have all papers relating to Courts Martial during General Anstruther's government of Minorca laid before the House, and complained of his still keeping his regiment, though he had been found guilty by the Privy Council. Sir Harry Erskine again disclaimed revenge, but, with heaping new aggravations, said he had still more in reserve to urge against him; defied any retaliation on his uncle St. Clair, and affirmed that partialities had lately been exercised towards the Scotch—not favourable ones. Mr. Pelham replied to this; said he knew little of military promotions, but could observe from the Newspapers, that there were at least as many Erskines and Dalrymples preferred as of any English name; that he disliked proceeding parliamentarily in this business, but would engage to have Anstruther tried by a Court Martial. Mr. Pitt gave strongly into a Parliamentary Inquiry. Mr. Fox was as warm against it, and said that if Sir Harry Erskine had not openly disclaimed revenge, he should have much suspected him of harbouring the bitterest, especially as Sir Harry had too much parts to have accused out of ignorance. He urged the impropriety of trying a man after an Act of Grace had passed, which that he did not mention from prejudice would appear from his having voted at Council for condemning Anstruther. The Attorney and Solicitor Generals spoke to the same point of Law. Fazakerely endeavoured to show that pardons from the Crown were not pleadable against impeachments, which were now threatened by Lord Egmont and others. The Attorney in answer showed that the Act of Grace was the act, not of the Crown singly, but of the whole Legislature. Colonel Haldane, who had been one of the warmest against Murray, talked high for inquiries, more necessary, he now said, than prosecutions on elections. Mr. Conway temporized, proposed a middle way; the House was going to divide, when Mr. Fox moved for some fewer papers that would serve the purpose, and that Sir Harry Erskine might have two days to prepare a charge in form; but desired it might be delivered in before the papers in question were brought, that they might not be assisting to the composition. The House sat till past nine without dividing.

5th.—George Townshend presented a vehement petition from one Don Juan Compagni, a Minorchese, who had been barbarously treated by Anstruther; had had his sentences reversed by the Council here; but having run in debt while he attended the event of his suit, had applied without success to the Treasury for money to carry on the prosecution: this was the scope too of the petition, though Mr. Townshend said it was only presented to be in the eye of the House when the other trial should come on, and moved to have it lie upon the table. Mr. Pelham owned he had refused money from the Treasury, and observed upon the impropriety of suffering such petitions, as it would encourage the like from all our Governments and Plantations: that for his part he would not oppose it, unless somebody else did, and then he should be for rejecting it. Lord Duplin and Harding spoke against the want of order in it, as the accused was a member, as the petition would appear at length in the votes, a heavy accusation! and as the money must be granted without hearing either the cause or the defendant; or if heard, you might find a crime, and could not find a punishment.

Mr. Pitt spoke warmly for the petition, on the fitness of granting two or three thousand pounds to a poor man oppressed by military law, and of so good a family as the Compagnis, (so deeply was Mr. Pitt versed in Minorchese genealogies!) and declared he would support such a cause to the last drop of his blood. Mr. Fox ridiculed this warmth; observed how little foundation there was for believing the allegations of the petition, and then said he discovered much persecution in this affair; that good men would join in the persecution if they thought Anstruther guilty; others would, because he had been guilty of what he did not think bad (the vote on Porteous's case); and that it was Anstruther-guilt, as much as the guilt of the Governor, that had blown up this vengeance; and then he moved for rejecting the petition, or for the Orders of the Day. Pitt disclaimed warmth, but with so much coolness and endeavours to be cool, that it only proved him more angry. Colonel Haldane defended the Scotch; Oswald still more, and called on Fox to charge them. Mr. Fox said he scorned prudence when it was honesty to speak out; urged the notoriety of the national inveteracy to the General, to a degree, that a petition on a contested election having been presented against him soon after his vote of offence, all the Scotch members had to a man voted against him; and said, that as he himself had been warm on the affair of Porteous's murder, a Scotch General Officer had told him at the time, "young man, this will never be forgiven you."

This pique created a constant opposition between Fox and Oswald, a man who was master of a quickness and strength of argument, not inferior to Fox, or any speaker in the House. The rapidity of his eloquence was astonishing; not adorned, but confined to business. He had come into Parliament about the time of Sir Robert Walpole's fall, and had consulted a friend, whether the Minister or the Opposition were likely to prevail. His friend recommended him to the former; his own sagacity conducted him to the latter, which being soon after victorious, he reproached his friend with the scrape into which he had near drawn him. On the change he was made a Commissioner of the Navy, which he resigned on the New Place Bill, to keep his seat; but wavering in his connections, had no new preferment. Mr. Conway spoke for the Orders of the Day; but asking if the intention was to hear the cause, and Pitt telling him it was, he then spoke and voted for the petition. Lord Egmont made a very fine and inflammatory speech for it, and said the nation would so much resent its being rejected, that no man who voted for the rejection would dare to show his face. Mr. Pelham took this up, said he would serve the King and his line faithfully, in place and out of place too, without opposing from resentment, and then should always dare to show his face anywhere. Pitt then endeavoured to prevent a division, but was disregarded; and towards seven o'clock it was carried by 97 to 58 for reading the Orders of the Day. Lord Ankram, Carneguy, Hope Weir, and M'Cleod, voting in the majority, and no English Whigs but Pitt, Conway, and the three Grenvilles in the minority. When the House was up,

Pitt, in a dispute with Mr. Pelham, defended parliamentary inquiries, and said, "he would never consent to lop the bough on which he stood."

The King asked Mr. Fox "with whom it was that Pitt meant to ingratiate himself? was it with Lord Egmont?" and he told the Duke of Bedford that he would not, even if addressed by the House, take away Anstruther's regiment, who had got his favour by the vote that had so much offended his countrymen. The General, after that vote, had been obliged on his return to Scotland, to pass in disguise to his own estate, and crossing a firth, he said to the waterman, "This is a pretty boat; I fancy you sometimes smuggle with it." The fellow replied, "I never smuggled a Brigadier before."

Pitt's behaviour, who at this time had the chief influence with the Duke of Newcastle, had extremely offended both the King and the Whigs. The tide of popularity was running with the Duke of Bedford and Mr. Fox; and without the great event[59] that soon after happened, possibly the charm might have been broken, that held a whole nation enchanted to such phantoms, either of honesty or abilities as the two Pelhams.

The 7th was appointed for the Naturalization Bill, but the House adjourned to attend at Drury-lane, where Othello was acted by a Mr. Delaval and his family, who had hired the theatre on purpose. The crowd of people of fashion was so great, that the Footman's Gallery was hung with blue ribbands.

8th.—The Bill was read in the Committee. Mr. Fox spoke against it, but said he was open to conviction. Mr. Pelham mentioned the forfeited estates in Scotland, which might be improved by a colony of Foreigners. Mr. Fox declared himself convinced by this argument. Pitt ridiculed Fox's conviction, and did it well. The Bill was carried in the Committee by 123 to 52. While Pitt was speaking, Fox said to one who sat next to him, "He is a better speaker than I am; but, thank God, I have more judgment!"

Lord Halifax had been soliciting to have a fifty and a sixty gun ship sent to Nova-Scotia, upon a report that the French were sending a fleet thither: the Admiralty had refused, for fear of drawing on a new war. The

---

[59] The death of the Prince.

Board of Trade presented a long Memorial to promote their demand, which the Duke of Bedford carried to the King; the Duke of Newcastle was present, but said not a word. The Duke of Bedford said to the King, "Sir, this paper is too long for your Majesty to read, but I will tell you the purport of it: it is a project of the same faction, who have endeavoured to increase the Navy this year: I have desired your Majesty's servants to meet at my House next Wednesday; I believe they will not think it proper to come into this proposal." "No," replied the King, "they are the most troublesome, impracticable fellows I ever met with; there is no carrying on the measures of Government with them." Mr. Pelham wrote the Duke of Bedford word, on his summons, that he would wait upon him, but did not believe[60] he should think Lord Halifax's proposal fit to be complied with.

11th.—A proposal came from the South Sea Company for lowering their interest after a term of seven years. Mr. Pelham moved to accept it, provided they gave up all demands on the King of Spain. Belchier desired time till the next General Court; but the resolution passed.

Lord Duplin[61], who, considering how fond he was of forms and trifles and being busy, was not absolutely a bad speaker, opened in a long deduction the affairs of Nova-Scotia, and moved for a sum of money for carrying on that new Colony, the establishment of which had been eagerly revived by Lord Halifax on his coming to the head of the Board of Trade, and his friend Colonel Cornwallis[62], sent thither as Governor, who was a brave, sensible young man, and of great temper and good-nature. Vyner alone opposed the Motion; the Opposition favoured it, and Th. Pitt spoke much against ever giving up that Colony to France.

Sir Henry Erskine then presented his charge against General Anstruther, which he called only a state of his own case. It was very trifling in comparison of what had been expected from the parade of his first accusation; his grievances barely comprized in a confinement of six weeks before and during his trial, and of a few days after it. George Townshend moved to address for the proceedings of that Court-Martial.

---

[60] Yet, as it will appear afterwards, Mr. Pelham supported the demand of the Board of Trade against the Duke of Bedford.
[61] Thomas Hay, eldest son of George, Earl of Kinnoul, one of the Lords of Trade.
[62] Edward, brother to Lord Cornwallis, and Groom of the Bedchamber to the King.

Mr. Pitt desired there might be no Motion till the House came to some determination how to proceed. Mr. Fox read a letter from Anstruther, to say that he was laid up with the rheumatism, but would attend as soon as possible, and would send in an answer to the charge. It was agreed to send him a copy of what they were in doubt whether to call a charge, or a complaint, or simply a paper. Mr. Fox called upon Erskine to prove the accusation, which he said he was ready to do. Fox then said, that General Anstruther desired to inform the House that he had the copy of the Court-Martial in his own possession, and would send it whenever they pleased; though it was not necessary to preserve sentences of acquittals, nor were they ever sent to the War-office. Notwithstanding this voluntary offer, the House sat debating for two hours on the method of coming at this copy, and whether they should address the King, or order Anstruther to send it by their own authority. Joddrell, the Prince's Solicitor, flamed, and Lord Egmont still more, on this notice of records of Courts-Martial not being preserved. The House sat till eight, but came to no division.

10th.—The King would not go to Chapel, because Secker, Bishop of Oxford, was to preach before him. The Ministers did not insist upon his hearing the sermon, as they had lately upon his making him Dean of St. Paul's. Character and popularity do not always depend upon the circumstances that ought to compose either. This Bishop, who had been bred a Presbyterian and Man-midwife, which sect and profession he had dropt for a season, while he was President of a very free thinking club,[63] had been converted by Bishop Talbot,[64] whose relation he married, and his faith settled in a Prebend of Durham: from thence he was transplanted, at the recommendation of Dr. Bland,[65] by the Queen, and advanced by her [who had no aversion to a medley of religions, which she always compounded into a scheme of heresy of her own], to the living of St. James's, vacant by the death of her favourite Arian, Dr. Clarke, and

---

[63] Here is my evidence. Mr. Robyns said he had known him an atheist, and had advised him against talking so openly in coffee-houses. Mr. Stevens, a Mathematician, who lives much in the house with Earl Powlett, says, Secker made him an atheist at Leyden, where the club was established.
[64] Bishop of Durham, father to Lord Chancellor Talbot.
[65] Dr. Henry Bland, Dean of Durham and Provost of Eton, a great favourite of Sir Robert Walpole.

afterwards to the Bishoprics of Bristol and Oxford.[66] It is incredible how popular he grew in his parish, and how much some of his former qualifications contributed to heighten his present doctrines. His discourses from the pulpit, which, by a fashion that he introduced, were a kind of moral essays, were as clear from quotations of Scripture, as when he presided in a less Christian society; but what they wanted of Gospel, was made up by a tone of fanaticism that he still retained. He had made a match between a daughter of the late Duke of Kent[67] and a Doctor Gregory, whose talents would have been extremely thrown away in any priesthood, where celibacy was one of the injunctions. He had been presented with a noble service of plate for procuring a marriage between the heiress[68] of the same Duke of Kent and the Chancellor's son, and was now forced upon the King[69] by the gratitude of the same Minister, though he had long been in disgrace for having laid his plan for Canterbury in the interest he had cultivated at the Prince's Court. But even the Church had its renegades in politics, and the King was obliged to fling open his asylum to all kind of deserters; content with not speaking to them at his levee, or listening to them in the pulpit!

12th.—Potter produced several Physicians and Masters of Workhouses to prove the fatal consequences of spirituous liquors, which laid waste the meaner parts of the town, and were now spreading into the country. Sir Joseph Jekyll had formerly carried through a Bill against Gin, but with such danger from the populace, that the Act had been established merely by military force, and with little success, as informers against the retailers of it had seldom escaped the vengeance of the mob. Mr. Sandys,[70] on succeeding Sir Robert Walpole, had repealed this Act to increase the Revenue; but being one of the acts of his short reign, to which he had risen by deserting his party, he was as ill-treated by the faction as the prohibition

---

[66] He was nominated to the Archbishopric of Canterbury, March 28, 1758.
[67] Lady Mary Grey.
[68] Annabella, daughter of the Lord Glenorchy, by the eldest daughter of Henry, the last Duke of Kent. On this match with the Chancellor's son, she was created Marchioness de Grey.
[69] He was made Dean of St. Paul's by the Chancellor's interest about this time.
[70] Samuel Sandys, a republican opposer of the Court, was made Chancellor of the Exchequer, in the room of Sir Robert Walpole, in 1742, but was turned out in less than two years, and made Cofferer and a Baron, and entirely laid aside on the disgrace of Lord Granville.

had been by the lower people. Lord Hervey,[71] who had turned patriot at that season on being turned out of place, had made three remarkably fine orations against the repeal; and Sir Charles Williams had made a couple of ballads[72] with much wit, to ridicule both Sandys and Lord Hervey. Mr. Pelham spoke now against the appearance of the Physicians, &c. as he believed no remedy could be found for the evil, and yet imposing new duties would greatly diminish the Revenue: but they were examined.

18th.—Mr. Fox acquainted the House that Mr. Moncrief attended without, who was called in, and delivered the original copy of the Court-Martial from General Anstruther; and (as he was not able to come in person, being above seventy, and laid up with a rheumatism and pain in his bowels) an answer to Sir Henry Erskine's complaint, in which he acknowledged the facts, but denied the aggravating circumstances. That day se'nnight was appointed to consider the charge and answer, and the Minutes of the Council; after Sir Harry Erskine had declared he would say no more, though if he chanced to prove more, it would be but the more conspicuous: to which Mr. Fox replied, that it would be fairer to acquaint Anstruther with that *more*. Mr. Fox then moved, at Anstruther's desire, for a copy of a Resolution of Council against Colonel Pinfold, a former Governor of Minorca, who had been condemned to make satisfaction to the oppressed parties, and had. Anstruther would have done the like, but was prevented.

The Prince was dangerously ill.

19th.—The Council, which had been postponed, was held at Bedford-house, whither the Duke of Newcastle would have carried Lord Halifax and Lord Anson, but the Duke of Bedford refused to admit them. It was proposed to hear the whole Board of Trade upon their Memorial; but the Duke of Bedford said, that this proposal of stationing two men of war at Nova Scotia, upon the notion of a French fleet going thither, had not been mentioned in a long letter that he had received from that Board in January

---

[71] John, Lord Hervey, eldest son to the Earl of Bristol, was removed from the post of Lord Privy Seal, to make way for Lord Gower, in 1742, and took the place in Opposition which Lord Gower had left.

[72] One of them was printed; the subject, Jekyll's Ghost appearing to Sandys, in imitation of William and Margaret: the other was the same Ghost appearing to Lord Hervey.

last, since which period there had been no letters from Governor Cornwallis. Nobody agreed with the Duke but Lord Sandwich, not even his father-in-law, Lord Gower, who had been with him an hour before the rest arrived, and said to him, "Now we have caught Lord Halifax in a trap;" (but he himself was intangled in Mr. Pelham's snares, and did not know it!) nor the Duke of Marlborough, though his friend and brother-in-law, and though his connection with Mr. Fox had made the Duke of Bedford flatter himself with his support: but both the Duke and Lord Sandwich were too sanguine about Mr. Fox, who had declared to them, that if it came to a rupture, he must adhere to Mr. Pelham. He had repeated this to Lord Sandwich in the summer, when commissioned by him to carry a reconciling message to Mr. Pelham. Mr. Fox had made the same declaration of his unavoidable connection with Mr. Pelham to the Duke of Cumberland: but the Duke of Bedford was not only apt to forget what he did not care to hear, and even to forget his own change of opinion, but would and did often believe the very reverse. He told the two brothers that this was designed as a hostile measure against him, which they then denied.

20th.—Potter[73] opened in an able manner his scheme for an additional duty of two shillings on spirits, to be collected by way of Excise. He was a young man of the greatest goodnature, though he had set out with two of the severest speeches[74] that ever were made against the Ministry and the Grenvilles, and with the greatest applause; but his goodnature had kept up

---

[73] Thomas Potter, second son to the late Archbishop of Canterbury, and Secretary to the Princess of Wales.
On Sunday, June 17, 1759, died Thomas Potter, Esq., joint Vice-Treasurer of Ireland, Principal Registrar of the province of Canterbury, Recorder of the city of Bath, and member in the present Parliament for Okehampton in Devonshire.—(Public Journals.)

[74] The first was on a petition for setting aside Mr. W. Pitt's election at Seaforth, where the Duke of Newcastle had appeared at the poll, contrary to the resolution of the House of Commons against Peers interfering in elections. It was printed in the London Magazine, and old Horace Walpole published a letter to him upon it. The other speech was on the famous bill for removing the Assizes from Aylesbury to Buckingham, on a contest between the Lord Chief Justice Willes and the Grenvilles. Potter talking upon his plan for suppressing Gin, told a near relation of Sir Robert Walpole, that he would imitate that Minister, and expose himself to all the unpopularity of the Excise Scheme. When Mr. Fox was told of this speech, he said it put him in mind of Sir Godfrey Kneller, who, when his gardener was cursing himself, said to him, "God d—n *you!* God d—ns Kings and Princes and great men; God no d—n such poor fellows as you."

to its character much more than his parts. He was not bashful nor void of vanity, and had now flattered himself that he should figure like Sir Robert Walpole by attempting to re-establish the defeated Excise Scheme; not reflecting that the opposition to that project was levelled at the Minister, not occasioned by the pretended inconveniences and dangers of it. Mr. Pelham spoke greatly against it, and for suppressing unlicensed houses, and for a visitation by parish officers. He was seconded by the Solicitor General. Alderman Baker, a man rather busy and confident than very able, fluctuated between both schemes: but Mr. Pelham desiring a respite till the morrow se'nnight for further deliberation, it was agreed to.

The Prince of Wales had been ill of a pleurisy, but was so well recovered as to attend the King to the House of Lords on the 12th, where he was very hot. He went to Carlton-house to unrobe, put on only a light frock, and went to Kew, where he walked some time, and returning to Carlton-house, laid down upon a couch for three hours in a ground room next to the garden, caught a fresh cold, and relapsed that night. He had had a blow upon his stomach in the summer by a fall, from which he had often felt great pains. Dr. Wilmot, Taylor, and Leigh attended him, and Hawkins the Surgeon. On Monday, 18th, a thrush appeared; however, he was thought better. On Wednesday night, between nine and ten o'clock, Wilmot and Hawkins were with him; he had a fit of coughing. Wilmot said, "Sir, you have brought up all the phlegm; I hope this will be over in a quarter of an hour, and that your Royal Highness will have a good night." Hawkins went out of the room, and said, "Here is something I don't like." The cough continued; the Prince laid his hand upon his stomach, and said, "*Je sens la mort.*" Pavonarius, his favourite German valet-de-chambre, who was holding him up, felt him shiver, and cried, "Good God! the Prince is going!" The Princess, who was at the feet of the bed, snatched up a candle, but before she got to him, he was dead! An imposthume had broken, which, on his body being opened, the Physicians were of opinion had not been occasioned by the fall, but from a blow of a tennis-ball three years before.

Thus died Frederick Prince of Wales! having resembled his pattern the Black Prince in nothing but in dying before his father. Indeed it was not his fault if he had not distinguished himself by any warlike achievements. He had solicited the command of the Army in Scotland during the last Rebellion; though that ambition was ascribed rather to his jealousy of his brother than to his courage. A hard judgment! for what he could he did! When the Royal Army lay before Carlisle, the Prince, at a great supper that he gave to his Court and his favourites, as was his custom when the Princess laid in, had ordered for the dessert the representation of the citadel of Carlisle in paste, which he in person, and the Maids of Honour, bombarded with sugar plums! He had disagreed with the King and Queen early after his coming to England; not entirely by his own fault. The King had refused to pay what debts he had left at Hanover; and it ran a little in the blood of the family to hate the eldest son: the Prince himself had so far not degenerated, though a better natured man, and a much better father, as to be fondest of his second son, Prince Edward. The Queen had exerted more authority, joined to a narrow prying into his conduct, than he liked; and Princess Emily, who had been admitted into his greatest confidence, had not forfeited her duty to the Queen by concealing any of his secrets that might do him prejudice.

Lord Bolingbroke, who had sowed a division in the Pretender's Court, by the scheme for the father's resigning his claim to the eldest boy, repeated the same plan of discord here, on the first notice of the Prince's disgusts; and the whole Opposition was instructed to offer their services to the Heir Apparent against the Crown and the Minister. The Prince was sensible to flattery, and had a sort of parts that made him relish the sort of parts of Lord Chesterfield, Doddington, and Lyttelton, the latter of whom being introduced by Doddington, had wrought the disgrace of his protector. Whoever was unwelcome at St. James's was sure of countenance at the Prince's apartments there. He was in vain reprimanded for this want of respect. At last, having hurried the Princess from Hampton Court, when she was in actual labour, to the imminent danger of hers and the child's life,[75] without acquainting either King or Queen, the formal breach ensued;

---

[75] It was (Lady Augusta) the eldest, "afterwards Duchess of Brunswick." As it was necessary to have the Privy Councillors present at the birth of an Heir-Apparent to the Crown, which was prevented by this rash step, the Prince sent messengers, as he was upon the road, to

he having added to this insult, a total silence to his mother on her arriving immediately to visit the Princess, and while he led her to her coach; but as soon as he came in sight of the populace, he knelt down in the dirt and kissed her hand with the most respectful show of duty. He immediately went all lengths of opposition and popularity till the fall of Sir Robert Walpole, when he was reconciled to, though never after spoken to, by the King.

On Lord Granville's disgrace, he again grew out of humour; but after having been betrayed and deserted by all he had obliged, he did not erect a new standard of opposition, till the Pelhams had bought off every man of any genius that might have promoted his views. Indeed, his attachment to his followers was not stronger than theirs to him. Being angry with Lord Doneraile[76] for not speaking oftener in the House of Commons, he said, "Does he think I will support him, unless he does as I would have him? Does not he consider that whoever are my Ministers, I must be King?" His chief passion was women, but like the rest of his race, beauty was not a necessary ingredient. Miss ****, whom he had debauched without loving, and who had been debauched without loving him so well as either Lord Harrington or Lord Hervey, who both pretended to her first favours, had no other charms than of being a Maid of Honour, who was willing to cease to be so upon the first opportunity.

Chiswick and Lambeth, to fetch Lord Wilmington and the Archbishop of Canterbury; but they arrived too late. The Princess was put into a bed that had not been prepared, for which the Prince and Lady Archibald Hamilton were forced to air the sheets. The Queen followed them early in the morning, and asked Lady Archibald, "how she dared to bring away the Princess in that manner?" who turned to the Prince, and said, "You see, Sir, I told you it would be laid upon me."

[76] Arthur St. Leger, Lord Viscount Doneraile, Lord of the Bedchamber to the Prince, died of a consumption at Lisbon in 1750. He was a young man of great parts, but of no steadiness in courage, conduct, or principles. He made a celebrated speech against the Pelhams, on the affair of the sixteen new regiments that were to be raised by some Noblemen during the Rebellion. These Lords had offered to raise them at their own expense, but made a notorious job of it, at the same time that the Earl of Kildare, who really meant it, was not permitted, as Lord Doneraile by his authority acquainted the House of Commons, and concluded with saying, that "the Ministry were either too weak to do a right thing, or too good-natured to refuse a wrong one."

One of his favourites, Lady Archibald Hamilton[77] had been neither young nor handsome within his memory. Lady Middlesex[78] was very short, very plain, and very yellow: a vain girl, full of Greek and Latin, and music, and painting, but neither mischievous nor political. Lady Archibald was very agreeable and artful, but had lost his heart, by giving him William Pitt for a rival. But though these mistresses were pretty much declared, he was a good husband, and the quiet inoffensive good sense of the Princess (who had never said a foolish thing, or done a disobliging one since her arrival, though in very difficult situations, young, uninstructed, and besieged by the Queen, Princess Emily, and Lady Archibald's creatures, and very jarring interests), was likely to have always preserved a chief ascendant over him.

Gaming was another of his passions, but his style of play did him less honour than the amusement. He carried this dexterity[79] into practice in more essential commerce, and was vain of it! One day at Kensington that he had just borrowed five thousand pounds of Doddington, seeing him pass under his window, he said to Hedges[80] his Secretary, "That man is reckoned one of the most sensible men in England, yet with all his parts, I have just nicked him out of five thousand pounds." He was really childish, affectedly a protector of arts and sciences, fond of displaying what he knew: a mimic, the Lord knows what a mimic!—of the celebrated Duke of

---

[77] Jane, daughter to Lord Abercorn, and wife of Lord Archibald Hamilton, was Mistress of the Robes to the Princess of Wales, and for some years governed absolutely at the Prince's Court. She had contrived to have the Princess told, before her arrival in England, that Lady **** was his mistress, to divert any suspicions from herself; and had planted so many of her own relations about her, that one day at Carlton-house, Sir William Stanhope called everybody there whom he did not know, *Mr. or Mrs. Hamilton*. Lady Archibald quitted that Court soon after Mr. Pitt accepted a place in the Administration.

[78] Grace, daughter to the Lord Viscount Shannon, and wife of Charles Sackville, Earl of Middlesex, Master of the Horse to the Prince. She succeeded Lady Archibald Hamilton as Mistress of the Robes.

[79] The following remarkable anecdote was told me by Mr. Fox, who said the King himself told it him, and that the late Lord Hervey had told him the same particular from the Queen. One day, when the Prince was but a boy, his Governor was complaining of him: the Queen, whose way (as the King said) was to excuse him, said, "*Ah! je m'imagine que ces sont des tours de page.*" The Governor replied, "*Plût à Dieu, madame, que ces fûssent des tours de page! ces sont des tours de laquais et de coquins.*"

[80] Charles Hedges had been Minister at Turin, and was Secretary to the Prince. He was a man much in fashion, and a pretty Latin poet.

Orleans, in imitation of whom he wrote two or three silly French songs.[81] His best quality was generosity; his worst, insincerity, and indifference to truth, which appeared so early, that Earl Stanhope wrote to Lord Sunderland from Hanover, what I shall conclude his character with, "He has his father's head, and his mother's heart."

The Princess staid four hours in the room after he was dead, before she could be quite convinced of it. At six in the morning they put her to bed; but she rose again at eight, and sent for Dr. Lee, and burnt, or said she burnt, all the Prince's papers. As soon as he was dead, Lord North was sent to notify it to the King, who was playing at cards. He immediately went down to Lady Yarmouth, looking extremely pale and shocked, and only said, "*Il est mort!*" He sent a very kind message to the Princess, and another the next morning in writing by the Lord in Waiting, Lord Lincoln. She received him alone, sitting with her eyes fixed; thanked the King much, and said she would write as soon as she was able; in the meantime, recommended her miserable self and children to him.

The King and she both took their parts at once; she, of flinging herself entirely into his hands, and studying nothing but his pleasure, but with winding what interest she got with him to the advantage of her own and the Prince's friends: the King of acting the tender grandfather; which he, who had never acted the tender father, grew so pleased with representing, that he soon became it in earnest. When he was called the morning after the Prince's death, they found him drest, walking about his room, and extremely silent. Princess Emily, who had no great reason to flatter herself with much favour if her brother had lived to be King, sent immediately for the Duke from Windsor, who, on receiving the news, said to Lord Sandwich with a sneer, "It is a great blow to this country, but I hope it will recover it in time!" He little thought that himself was to receive the greatest shock from it! He sent a compliment by Lord Cathcart to Prince George, who cried extremely. As soon as the Prince's death was published, elegies were cried about the streets, to which they added, "Oh, that it was but his brother!"[82] and upon Change and in the city, "Oh, that it was but the

---

[81] Vide the Appendix, D and E.
[82] Vide Appendix.

butcher!"[83] In short, the consternation that spread on the apprehensions that the Duke would at least be Regent on the King's death, and have the sole power in the meantime, was near as strong as what was occasioned by the notice of the Rebels being at Derby.

The Houses met the next morning, but adjourned without doing anything.

The Duke of Bedford proposed to the King to remove Dr. Ayscough from the young Princes, which he much approved, and nobody but the Cobham cousins[84] disliked, who had just patched up their peace with the Prince by his intervention. Lyttelton, whose sister he had married, solicited Mr. Pelham to save him. Mr. Pelham answered, "I know nothing of Dr. Ayscough—oh, yes, I recollect, a very worthy man told me in this room two years ago that he was a great rogue!" It was Lyttelton himself who had quarrelled with him about an election business. Ayscough, who was an insolent man, unwelcome to the Clergy on suspicions of heterodoxy, and of no fair reputation for integrity, had been placed by Lyttelton and Pitt with the Prince, into whose favour he had worked himself, chiefly by partialities to Prince Edward; and managed his Privy Purse and his election affairs. The Princess, finding that Prince George, at eleven years old, could not read English, though Ayscough, to make amends, assured her he could make Latin verses, had already introduced a new Preceptor, one Scot, recommended by Lord Bolingbroke, who had lately seen the Prince two or three times in private.

22d.—The King sent a Commission to pass the Mutiny Bill. Lord Egremont in the House of Lords, and Lord Hilsborough in the Commons, moved the Address of Condolence; and then the Lords adjourned to Wednesday, and the Commons till Monday. Lord Egremont, who was son to the great Sir William Windham, and grandson to the old Duke of Somerset, whose prodigious pride he inherited, more than his father's

---

[83] This nickname was not given in the sense it was formerly; "Le boucher etoit anciennement un surnom glorieux qu'on donnoit à un general après une victoire, en reconnoissance du carnage qu'il avoit fait de trente ou quarante mille hommes."—Essais Histor. sur Paris, de Saintfoix, tom. 2, p. 63.

[84] Sir George Lyttelton, whose sister Ayscough had married, and the three Granvilles, were nephews to Lord Cobham. W. Pitt's brother had married Lyttelton's sister.

abilities, though he had a great deal of humour, had formerly been a personal favourite with the Prince, but had slighted that intimacy when Lord Granville his patron would not co-operate in the Prince's last Opposition.

Lord Hilsborough was a young man of great honour and merit, remarkably nice in weighing whatever cause he was to vote in, and excellent at setting off his reasons, if the affair was at all tragic, by a solemnity in his voice and manner that made much impression on his hearers.

At seven o'clock of the very morning after the Prince expired, Lord Egmont sent cards to several of the Opposition, desiring them to meet at his house, to consult on the measures proper for them to take on the present conjuncture. Many of them came. He did not make any formal oration, but whispered most of them something about taking upon themselves the protection of the Princess and her children. The meeting passed in a sort of dumb confusion and uncertainty, and broke up without taking any measures at all.

An Order of Council was made to omit the name of the Prince of Wales in the prayers. As no rank was yet given to Prince George, it created murmurs. Though the House sat, nothing was done but private business. On the 26th, Colonel Haldane moved, as the Prince's servants did not yet attend the House, that Anstruther's affair might be postponed till after Easter, which was agreed to, though the General was present, and earnest to have it heard sooner.

28th.—A Council was held at the Cockpit, on the Nova-Scotia affair. They divided: the Chancellor, Mr. Pelham, the Dukes of Newcastle, Grafton, Dorset, and Argyle, were for complying with the request of the Board of Trade; the Duke of Bedford and Lord Sandwich, who had now got the Duke of Marlborough and Lord Gower on their side, against it.

The German politics went ill. What Allies we had there wanted more money. The Elector of Cologne, who had signed a treaty with the King, refused to execute it, and united with France. That Court used continual evasions with us, on the evacuation of Tobago, and the contested islands in the West Indies, and gave great disturbance to our Colony of Nova-Scotia.

In the east, they were driving us out of our Settlements; and upon the coast of Africa seizing our forts, raising others, inveigling away our Allies, and working us out of our whole Negro and Gold-Coast trade. The British Minister at Paris, Lord Albemarle,[85] was not a man to offend the haughtiness of that Court, or the pusillanimity of his own, by mixing more sturdiness with his Memorials than he was commissioned to do. It was convenient to him to be anywhere but in England: his debts were excessive, though he was Embassador, Groom of the Stole, Governor of Virginia, and Colonel of a regiment of Guards. His figure was genteel, his manner noble and agreeable: the rest of his merit, for he had not even an estate, was the interest my Lady Albemarle had with the King through Lady Yarmouth, and his son, Lord Bury, being the Duke's chief favourite. He had all his life imitated the French manners, till he came to Paris, where he never conversed with a Frenchman; not from partiality to his own countrymen, for he conversed as little with them, living entirely with a Flemish Columbine, that he had brought from the Army. If good breeding is not different from good sense, Lord Albemarle, who might have disputed even that maxim, at least knew how to distinguish it from good nature. He would bow to his postilion, while he was ruining his tailor.

31st.—The King went to see the Princess. A chair of state was placed for him, but he refused it, and sat by her on the couch, embraced, and wept with her. He would not suffer the Lady Augusta to kiss his hand, but embraced her, and gave it to her brothers, and told them, "They must be brave boys, obedient to their mother, and deserve the fortune to which they were born."

---

[85] William Anne Van Keppel, the second Earl of Albemarle.

Chapter 4

April 2d.—Mr. Cooke moved in a very thin House, and late in the day, to have Mr. Murray taken into the custody of the Serjeant at Arms, on account of his bad health. It was agreed to, and ordered that the Speaker should give permission to whomever he thought proper to visit him.

Lord Lincoln was made Auditor of the Exchequer, in the room of the Earl of Orford,[86] who was just dead. Mr. Pelham had affected to be willing to retire with this post, which is at least eight thousand pounds a year, and a sinecure for life. The King desired him not to take it himself, and that dutiful Minister obeyed; that is, he held it in the name of Lord Lincoln,[87] who was his nephew and son-in-law, adopted heir to the Duke of Newcastle, and the mimic of his fulsome fondnesses and follies, but with more honour and more pride. As the Duke, his uncle, was a political weathercock, he was a political weatherglass; his quicksilver being always up at insolence, or down at despair. Lyttelton asked to be Cofferer, if Lord Lincoln resigned it. Mr. Pelham told him that, from his and Pitt's behaviour this winter, the King would do nothing for him.

3rd.—Palmer the deputy Serjeant-at-arms, reported to the House that Dr. Lamont, who the day before had represented Murray as ill of the jail distemper, told him that the prisoner had been in a sweat, and must not be

---

[86] Robert Walpole, the second Earl of Orford, Auditor of the Exchequer, Master of the Foxhounds, Ranger of Richmond New Park, and Knight of the Bath, died in March, 1751.

[87] Henry Clinton, Earl of Lincoln, Cofferer, and one of the Lords of the Bedchamber to the King. His mother was sister to the Duke of Newcastle and Mr. Pelham; and he married Mr. Pelham's eldest daughter, and had the Duke of Newcastle's estate entailed upon him. He was created a Knight of the Garter in 1752; became Duke of Newcastle in 1768, and died 1794.

removed; besides, that there was danger of the motion causing a return of his vomiting; and that on acquainting Mr. Murray with the indulgence of the House, he replied, "He would not come out of Newgate, and that it was mean and paltry in that puppy, his brother, or any of his friends to petition for his enlargement." The House sent for Dr. Lamont, examined him again, and then voted a total revocation of the preceding indulgence.

4th.—The King went again to see the Princess, and settled with her the new Governor and Preceptors for the children. Lord North[88] had lately been entrusted with the care of Prince George, with the promise of an Earldom; an amiable worthy man, of no great genius, unless compared with his successor. The Pelhams, who had now laid a plan of perpetuating that power, which by so many accidents had dropped into their hands, determined to beset the young Prince entirely with their own creatures. Lord North was removed to make way for Lord Harcourt,[89] who wanted a Governor himself, as much as the Duke of Newcastle was likely to do by parting with Stone, who was to be the real engine of their policy, while Lord Harcourt, who was civil and sheepish, did not threaten them with traversing their scheme, or teaching the young Prince other arts than what he knew himself—hunting and drinking. Stone,[90] lately grown a personal favourite with the King during the journeys to Hanover, was a dark, proud man, very able and very mercenary. The other Preceptor was Hayter, Bishop of Norwich, a sensible, well-bred man, natural son of Blackbourn, the jolly old Archbishop of York, who had all the manners of a man of quality, though he had been a Buccaneer and was a Clergyman; but he retained nothing of his first profession except his seraglio. Lord Hartington had been offered the government of the Prince, but declined it.

The late Prince's debts, which were supposed very great, were extremely denied, and concealed as carefully as they would have been vaunted by those who had laid that foundation of their future advancement,

---

[88] Francis Lord North and Guildford, one of the Lords of the Bedchamber to the Prince; created Earl of Guildford in 1752.

[89] Simon Lord Viscount Harcourt, one of the Lords of the Bedchamber to the King; created Earl in 1751.

[90] Andrew Stone, son of a banker, private secretary to the Duke of Newcastle. His younger brother had lately been raised to the Primacy of Ireland.

if he had lived to be King. The Hanoverians, who were said to have lent him considerable sums, took care not to be the most clamorous for repayment. All who had flattered themselves with rising in his reign, by being so insignificant at present as to have no other support, were extremely disappointed at losing their only prospect. Some Peerages were still-born, more First-ministerships, and sundry regiments and inferior posts. Drax, his Secretary, who could not write his own name; Lord Baltimore, who, with a great deal of mistaken knowledge, could not spell; and Sir William Irby, the Princess's Polonius, were to be Barons. Doddington,[91] it is said, had actually kissed his hand for the reversion of a Dukedom. This man, with great knowledge of business, much wit, and great parts, had, by mere absurdity of judgment, and a disposition to finesse, thrown himself out of all estimation, and out of all the great views which his large fortune and abilities could not have failed to promote, if he had but preserved the least shadow of steadiness. He had two or three times alternately gone all lengths of flattery with Sir Robert Walpole and the Prince of Wales. The latter and he had met again at last in a necessary connection, for no party would have anything to do with either.[92]

---

[91] George Bubb Doddington had distinguished himself early in business, and was at the Court of Spain very young with Sir Paul Methuen, who left him there to sign the treaty of Madrid. He flattered Sir Robert Walpole extravagantly, and wrote that epistle to him, from whence Pope quoted the famous line, where he calls him the bard,
In power a servant, out of power a friend.
However, being refused a Peerage, the great object of his ambition, he broke with the Minister, and attached himself to the Prince of Wales, but was undermined by Lyttelton. He renewed his connexions with Sir Robert Walpole, and was made a Lord of the Treasury; but deserted him again on his decline, and contributed greatly to carry the western elections in 1741, against the Court. He continued in Opposition during Lord Granville's administration; but came into place again on the Coalition, and was Treasurer of the Navy. However, he again quitted the Court, and renewed his engagements with the Prince, and had a new place erected for him at Leicester House, that of Treasurer of the Chambers, for which, when he went to kiss hands at St. James's, the King burst out a laughing in his face. The Prince's family were exceedingly averse to receive him again amongst them, and treated him with great contempt, which made Nugent, but a little before the Prince's death, tell the Princess, that he thought, considering Doddington was united with them, that he was too ill treated there. She replied with warmth, "However the Prince himself treats him, depend upon it he can never forgive him. He knows that even since his coming this last time into his service, he has said of the Prince, *Il a une telle tête, et un tel cœur, qu'on ne peut rien faire avec lui.*"—(Vide Appendix.)

[92] On the birth-day of the Prince of Wales, in 1759, Doddington standing in the circle, the Princess passed him without speaking; the Prince just spoke to him, but affected to cough,

Lord Chief Justice Willes was designed for Chancellor. He had been raised by Sir Robert Walpole, though always brow-beaten by haughty Yorke, and hated by the Pelhams, for that very attachment to their own patron. As Willes's nature was more open, he returned their aversion with little reserve. He was not wont to disguise any of his passions. That for gaming was notorious; for women, unbounded. There was a remarkable story current of a grave person's coming to reprove the scandal he gave, and to tell him that the world talked of one of his maid servants being with child. Willes said, "What is that to me?" The monitor answered, "Oh! but they say that it is by your Lordship." "And what is that to you?" He had great quickness of wit, and a merit that would atone for many foibles, his severity to, and discouragement of that pest of society, Attorneys: hence his Court was deserted by them; and all the business they could transport, carried into the Chancery, where Yorke's filial piety would not refuse an asylum to his father's profession.

The Council forgetting that it was the Duke's birth-day, appointed the 15th for the Prince's funeral, but changed it to the 13th, when it was performed with the usual state.

Dr. Lee[93] was made Treasurer to the Princess, against the inclination of the Pelhams; but the Duke of Newcastle soon began to pay such court to

---

and walked on; the little Princes, less apprized of his history, and accustomed to see him there, talked a good deal to him. Charles Townshend, who stood behind and observed this scene, leaned forward, and in a half whisper, cried, "Doddington, you are d—d well with the youngest."

[93] It was common for the Prince, after dinner, to toast to Dr. Lee's being soon Chancellor of the Exchequer.

December 19th, 1758.—Yesterday morning, died suddenly, in his chair, at his house in St. James's-square, the Right Hon. Sir George Lee, Knight, Doctor of Laws, Dean of the Arches, Judge of the Prerogative Court of Canterbury, member of Parliament for Launceston, in Cornwall, and one of his Majesty's Most Honourable Privy Council.

Sir George Lee was the fifth son of Sir Thomas Lee, of Hartwell, in Buckinghamshire, Bart., by Alice, daughter and heir of Mr. Hopkins, of London, merchant; and youngest brother to the late Lord Chief Justice Lee. He represented the borough of Brackley in the seventh, eighth, and ninth Parliaments of Great Britain, and on the 16th of December, 1741, was elected Chairman of the Committee of Elections in the honourable House of Commons by a majority of two only against Giles Earle, Esq.; and upon the change of the Ministry in March following, was appointed a Lord of the Admiralty, which vacating his seat in Parliament, he was in July following chosen for Devizes. In the tenth Parliament he served for Leskard, in Cornwall.

him, and he to be so pleased with it, that they were satisfied. He was a man of great integrity, and had preserved it through all the late changes. His election to be Chairman of the Committee of Privileges and Elections was the first instance of Sir Robert Walpole's declining power; he had been made a Lord of the Admiralty by Lord Granville and Lord Bath, and had resigned with the former, notwithstanding great offers from his antagonists. The Prince had designed him for Chancellor of the Exchequer, a post for which he was little qualified; for though he was a speaker of great weight in Parliament, which was set off with a solemn harmonious voice, and something severe in his style, his business of civilian had confined him to too narrow a sphere for the extensive knowledge of men that is requisite to a Prime Minister.

16th.—Lord Waldegrave[94] was made Warden of the Stannaries in the room of T—— P——, a bad man; never was ill-nature so dull as his, never dullness so vain. Lord Waldegrave on the contrary, had complaisance enough to have covered folly or ill-nature, though in him it only concealed a very good understanding, and made his good-nature the less observed. He was a personal favourite of the King, who had long wished for an opportunity to serve him. Potter resigned his employment of Secretary to the Princess, which was restored to Cresset, who was her chief favourite, and related to the Royal Family by a Duchess of Zelle,[95] who had come from somewhere in the provinces of France. Scott was continued a Subpreceptor.

The Naturalization Bill was thrown out at nine o'clock at night on the third reading, by 129 to 116. The Duke of Bedford's people had staid away; the Wiltshire members, the Welsh, and the Tories to a man were against it. Pitt and Fox had again some sparring: people could not help

---

Upon the establishment of the Princess of Wales's Household, he was in April, 1751, appointed Treasurer to her Royal Highness, which he resigned in the year 1757.

In December, 1751, on the decease of Dr. John Bettesworth, he was appointed, by Archbishop Herring, Dean of the Arches, and Judge of the Prerogative Court of Canterbury, and in February following his Majesty was pleased to confer upon him the honour of Knighthood.

[94] James, Earl Waldegrave, one of the Lords of the Bedchamber.

[95] Eleonora D'Esmurs, daughter of Alexander D'Olbreuse, a private French gentleman, was married to George William, Duke of Zelle, father of Sophia Dorothea, wife of King George the First.

smiling to see Cæsar and Pompey squabbling, when they had nothing to say.

Pitt[96] was undoubtedly one of the greatest masters of ornamental eloquence. His language was amazingly fine and flowing; his voice admirable; his action most expressive; his figure genteel and commanding. Bitter satire was his forte: when he attempted ridicule, which was very seldom, he succeeded happily; when he attempted to reason, poorly. But where he chiefly shone, was in exposing his own conduct: having waded through the most notorious apostasy in politics, he treated it with an impudent confidence, that made all reflections upon him poor and spiritless, when worded by any other man. Out of the House of Commons he was far from being this shining character. His conversation was affected and unnatural, his manner not engaging, nor his talents adapted to a country, where Ministers must court, if they would be courted.

Fox,[97] with a great hesitation in his elocution, and a barrenness of expression, had conquered these impediments and the prejudices they had raised against his speaking, by a vehemence of reasoning, and closeness of argument, that beat all the orators of the time. His spirit, his steadiness, and humanity procured him strong attachments, which the more jealous he grew of Pitt, the more he cultivated. Fox always spoke to the question, Pitt

---

[96] William Pitt, younger brother of Thomas Pitt, of Boconnok, in Cornwall, was originally a Cornet of Horse, and broke by Sir R. Walpole at the time of the Excise, when his kinsman, Lord Cobham, lost his regiment for opposing that scheme. He was then made Groom of the Bedchamber to the Prince of Wales. The old Duchess of Marlborough left him ten thousand pounds, and her grandson, Mr. Spencer, entailed the Sunderland estate upon him after his own son. When Sir Robert Walpole resigned, and Mr. Pulteney was created an Earl, Mr. Pitt said, "He now knew his place in the House of Commons." He continued in Opposition, and distinguished himself greatly against the Hanover troops, and personally against Lord Granville, till the fall of that Minister. On the coalition, he pretended to desire nothing for himself; but as soon as his junto were placed in good employments, he began opposing again, till in a very short time he was made Vice Treasurer of Ireland, and was designed for Secretary at War, which the King (at the instance of Lord Bath) refusing to make him, occasioned the revolution of three days in 1746; soon after which he was made Paymaster of the Forces on the death of Mr. Winnington, the King persisting in not letting him have any place that could give him the entrée of his closet.

[97] Henry Fox, only brother to Lord Ilchester, had been bred a Tory, and was voted, upon a petition, out of one of Sir Robert Walpole's Parliaments; but being reconciled to the principles of the Court, by the friendship of his brother with Lord Hervey, to whom Mr. Fox was second in his duel with Mr. Pulteney, he was made Surveyor of the Works, and on Mr. Pelham succeeding to the head of the Treasury, Mr. Fox was made a Commissioner of that board, and was at this time Secretary at War.

to the passions: Fox, to carry the question; Pitt, to raise himself: Fox pointed out, Pitt lashed the errors of his antagonists: Pitt's talents were likely to make him soonest, Fox's to keep him First Minister longest.

17th.—The Earls of Harcourt and Hertford moved an Address of Condolence to the Princess in the House of Lords; Lord Downe in the Commons.

18th.—Lord Sussex, Lord Robert Bertie, and Lord Downe were appointed Lords of the Bedchamber to Prince George; Peachy, Digby, and Schutz, Grooms. Old John Selwyn[98] (who had succeeded to the confidence of Lord Townshend, Sir Robert Walpole, and Mr. Pelham, as they succeeded one another in power, and had already laid a foundation with Mr. Fox) was appointed Treasurer to the Prince, as he and his son were already to the Duke and Princesses. He was a shrewd silent man, humane, and reckoned very honest—he might be so—if he was, he did great honour to the cause, for he had made his court and his fortune with as much dexterity as those who reckon virtue the greatest impediment to worldly success.

Anstruther's affair came on. George Townshend moved to address the King to enforce the sentence of the Privy Council, and oblige him to make compensation to those he had oppressed and despoiled. Mitchell opposed the Motion; Pitt spoke well in behalf of it, and it was agreed to without a division; and the further consideration deferred to the Wednesday following.

Sir John Molesworth and Sir Robert Burdett, two Tory members, complained to the House of having been carried by a Constable to St. Martin's roundhouse as they were walking home, and kept there all night. At five in the morning, Carne, the High Constable, who had been very active against Lord Trentham, offered to release them on promise of their taking no revenge, which they refused. The Constable was taken into custody, and Carne too, after a short debate, the Whigs being very zealous

---

[98] He had been Aide-de-camp to the Duke of Marlborough, and a Colonel of Foot, but was obliged to sell his regiment when his Patron was disgraced. On the accession of the Hanover family, he was made Comptroller of the Customs, then Groom of the Bedchamber to the present King, Treasurer to the Queen, and on the resignation of Sir Charles Hanbury Williams, Paymaster of the Marines. He died at the end of the year 1751.

to vindicate the honour of the Tory members against a Tory High Constable. He was released the next day.

Bathurst[99] and Joddrell were continued Attorney and Solicitor to the Princess. Bathurst was an unpleasant, but sometimes a good speaker. Joddrell was a very rising man, but died soon after, and was succeeded by Henley, who was a lawyer in vogue, but his abilities did not figure in proportion to the impudence of his ill-nature. Douglas and Boone (in the room of Sir John Cust, who was soon after restored on the death of Douglas) were named to the Green Cloth, and Bloodworth had the sole direction of the Stables. The King offered the Princess a Master of the Horse, but told her it must be a Nobleman, and there was one to whom he had an objection: This was Lord Middlesex.[100] She desired none; if she had been disposed to contend, it would not have been of all men in favour of the Lord in question. His figure, which was handsome, had all the reserve of his family, and all the dignity of his ancestors. He was a poet, too, because they had been poets. As little as he came near them in this talent, it

---

[99] Henry, a younger son of Allen, Lord Bathurst.
[100] January 6, 1769.—Yesterday died at his house in St. James's Street, his Grace Charles Sackville, Duke of Dorset, in the 58th year of his age. His Grace received the first rudiments of his education at Westminster School, in which he was introduced by the late celebrated Prior, and there gave strong indication of genius. The Duke afterwards visited France and Italy, with the latter of which countries he was particularly delighted, being accompanied by the late learned and very benevolent Mr. Spence, who cherished the love which his Grace naturally bore to the Polite Arts. At his return from his travels, he encouraged learning and learned men. The Duke was honoured with the esteem and affection of the late much-lamented Prince Frederick, and it was thought that his Grace would have made a very considerable figure in the State. He was skilled not only in the learned languages, but also in the modern. He had not the talent of speaking in public, so was not distinguished in the House of Commons; but he was a fine prose writer, of which (among other pieces) his Treatise concerning the Militia is a proof. Some few printed specimens of his poetry show his happy talent for that engaging art; and especially the manuscript pieces left behind him, which, it is hoped, will not be lost to the world. The Duke had laboured, during many years, under a complication of distempers, and was carried off in a fit. The excruciating pains with which he had been long afflicted made life uncomfortable; however, those who were acquainted with his former days, image to themselves the learned, the polite, and entertaining companion, whose affability was very attractive, as it threw off (in his presence) all distinction, that of superior merit excepted. But, alas! sickness, disgust, and disappointment, are apt to sour the sweetest dispositions.— (Public Journals.)
His Grace is succeeded in title and estate by the Hon. John Frederick Sackville (son of the late Lord John Philip Sackville, second son of Lionel Cranfield, first Duke of Dorset), and Knight of the Shire in the present Parliament for the county of Kent.

was what he most resembled them in, and in what he best supported their honour. His passion was the direction of operas, in which he had not only wasted immense sums, but had stood lawsuits in Westminster Hall with some of those poor devils for their salaries. The Duke of Dorset had often paid his debts, but never could work upon his affections; and he had at last carried his disobedience so far, in complaisance to, and in imitation of the Prince, as to oppose his father in his own boroughs. That Duke,[101] with the greatest dignity in his appearance, was in private the greatest lover of low humour and buffoonery. He had early lost the hearts of the Whigs by some indirect connections with Lord Oxford in the end of Queen Anne's reign; and he was never thought to have wanted a tendency to power, in whatever hands it was, or was likely to be lodged.

The people had idly imagined that advantage would be made of the youth of the Prince's children to raise the Duke to the Throne. Nobody had doubted but he must be Protector if the King should die during their minority. All the precedents ran in his favour, except two Acts which had never taken place, made in the reign of King Henry the Eighth, for appointing Anne Boleyn and Jane Seymour Regents during the eventual minorities of their respective children. No woman had ever yet been Regent in a minority. Even the Black Prince's widow, though of the most distinguished virtue and character, though an English woman, and of the Blood Royal of England herself, was passed over, and her son regented by his uncles. The King, who never thought of disturbing the right order of succession, and who grew a little jealous of the Duke the moment he had lost his other son, had, immediately on the Prince's death, proposed to have the future Regency settled by Parliament.

The Duke of Bedford, though connected with, and wishing well to the Duke, and upon no terms with the Princess, had the honesty to be the first man that declared for her being Regent. The Pelhams took care not to

---

[101] Lionel Cranfield, first Duke of Dorset, had gone through most of the great posts, and was at this time Lord President, Lord Lieutenant of Ireland, Constable of Dover Castle, and Knight of the Garter.
He had voted once or twice with the Tory Ministry, when coming one day into the Kit Cat Club (it was about the time that the Portuguese had abandoned the Army of the Allies in Spain) Earl Berkeley, a boisterous zealous Whig seaman, cried out, "God d—n you, Sir, no Portuguese! I will keep company with no Portuguese!"—(Vide Appendix.)

disagree with him on this article. The Duke[102] had broke entirely with the Duke of Newcastle towards the end of the war, when Lord Sandwich having been ordered to communicate a new plan to Count Kaunitz, had desired to be excused, but the orders being repeated, he had obeyed artfully. The Duke thought him in the wrong, and had received his consent to say everything that might reconcile him to the Duke of Newcastle, but that he thought himself in the wrong. The Duke of Newcastle had neither accepted nor refused the Duke's mediation, who was not apt to pardon slighter offences than contempt. He loved indiscriminate submission; flattery did not come up to his ideas of obedience, and consequently he overlooked it: but the least opposition he never forgave. With the most heroic bravery, he had all the severity that levels valour to cowardice, and seemed to love war for itself, without feeling the passions that it gratifies.

It is certain that his martial genius did not proceed from love of glory, nor much from ambition. Glory he despised, saying, "That when he was most popular, the satisfaction was allayed, by thinking on Admiral Vernon!"[103] and he had taken every step to make himself unpopular both

---

[102] The Duke of Cumberland.

[103] Edward Vernon, a silly, noisy Admiral, who, towards the beginning of the war with Spain, was rash enough to engage to take Porto Bello with six ships only, and rash enough to accomplish his engagement; which made him so popular, that, notwithstanding his failing soon afterwards in an attempt upon Carthagena, and after that, more blameably upon Cuba, by his dissensions with General Wentworth, he was chosen into Parliament for several places, had his head painted on every Sign, and his birth-day kept twice in one year. Yet as his courage was much greater than his sense, his reputation was much greater than his courage. One should have thought that the lightness of his head would have buoyed up his heart in any extremity! He had withdrawn himself but very awkwardly from two or three private quarrels, and lost his public character with still greater infamy; for being out of humour with the Admiralty, he published a series of letters and instructions from that Board in the very heat of the Rebellion, by which he betrayed our spies—[It was believed that one of them was actually hanged in France, he being never heard of after this transaction]—and intelligence to the French, and was removed from all command with ignominy. He raised great wealth by the war, and by his economy, and was at last chosen one of the Directors of the New Herring Fisheries, which occasioned the following epigram:—

> Long in the senate hath brave Vernon rail'd,
> And all mankind with bitter tongue assail'd;
> Sick of his noise, we wearied Heav'n with pray'r,
> In his own element to place the tar:
> The gods at length have yielded to our wish,
> And bad him rule o'er Billingsgate and fish.

October 31, 1757.—Sunday last, died at his seat, at Nacton, in Suffolk, Edward Vernon, Esq., member of Parliament for Ipswich, and elder brother of the Trinity-house. In the sixth

with the people and the Army; and thought it so much beneath his rank to have any share in the Ministry, that he would not be of the Cabinet Council, and even when desired to attend their consultations for the Expedition to Port L'Orient, he would not vouchsafe to give his opinion, but confined himself to answering their questions. His strongest principle was the dignity of the Blood Royal, and his maxim to bear anything from his brother if he had lived to be King, rather than set an example of disobedience to the royal authority. These prejudices and this pride were the swellings of his heart and temper, not the errors of his head, for his understanding was strong, judicious, and penetrating, though incapable of resisting partialities and piques, of which he was susceptible from the slightest merit, or most trifling offence. He was as angry at an Officer's transgressing the minutest precept of the military rubric as at deserting his post, and was as intent on establishing the form of spatter-dashes, or the pattern of cockades, as on taking a town, or securing an advantageous situation.

The misfortunes[104] the nation had suffered from his inexperience while he commanded in Flanders had been amply atoned by his defeating the Rebels in Scotland; but that victory made him in the end more unpopular than all his defeats; for the Scotch, the Jacobites, and his brother's jealousy never rested till they had propagated such stories of his tyranny and

---

and seventh Parliaments of Great Britain he represented the borough of Penryn, in the eighth the town of Portsmouth. On the 20th of July, 1739, he sailed from Portsmouth for the West Indies with nine men-of-war and a sloop; and on the 5th of November following sailed from Jamaica with the Burford, Hampton Court, Princess Louisa, Strafford, Norwich, and Sheerness; and on the 21st of the same month took the fort of Porto Bello; as also Gloria Castle, and Castle of St. Jeronimo, with five ships only (the Sheerness being then cruising off Carthagena), with the loss of only seven persons killed, and twelve wounded. In this expedition the principal engineer in the mining work was Captain (now Admiral) Knowles of the Diamond, assisted by Captain (now Admiral) Boscawen, who desired he might serve in this expedition as a Volunteer, his ship the Shoreham not being then fit for the sea. For this service the Admiral had the Thanks of both Houses of Parliament, was presented with the Freedom of the city of London in a gold box; and in the ninth Parliament of Great Britain, summoned to meet the 25th of June, 1741, was returned for the city of Rochester and borough of Ipswich, but made his election for Ipswich, which he also represented in the last, and in the present Parliament. After the affair of Porto Bello, he took Chagre, and continued in his Majesty's service till the year 1748, when several matters which had passed between the Lords of the Admiralty and Mr. Vernon being laid before his Majesty, he was struck off the list of Flag Officers. (Public Journals.)

[104] He lost the battles of Fontenoy and Laffelt against Marshal Saxe, and all Flanders.

severity, as entirely lost him the hearts of the nation. He bore that hatred mildly, and said, "That so far from resenting it (though he did not know, since he came from Flanders, that he had deserved either praise or blame) he should always with gratitude remember the behaviour of the English, who received him with transports after the battle of Laffelt, instead of impeaching him." It is said, that after the loss of that day, an English captive telling a French Officer, that they had been very near taking the Duke prisoner, the Frenchman replied, "We took care of that; he does us more service at the head of your Army." General Legonier,[105] who, by an action of the most desperate gallantry, had prevented the total destruction of our troops in that battle, and almost made Marshal Saxe doubt of his victory, was never kindly treated by the Duke afterwards. Hawley,[106] his executioner, who had been beat at Falkirk by his own arrogance and obstinacy, was always in his favour. He despised money, fame, and politics; loved gaming, women, and his own favourites, and yet had not one sociable virtue.

The Pelhams taking advantage of this national antipathy to the Duke; of their own superiority in Parliament, which was now enforced by the greatest part of the late Prince's faction; and of a Hanoverian regulation, by which the nearest male relation must be Administrator of that Electorate during a minority, and consequently the Duke's presence necessary there, even if the King of Prussia should not pretend to the Government in case of his absence, yet as so formidable a neighbour would be too dangerous to an infant Elector, an apprehension that they well knew would easily make its way into the King's breast, where hatred and fear of his nephew were already sufficiently implanted; by these arts and insinuations they worked upon the King to nominate the Princess, Regent, with a Council; and the Lord Chancellor was deputed from the King to communicate the plan to the Duke. He went in a great fright: the Duke read the scheme, and asked if he must send an answer. The Chancellor hesitated, and did not make a direct reply. However, the Duke desired "He would return his duty and thanks to the King for the communication of the plan of Regency;" and

---

[105] Sir John Legonier was a French Protestant and Knight of the Bath.
[106] General Hawley was so severe, that he was called in the Army the Chief Justice.

Chapter 4

said, "For the part allotted to me, I shall submit to it, because he commands it, be that Regency what it will!" The Duke bad Mr. Fox tell Mr. Pelham this answer, and remember the word *submit*; adding, "It was a material word; the Chancellor will remember it, however he reports it."

The Duke felt the force of this treatment in the most sensible manner, and lamented himself in moving terms with his intimates, wishing "the name of William could be blotted out of the English annals;" and saying, "He now felt his own insignificance, when even Mr. Pelham would dare to use him thus!"

From this moment he openly declared his resentment to the two brothers, and professed being ready to connect with, nay, to forgive any man, who would oppose them, even Lord Granville, who was not at all unwilling to overset their power, though till that could be done conveniently, he thought it as well to unite with them. Lord Granville had, during his short and precipitate Ministry, offended the Duke, not only by negotiating a match for him with the King of Denmark's sister, to favour some of the King's German views, but had treated him roughly enough, on his expressing an aversion to that marriage, and had told him, he must be taught his duty to his father. The Duke consulted Sir Robert Walpole, then retired from business, how to avoid this wedding. Sir Robert advised him to seem willing to consent, provided the King would immediately make him a large settlement. The Duke took the advice, and had no reason to repent it. The King would not part with his money, as Sir Robert Walpole had foreseen, even to purchase advantages for Hanover.

A mortification of a slighter sort followed soon after the Regency Bill, that showed the Duke in what light he had appeared at his brother's Court. Prince George making him a visit, asked to see his apartment, where there are few ornaments but arms. The Duke is neither curious nor magnificent. To amuse the boy, he took down a sword and drew it. The young Prince turned pale and trembled, and thought his uncle was going to murder him. The Duke was extremely shocked, and complained to the Princess of the impressions that had been instilled into the child against him.

23rd—Mr. Pelham proposed some further restrictions on the sale of Gin; slight ones indeed for so enormous an evil! They were ratified.

24th.—General Anstruther's cause came on, and several witnesses attended, according to the orders of the House. Sir Henry Erskine moved to call in Brigadier Ofarel. Sir William Yonge objected to it, saying, "He knew that what he was going to propose would be disagreeable both to the gentleman who had brought the charge, and to the gentleman accused; but that it concerned the honour of the whole House, and therefore he must first desire to know of the gentlemen of the Law, whether the crimes specified were not comprehended within the pardon of the late Act of Grace." Sir Henry Erskine protested that he had no vindictive motive, but that he must desire to have his cause heard; and asked whether the Act of Grace was not known, or had not been mentioned before, that now he was prepared to prove his accusation, he was to be put off in this injurious manner? General Anstruther agreed with him in desiring to have the cause heard, which he affirmed was a malicious, false, and scandalous accusation, particularly in charging him with subornation of witnesses, of which, he said, none could be guilty but they who charged it on others.

The Attorney-General said, "He must enter his protest against complaints in these circumstances; that there were two very striking in this complaint; one, that the charge exhibited was of a private nature; the other, that the facts alleged were previous in time to the Act of Indemnity. That the House of Commons is not a Court of Appeal; that this 'is' a case of false imprisonment; that there are neither general nor particular words in the Act of Grace to except it; that no punishment can follow, even if the General should be convicted, and we should address for it. That the two Houses of Parliament can have no mental reservation to pardon for the King, and not for themselves; and, lastly, that the House of Commons is not a Court of Inquiry into the characters of its own members." Sir Henry Erskine said, "That he supposed Anstruther had been apprised of this objection, or he would not have used such epithets on the charge, if he had believed the witnesses would be heard, who would prove the allegations; but that he yet could furnish crimes, from which the Act of Grace would not screen him."

Lord George Sackville[107] said, "The Officers were concerned to have this affair inquired into; that if the General did not disculpate himself, could Officers with honour serve under him? that he was sensible of the difficulty of not being able to punish him; and therefore would give his negative to calling in Ofarel, but proposed to have Anstruther tried by a Board of General Officers." Henley (the profession out-weighing the faction in him) declared the House could exercise no jurisdiction in this case, where the crimes were misdemeanours; and that even if both parties should consent to go before a Judge, he would be bound ex-officio to dismiss the complaint. Lord Strange,[108] a busy young Lord, very disinterested, often quick, as often injudicious, and not the less troublesome for either, proposed at least to declare, that the Act of Grace was the reason of not proceeding; and that if the House would take no cognizance of this affair, it might be heard by the Board of Officers. Nugent, too, was tender of infringing the Act of Grace, and sorry if he had been one to call improperly on Sir Harry to make the charge. He said, "He had been told that offences against the Mutiny Bill were to be pardoned only from the year 43, but that the crimes in question were antecedent to that era; if not, that the accused must plead the Act. That for himself he should vote for Lord George's Motion."

Anstruther said, "I plead nothing as to the Act of Grace, but desire the House to take it into their consideration." Sir Richard Loyd, a lawyer, said, "This was a misdemeanour, and a pardoned one; that the prosecution of it now would affect numbers. An angry court would have acted so formerly; should a House of Commons act with such narrow microscopic eyes? We want no pardon; many of our constituents may. An Act of Grace does not merely take away punishment, but restores a criminal so fully, that to call a pardoned Rebel perjured, he would have an action. But it is said, we may inspect: for what end, if no consequence can follow? The Clergy took this up once, on the misbehaviour of one of their own body, from whom they would have taken orders, saying, they could not serve with him; but the King's Bench deeming it a punishment, would not suffer it. In the reign of

---

[107] Youngest son to the Duke of Dorset, and Colonel of a regiment.
[108] Eldest son of the Earl of Derby.

James II a Mr. Bayne was sequestered by the House for his unworthiness; but was restored to his seat by an Act of Grace. If you have a mind to hear angry words for some hours, without doing anything, you certainly may, but his offence is neither against the Mutiny Bill, nor within the excepted term; nor can he, being included within the Act of Grace, wave the advantage of it." He concluded, begging pardon of the House with a sneer, for endeavouring to stop an inquiry.

Mr. W. Pitt said that if he had wanted information upon the Act of Grace, he should have fully received it, though he had never thought of infringing that; but that he had been desirous of inquiring into the nature of the General's tyranny, in order to new model the Mutiny Bill, if it were necessary. That he wanted to see the minutes of the Court-Martial for information, not for foundation of a criminal prosecution. That without the impediment of the Act of Grace, he should be against calling in Ofarel, as the business of the House was not to hear causes that are without our jurisdiction, but to find deficiencies in our laws, and remedies for them. That, if this infringed the liberty of two members, at least it was relative to what had happened before they were so. That he had perceived there was something in the dark, yet had not been the loudest to call for what others, whose situation was more connected with military matters, might know better. That to send this to a Board of Officers would be constituting the crime anew: that all he desired was, that Governors in our Plantations and Foreign Garrisons might know that the prosecution of this affair was stopped by the Act of Grace, and might tremble for the future. The hint towards the latter end of the speech was levelled at Fox, the Secretary at War, an employment that Pitt professed wishing to have preferably to Paymaster, though the latter 'was' so much more considerable in profit, as it would give him an introduction to the closet; the very reason why the King had refused it to him. Pitt was so much mortified at the King's never speaking to him, that above a year before this the Pelhams had with great difficulty obtained a word to him at the levee.

Sir John Mordaunt, an Officer of gallantry, with some wit, said, he had early spoke his mind for hearing this cause, and had come determined to hear the witnesses, but had changed his opinion, because of the impropriety there would be of letting him continue a member if he was proved guilty, an objection that would hold equally against trying him by a Board of General Officers; a trial that he disliked, as to clear the reputation of soldiers, he wished to have them tried by any but Officers. That he saw the Crown would be under the same difficulties as the House, and therefore he agreed with Lord Strange's motion for declaring the Act of Grace the impediment. Fazakerley, a tiresome Jacobite lawyer, was clear that he was comprized within the general pardon; and yet for the honour of the House was for doing something, and that something was to try him, that the King might not trust him any longer.

Mr. Pelham said, "That if he were for trying him by a Board of Officers, he should not be hindered by the Act of Grace, which had been originally his opinion as the properest way of carrying the cause before the King; but that it must now rest here, as all the lawyers were agreed on its being a violation of the general indemnity. That so far from desiring with Fazakerley that the King should remember it, he wished the whole case could be obliterated; and that this might go no further between the two persons, whom he begged to bury in oblivion their private resentments, as the House was obliged to do those of the public." The Speaker took up this, observed on the harsh words that had passed, and desired they would be publicly reconciled. Sir Henry Erskine answered, "The General gave the offence." The General replied, "I gave no offence: I said the accusation was false and malicious; does not my very denial of the charge say the same?" The Chair insisted on their engaging to carry this quarrel no further; to which Anstruther answered, "I shall take no further notice." The Speaker said, "Do you give your honour?" Anstruther; "I do." Sir Harry Erskine said pertly, "I thought he would have made an apology." Sir William Yonge interrupted him, and told him, he must not enter into a discussion of what had passed; and the Chair insisted on Sir Harry's giving the proper assurances; on which Sir Harry at last said dryly, "I give my honour in consequence." Lord Strange then repeated his Motion for a declaration of the reasons of not proceeding.

Mr. Fox told him, "He was sorry to hear such a Motion after so wise a conclusion; and that it would be giving a reason for all, which was not the reason of many. That the accusation was nothing before reduced to writing; that he still thought it a frivolous affair; that it could not be said Sir Harry was unwilling to present the charge, as he had repeated the accusation day after day; that Anstruther could call it nothing but false or true; that he had frequently been intreated by the General to get the cause heard; and would now give him a word of comfort, that he had thought him much more guilty before the charge was presented—'and' now did not think him guilty of a thousandth part of what he had been accused. That as to the Motion, no vote ever passes for a single reason; that this would be introducing a new practice; and he concluded with asking whether the House would permit Anstruther to enter upon the Journals a complaint against the charge?" Sir Henry Erskine said to that, "That there were accusations in the answer as well as in the charge." General Oglethorpe[109], of whom it was uncertain whether he was a Whig or a Jacobite, whether very brave or a coward, for he had fought several duels, and had run away in the Rebellion; very certain that he was a troublesome and tiresome speaker, though even that was now and then tempered with sense; took notice that if it were mentioned in the votes that the Act of Grace had been read apropos to this Debate, it would sufficiently explain without a further comment why the affair was dropped. Lord Strange owned himself content with this remark, and withdrew his Motion. The House adjourned at half an hour after eight.

---

[109] The great promoter of the Colony of Georgia, had been surprised and put to flight by a party of the Rebels at Clifton.

Chapter 5

April 25th.—Prince George kissed the King's hand on being created Prince of Wales.

26th.—Sir John Phillips moved the King's Bench for a Habeas Corpus for Murray, which was granted. Sir John was a man of a worse character than parts, though they were not shining. He had quitted Parliament on the desperate situation of the Jacobite cause, after having attempted during the last Rebellion to get the Subscriptions and Associations for the King declared illegal; and was now retired to Oxford, the sanctuary of disaffection.

The King sent a Message to both Houses to desire they would pass an Act for appointing the Princess Dowager of Wales, Regent, with proper limitations, in case he died before the Prince was eighteen. The Duke of Newcastle, seconded by the Duke of Devonshire, opened it in the House of Lords; Mr. Pelham, and the Chancellor's eldest son[110], in the Commons. Both the brothers made awkward and ill-placed panegyrics on the Duke; and Addresses of Thanks were voted.

27th.—Murray was brought by Habeas Corpus into the King's Bench; but, three Judges allowing the validity of a commitment by the House of Commons, he was remanded to Newgate.

May 1st.—The Regency Bill was to have been brought into the House of Lords, but was deferred, to be softened a little, upon objections made by the Bishop of London to the unprecedented powers that the Council had

---

[110] Philip Yorke. He had married the granddaughter and heiress of the Duke of Kent.

given themselves in it. The Chancellor drew it; and for the honour of his profession had contrived to show that a legal tyranny might be formed as despotic as the most usurped authority. And lest it should shock a free people, and draw an odium on the Government, he had submitted to bear the greatest share of the envy himself; for, though the Bill was directed to establish the power of the Pelhams, the Chancellor was likely to have the amplest share by his own voice, and those of his creatures, the Archbishop, the Chief Justice Lee, and my Lord Anson, his son-in-law, whom they designed for first Lord of the Admiralty, though on the original plan, that Officer was omitted in the Council of Regency, because they had not then determined to remove Lord Sandwich.

3rd.—A question was proposed to the House by Sir William Yonge, whether such members as were named to be servants to the new Prince of Wales were to vacate their seats, as their appointment was by the King. Stone and John Selwyn were of the number. It was agreed in the negative without a Motion.

7th.—The Duke of Newcastle opened the Regency Bill in the House of Lords, and it was read the first time without opposition.

10th.—The committee in the Lords on the Regency Bill. Earl Stanhope, whose studies were mathematical, and principles republican, to the honour of which, though without any parts, he had acted steadily in Opposition, when Jacobites and Royalist-Whigs, and men of all other denominations had changed for every other denomination, opposed the clause that gave the Regent a Council; an opinion that was rather more consistent with the effect of his principles, to oppose a Regal Government, than with his principles themselves; but it was carried by 98 against him, and the Earls of Thanet, Shaftesbury, Oxford, and Lichfield, the Viscount Hereford and Townshend, and the Lords Ward, Maynard, Foley, Romney, and Talbot.

Lord Bath then made as miscellaneous a speech as he used to do in the House of Commons; objecting to the not leaving the Regent power to displace any of the inferior Commissioners of Treasury or Admiralty; and weeping actual tears when he mentioned the possible event of the King's

Chapter 5

death. This duteous dew was followed by a joke on Harry Vane[111], formerly his tool and spy, now in that office to the Pelhams, and a wonderful Lord of the Treasury, who, whenever he was drunk, told all he knew, and when he was sober more than he knew, and whom Lord Bath said, on seeing there, he did not mean to propose removing. Then soaring up to a panegyric on the Princess, he observed, that female reigns in England had not been the least glorious, and yet the great Princess, who was likely to figure with the Elizabeths and the Annes, would not be empowered to reward merit, or to place, if she found such an one, a proper person at the head of the Treasury: that she even would not have authority to appoint her own son, Prince Edward, Lord High Admiral, nor to grant convoys to any merchants who solicited for them: that indeed she might tell the merchants she would use her interest with Parliament to get this Bill altered, and then she would protect them. He then (it is very true he said so) wished that all employments were for life, or *quam diù* those who held them *se benè gesserint*; and professed (it is even true that he professed) having been ashamed of the struggles he had seen for places, half of which he wished were to be diminished at the King's death, and the salaries to be applied to the Sinking Fund: that, having been lately in France, he had observed that the weight of their debt is the debts on employments. He concluded with declaring he liked the Bill, and did not mean to oppose it.

Lord Bath[112] is so known a character, that it is almost needless to draw him. Who does not know that Mr. Pulteney was the great rival of Sir

---

[111] Eldest son of the Lord Barnard, was made Vice-Treasurer of Ireland by Lord Bath, on the change of the Ministry, in 1742, from which place he was removed on the coalition, but not long after placed in the Treasury; and was afterwards created Earl of Darlington. He died March 6th, 1758.

[112] William Pulteney, Earl of Bath, had been persuaded by Sir Robert Walpole to apply himself to politics, in which, soon making a figure, he was appointed Secretary at War, when the Whigs came into power in the late King's reign; but towards the end of it he went into Opposition, at the head of which he continued till the fall of Sir Robert Walpole. That Minister persuaded the King, when he took leave of him, to comply with none of Mr. Pulteney's demands, unless he would quit the House of Commons and accept a Peerage, which he imprudently promising to do, though not without great reluctance, before the patent was passed, and raising his creatures,—Sandys, Sir John Rushout, Gybbon, Harry Vane, and Harry Furnese,—who were men of the meanest capacities, to the chief places, in preference to all the rest of the Opposition who had acted with him, they refused to follow

Robert Walpole, whose power he so long opposed, at last overturned, and was undone with it? Who does not know that his virtue failed the moment his inveteracy was gratified? Who does not know that all the patriot's private vices, which his party would not see while he led them, were exposed, and, if possible, magnified by them the instant he deserted them? Who does not know that he had not judgment or resolution enough to engross the power, which he had forfeited his credit and character to obtain? and who does not know that his ambition, treachery, irresolution, timidity, and want of judgment were baffled[113] and made advantage of by a man who had all those vices and deficiencies in a stronger proportion—for who does not know the Duke of Newcastle?

The Chancellor answered Lord Bath upon some points of form that he had mentioned in the drawing Commissions for the Boards of Treasury and Admiralty, but owned that it was indifferent to him whether that clause in the Bill were altered or not. Lord Bath confessed himself in a mistake, having concluded that a single alteration vacated the whole Commission. Dr. Maddox, Bishop of Worcester, who did not want parts, wanted them now, making a bad speech, and objected that the Princess, who might make a Lord Lieutenant of Ireland, would not have authority to make a Baron of the Exchequer there; and he proposed her having the disposal of all offices in general. The Duke of Newcastle, who had too much good-nature, or too much jealousy, to let anybody else be eminently ridiculous where he was

---

him in his politics, and persecuted him in Parliament, and with innumerable libels and satires. On the death of Lord Wilmington, he asked for the Treasury, to which Mr. Pelham was preferred, but to which he was named in the Ministry of three days. From that time he made no figure; he was immensely rich, from great parsimony and great successions, and had endeavoured to add another to them: the Duchess of Buckingham, natural daughter to King James II., designing to take a journey to Rome, to promote some Jacobite measures, and apprehending the consequence, made over her estate to Lord Bath, by a deed which he afterwards sunk, and pretended to have lost. On this, the Duchess, after forcing a release from him, struck him out of her will as one of her Executors; and many years afterwards, on marrying her grandson to Lord Hervey's daughter, she appointed Sir Robert Walpole one of her Executors. This happening soon after that Minister's fall, he said to Lord Oxford in the House of Lords, "So, my Lord, I find I have got my Lord Bath's place before he has got mine."

[113] After the revolution of three days, Lord Bath was going to print a Diary which he had kept, in order to show all the falsehoods, treacheries, and breaches of promise of the Duke of Newcastle and Mr. Pelham, he having minuted down their conversations with him on the fall of Sir Robert Walpole.

present, replied in a tone of raillery, "that the nomination of Bishops and Judges had been previously excepted, because the first thoughts of the compilers of the Bill had been directed to the security of our souls and properties, and had been taken from the Regent, because she might not know the true character of such Divines as were recommended to her." And, lest even this nonsense should wear the appearance of an argument, his Grace added, that he could not help remembering what had been said when the Act of Union passed, that there were already in the English House of Lords twenty-six immortal Peers, meaning his good Lords the Bishops, who he hoped would all deserve immortality.

Lord Talbot, a Lord of good parts, only that they had rather more bias to "extravagance" than sense, opposed the clause for continuing the Parliament for three years after the King's death; talked over the nature of Government, asserted that the contests arrived in England during minorities had not arisen from new elections; and said, that "they might make laws with relation to future Parliaments, but had no power to extend the duration of the present." Lord Talbot[114] was a sworn enemy to the Chancellor from some family jealousies, and soon after his father's death and Yorke's elevation, who had made a speech against some advantages that were demanded for the Prince of Wales, Lord Talbot said, "He should certainly submit to such high authority, if he had not in his hand an opinion directly contrary, which he could not help thinking of equal weight." It was expected that he was going to read a judgment of his father, but it was an opinion which the present Chancellor himself had given, when he was Attorney-General, on a parallel case referred to his and Talbot's judgment in the late reign, when the present King had figured in the character of a mutinous Prince of Wales.

Lord Granville replied to Lord Talbot, "That it was the parliamentary clause that gave stability to the whole Bill, and hoped we should even have enacted it without a message from the Throne. That Rebellions were best carried on during elections; that it had been the policy of Louis the Fourteenth to foment them here at that season; and that he had had an

---

[114] William, Lord Talbot, was eldest son of Charles Talbot, Lord Chancellor.

opportunity, when last Secretary of State, of knowing, among the secrets which had not come to light, that it had been an advice given in the Council of France during the very last Rebellion, to wait for a general election." He declared his approbation of the restrictions, not that they would, he hoped, be necessary in the present case, but as they would be a precedent for, and of service to posterity. The Bishop of London made no opposition, and the Bill was committed by 106 to 12, Lord Townshend voting for the latter clauses, and Lord Folkestone against them.

The Duke of Bedford was laid up with the gout and rheumatism, but was very eager to have gone to the House and opposed the whole tenour of the restrictions. His friends apprehending that it would undo him with the King (who had been made to believe that this act against his own son was of his own direction), used all their endeavours to dissuade him, and succeeded pretty easily after the first division, which had been composed of so few, and those such insignificant Lords. Lord Sandwich, who was not impatient to precipitate his own fall, voted, with the Duke's consent, for every part of the Bill.

13th.—The Lords read the Regency Bill the third time, and sent it to the Commons, who read it immediately. Mr. Pelham opened it, and moved for its being read a second time. Sir Francis Dashwood made several objections to it, and asked "What was the intent of the Duke's being the head of the Council of Regency? a question, he said, simply of curiosity, for he did not desire he should have any power. If this Bill was calculated to pare away the prerogative, he wished the Parliament would set about it roundly, and stickle for a new Magna Charta. He observed that there was no provision made, in case the Princess should die before the determination of her Regency; and he feared her being displeased with these very strict limitations." He attended the Bill no more, which he foresaw would pass by a great majority, after he had satisfied himself with declaring against it. He was a man of sense without eloquence, and of humour without good humour: naturally inclined to adventures, and had early in his life made a voyage to Russia, dressed like Charles the Twelfth, in hopes of making the Czarina Anne fall in love with him—an improper hero to copy, when a woman was to be captivated! Oglethorpe found more faults in the Bill;

Nugent commended it extravagantly. Lord Limerick too approved it, but observed a want of provision, in case the King died during a dissolution of Parliament, or before a new-elected one had sat.

The Attorney-General answered him, and the two other opponents, and declared his opinion, that a new chosen Parliament, even before a session, would answer the purposes described in the Bill: but the Solicitor-General thought that it must be the dissolved Parliament that should re-assemble. The Attorney[115] was a man of singular goodness and integrity; of the highest reputation in his profession, of the lowest in the House, where he wearied the audience by the multiplicity of his arguments; resembling the Physician who ordered a medicine to be composed of all the simples in a meadow, as there must be some of them at least that would be proper. T. Pitt and Sydenham spoke against the Bill; Dr. Lee in approbation of the Council, as a safeguard to the Regent, and treated the nomination to offices as a trifle. Henley spoke for the Bill, but agreeing with Lord Limerick's observation. Mr. Pelham then proposed to read it a second time on the morrow. T. Pitt asked for a longer day, and to have the Bill printed, and was seconded by Sir John Cotton; but on Mr. Pelham's opposing it, there was no division. The House sat till past seven.

14th.—The Regency Bill was read a second time, and opposed only by Mr. Delaval, in a very absurd speech, which he asked pardon for not having made the day before, which was the first of his sitting in Parliament.

16th.—The House went into the Committee on the Regency Bill, when Mr. Pelham, who had apprehended no considerable opposition, was in the Chair. T. Pitt moved to refer the King's Message to the Committee; Vyner to adjourn till the Bill could be printed; but as the House generally suffered him to be singular in his opinion, nobody seconded him now. Prowse, who affected to be in Opposition, what Mr. Pelham affected to be in power, candid, and who was, like Mr. Pelham, a man of some sense without parts, said, "That when this Bill should be passed, he supposed the King would not remove any of the great Officers who were to compose the Regency, as

---

[115] Sir Dudley Ryder.

they would tacitly have had the approbation of Parliament; indeed, of what must they be guilty to justify turning them out after this approbation?" That it would be quoted hereafter by ambitious subjects, who should want to engraft themselves upon the Regal Authority, that even this Parliament had strictly tied up the hands of a Princess, whom they affected so much to commend; that the Royal Power can't be divided into many hands; and that if this Bill passed, the nation ought *indeed* to pray for the King's life.

Lord Strange and Sir Roger Newdigate both spoke against the Bill; and Charles Yorke, second son to the Chancellor, a young lawyer of good parts, but precise and affected, for it. He said, "That there were but two instances of a Parliamentary Regency, those of Richard the Second and Henry the Sixth, and in both those, Councils had been established by Parliament; that the confusions of those minorities flowed from the advice of Parliament not being followed: that the Duke of Gloucester, on his brother's going to France, applied to Parliament for directions how to act, and was told by them, that his power was limited, and accordingly had only the title of Protector conferred on him: that this clause puts the Princess under a happy inability of doing wrong; and that it would quiet jealousies, if there be a subject among us who could create suspicion."

Fazakerley made remarks upon the Bill, without directly opposing it; and then Mr. Onslow (the Speaker) with a solemnity never more properly assumed, made a noble and affecting speech against it. "He professed that he would not have begun an opposition to the Bill, but could not avoid, when once it was opened, to declare that he thought the regulations dangerous; and that having so much studied the constitution, as it was his duty to do, he was obliged to speak his opinion. It was, that the Regal Power must not be divided; that control is dividing it; that it never ought to be controlled, except when abused; that instead of one King, we should have nine; that the Council might put a negative on what the Regent should propose; that to control, is to give the power to those who control; that if the Council refuse to make peace or war, the Regent must submit; that this control is placed in the hands of those she will not be able to control; that the best Regent we ever had, the Earl of Pembroke, in Harry the Third's time, was a single Regent; a good man, but his virtue was assisted by his undivided power. That he foresaw there would be dissensions among themselves; though he had a high opinion of those designed, yet will they not be men? Power corrupts the best understandings; factions in the Regency may derive themselves into both Houses, and those who should correct, may become parties in the grievance. In Edward the Sixth's time, though the reformation of religion was then in question, did it check the animosities in the Council? Even then, letters-patent were obtained in contradiction to an Act of Parliament, which had limited the Protector's authority. That though any members of the future Council will be removeable by address to Parliament, how will such address be obtained against the most turbulent? Nay, Parliament may be under a long prorogation, and the Regent, all helpless, will see nothing but factions in the Council that should assist her. How distressed will be her condition, how distressed the condition of her children, of the nation! I wish well," continued he, "to those who will have the power, a power that nobody will envy them! Though it has the appearance of establishing that power of which I am the most apprehensive! I must—I will speak my duty! It may be for the service of those who procure this Bill. Why, if the power of peace and war is to be delegated, why is it not entrusted to the Parliament? I hope we are not to address the Council for either! Nay, if we should submit to that humiliation, what, if they should slight, as they may, our application? What a solecism in this constitution to have Parliament contradicted by nine persons!"

He then made a solemn prayer for the King's life, as the only preservative against this plan of power, which, he said, if it ever took effect, would exceed all the evils that could be foreseen from a single Regent. For himself, he had nothing to ask, nothing to fear, and whenever he should cease to serve the House, he knew whither only he would go. He then entered upon that monstrous clause, which subjects to the penalties of a præmunire whoever shall attempt any alteration of this system after it be enacted. He argued with great weight on the prodigious danger of it, and mentioned a test proposed in 1675 to oblige members to take an oath not to attempt any alteration in the State. It held a Debate of seventeen days, and at last the House of Lords resolved, that such a test would not affect

Debates in Parliament, or restrain them. He said, that if members should meet privately to concert measures for the repeal of this law, it might be construed into a præmunire; and many lives had been taken away by construction. He concluded with an earnest asseveration of the uprightness of his intention, and a serious protest against the mischiefs of the Bill.

Mr. Pelham was inexpressibly shocked at this speech, though he had no reason not to have apprehended it. The Speaker had been at the private meetings on the Bill, where he disputed warmly with the Chancellor. Their cabal said that he acquiesced; that when he had given his reasons and found they had no weight, he had said no more—was that acquiescing? They even said that he agreed to the general plan on their softening some points, which at last they did not soften. On sketching out some correction of the most flagrant strokes of power, the Duke of Newcastle had said, "Now they had reduced the Bill to nothing!" The Speaker replied, "I wish it was! it would be better for you. If it is nothing, it is a reason for not doing it." This argument probably struck them, and so they did all they first intended. He told Mr. Fox, that they might have softened it with regard to the Duke, by declaring it was the tenour of the English constitution. Mr. Fox assured him, that the Duke had said, "My Lord Chancellor told me, no such declaration could be made, because circumstances might happen to make it inconvenient. That crisis," continued the Duke, "must be when I am out of the question."

The Speaker was master of an honesty, which though it would bend very much upon most occasions, especially when its warping would prop its reputation, was tough and steady when pushed to an extremity: and he would sometimes see that extremity as soon in trifles as in materials. His disinterestedness[116] was remarkable, and he was fond of exerting it. Popularity was his great aim, impartiality his professed means, universal adulation and partiality to whatever was popular, his real means of

---

[116] He resigned the beneficial place of Treasurer of the Navy just after Sir Robert Walpole's removal, because the Opposition said that his attachment to the Court arose from interest; yet that Minister always thought the Speaker not enough attached to him, and treated him very roughly, especially on his first visit after his disgrace. However, when the votes for the two last members of the secret committee were equal on the ballot for two of Sir Robert's friends and two of his enemies, the Speaker decided in favour of the former.

acquiring it. He was bigoted to the power of the House of Commons; and, like all zealots, ardent for his own authority, as intimately connected with the interests of his idol. He had much devotion from the House, few friends in it, for he was too pompous to be loved, though too ridiculous to be hated; had too much knowledge not to be regarded; too much dignity in his appearance not to be admired; and was too fond of applause not to miss it.

The Speaker was answered in a long deduction by the Attorney-General, and by Charles Yorke, who said, that on the first Regency Bill after the Revolution, ten Judges had given their opinions that the regal power may be both delegated and divided. Lord Strange asked shrewdly, "If it was probable that there would be no dissensions in the Council of Regency, which was to be composed of the present Ministry? Survey them; with what cordiality have they concurred in all measures for some years! May not it happen, that if the Regent should refuse[117] to employ some person recommended by them, the junto may threaten to *resign?* an insult, such as within my own time I have almost seen offered to a crowned head! We shall see all that repeated scramble for power, that I have two or three times seen acted over. Can the Duke be removed by address of Parliament? I won't say that he is most likely to do mischief, but certainly he is most capable of doing it. As to the præmunire clause, the person who drew it deserves to incur it."

Murray, the Solicitor-General, said, "He did not wonder there were but few precedents to direct them of a Prince thinking thus greatly of his own death, and providing for emergencies to arise after it: that the Law of England knows no minority: if the person of the minor King should be seized by force, his power would accompany the possession of his person: that this Bill creates a minority, and provides against the evils of it: that in private cases, no guardian has the whole power over an estate, that his ward will have when he comes of age; that no Prince, even in absolute governments, ever appointed a Regency without control; that all the members of the future Regency must be thought proper persons by the King; that the great officers specified must be named by him; and the four

---

[117] As was the case in 1746, when the King refused to make W. Pitt Secretary at War, and the whole Ministry resigned upon it.

others whom he is to appoint by his will must be entirely of his own choice; that there are but three acts of legislation which the Regent and the two Houses cannot perform—altering the established succession, the established religion in England, and the Presbyterian church government in Scotland; that members of Parliament are not restrained from taking measures to get this law repealed; that the prohibition is levelled against altering what shall be done by the Regency, not against altering the Bill, and clause of præmunire. He asked whether it was wished that the Regent should be made too powerful for the Council and both Houses of Parliament; and whether even a King ever made a Judge without the approbation of at least three of his Council? and he added, that it would be a solecism to say that the Council should be a check upon the Regent, and yet be removeable by her as easily as she pleased. That she would have a strong control upon them, as they would not have power even to make a Judge without her; nor be able to move anything without her concurrence. With regard to what the Speaker had urged on the delegation of the power of making peace and war, he asked, if there was no difference between entrusting it to a Council of seven hundred men, who take all the inhabitants of this country to their assistance, and a Council of twelve persons?"

Mr. Fox then declared himself for the Bill though he spoke against almost every part of it; and being afterwards told by Mr. Pelham peevishly, that Pitt's was the finest speech he ever heard, but that he (Fox) had not spoke like himself; he replied, "I know it; if I had, I should have said ten times more against the Bill;" but he objected that the præmunire clause was a little ambiguously worded, and that if the person who penned it was aware how wrong it was, he indeed deserved to incur all the weight of it. "Can fourteen persons[118]," said he, "have power, and not want more than their share? and if the Regent and her Council should proclaim the young King major a year before the time specified, would not a man in the street who hallooed at such proclamation be liable to a præmunire?" "The

---

[118] The different ways of reckoning the Council, as to be composed of nine, ten, or fourteen persons, arose from including, or not including the Duke, or the four to be named by the King's will.—Vide the Act.

crime," he added, "was too uncertainly described for such heavy punishment, and of all times a minority is the worst to subject the people to penal laws." He would have had the whole clause omitted, because every man, without being a lawyer, ought to know what the Regent can or cannot do. He asserted, that as the Chancellor is named in the Bill to be necessarily of the Regency, the putting the Great Seal in Commission would violate the Act. If they would not erase the whole clause, he proposed that the punishment annexed should be impeachment, as it could only be meant to come at great persons who should attempt to disturb the Settlement. Mr. Pelham, from the chair, told him angrily that this was not the clause then in debate, but the first clause, which passed without a division about seven o'clock.

Norris Bertie then spoke against the whole Bill, thinking penal laws dangerous in the hands of ten subjects equal to himself, and that he was serving his country while he delayed the Bill even by speaking. Sir John Barnard declared against appointing a Council, and affirmed that the consideration of the person intended for Regent ought to have weight in the Debate, though the contrary was asserted; that while she was controlled, we should have no kingly authority; the more preposterous, as he could foresee no inconveniences from the Princess's enjoying it; that the nation might want some of its great officers, unless she should always name such persons as should be agreeable to the junto, who would have means of inducing the Parliament to pass Acts disagreeable to her, at the same time, that without them she would not have power to dissolve or prorogue it. He concluded with desiring it should be known that he was utterly against the Council. Harding, a sensible knowing man, but who having been many years clerk to the House, was not well received as a speaker, said, "that the mischiefs of former Regencies arose from a neglect of proper restrictions; and he quoted Chancellor Oxenstiern, who, on the death of Gustavus Adolphus, had given his advice to the senate of Sweden to compose a mixed Regency, but not to appoint a sole Regent, or a Council of Regency without a Regent. He added, that in his opinion even the Duke might be removed from the Council." This frank delivery of his sentiments was the more honest, as he was actually the Duke's Attorney.

Nugent made a bombast speech about an angel; and then Lord Cobham (the only one of the cousin-hood who could not be turned out, having no place; Lyttelton and George Grenville had both without doors, like him) declared against the Council. He said, "He could not figure a weaker government than what they were chalking out; and as if there were not factions enough in the legislative power, they were laying a foundation for as many in the executive, and were destroying a Bill, which, if the Council clause were omitted, would be the most popular that ever was passed; that he had come to the House resolving to acquiesce even in this, as he thought it would be happy if it were universally assented to; but when others had made objections, he could not suppress his, which was to the Council, not to the continuance of the Parliament; that the House of Commons might perhaps address the Regent to remove some of the Council, while the House of Lords might vote an approbation of the same persons; at the same time that the Parliament could not be dissolved but by an irremovable Council, the usual way of putting a stop to differences between the two Houses. He then turned absurdly to an apology for himself, as people do who are fearful or conscious, and hoped his behaviour was free from reproach; that he did not like cutting the Government out into sippets; but desired to be understood to have a good opinion of some, of many that were to compose the Council; and hoped that those (he approved) would never be removed from her Royal Highness's ear; at the same time he believed that those who brought in the Bill did not foresee all the power of the Council; nor would he himself consent to the prolongation of the Parliament, if he thought it was calculated for bad purposes."

Lord Cobham[119] was the absolute creature of Pitt; vehement in whatever faction he was engaged, and as mischievous as his understanding would let him be, which is not saying he was very bad. He had kept less measures with Mr. Pelham than any of his connection, and had not spoke to him above once for the last six months. He was more a gentleman than his brother George[120], who was a pedant in politics, but less deceitful.

---

[119] Richard Grenville, Lord Cobham, and since Earl Temple.
[120] Grenville, a Lord of the Treasury.

James[121], the youngest of the three, had all the defects of his brothers, and had turned them to the best account. All of them were troubled with a redundancy of words peculiar to their family, though without the energy of Pitt's language, or the hyperbole of Lyttelton's.

Martin spoke for the clause, and said, "the King could not have a separate interest from his people, the Princess might; witness Queen Isabella and her[122] minion Mortimer: that if this precedent were established, it could not hereafter be set aside, if the young King's mother should happen to be a bad woman; and that, if the conduct of the Princess were a foundation for entrusting her with the sole power, it was so amiable and estimable, that the argument would go to giving her absolute power." Sir John Cotton disapproved of the latitude given to the King, of naming four persons to be of the Council by a testamentary disposition, and of whom the House could know nothing. Pitt declared he had no objection to the Council, as he could find no traces of a Regent without control; and then (as if all mankind had forgot his ingratitude to the Prince, as he had his obligations to him) he pronounced the present case doubly aggravated by the loss of the most *patriot* Prince that ever lived, to whom he had such infinite obligations, and such early attachments, which he was proud to transfer to his family. Then turning to the King, whom he regarded with wonder for exerting a fortitude which Edward the Third had not been master of, he blessed the Crown when it was the first to lessen the royal authority, as it had been in the present case, by pointing out these limitations, so expedient, as dangers were to be foreseen from abroad— from at home, if we considered the great person who might have become sole Regent. What a precedent would that have been for futurity, if hereafter any ambitious person should think less of protecting the Crown than of wearing it! With regard to the Princess, the limitations were of no consequence, for let her but hint to Parliament at any improper negative given by the Council to her recommendation, an address would immediately be offered to her to remove them. He desired, if that event

---

[121] Grenville, Deputy Paymaster, and one of the Lords of Trade.
[122] It is remarkable that, in the next reign, Martin became a distinguished tool of the Princess's minion, Lord Bute.

should ever happen, to be put in mind of what he now said, and he would second the Motion.

Fox replied, "that it was an absurd notion not to give the Princess the whole power of royalty, because she was not called Queen; and he hoped that the nation was not only safe from the characters of the persons who were to compose the Council, but from the constitution; and if that, and the laws already in force, were not sufficient to circumscribe the Regent, our liberties would not be safe; that if those laws would not be efficient under a Regent, how are they so under a King? That as to the precedents that had been alleged, they were urged ridiculously; must this be assented to because it was so in the days of Harry the Third, when the constitution was totally unlike what it is now? Half of the Regency nominated by Henry the Eighth were Papists, half Protestants; was that disposition preferable to a single Regent? No; it was formed for dissension; nor is there one reason to be drawn from precedent, or from the nature of our constitution. Should we follow the example of the Barons? The only reason to imitate them would be, that the times are unlike. Oxenstiern's advice too is totally unapplicable: not," continued he, "that I believe the Council will obstruct the Regent's measures; I believe they will assist her: but if they should not, whoever should advise her to make a speech to Parliament to accuse her Ministers, would be guilty of a præmunire." Pitt answered, "That the tendency of such a speech would not be to alter the plan of Regency, but to check a faction; that what he had said regarded the clause of non-amotion; and that he was of Mr. Fox's opinion, who must have mistaken all his speech, or he all Fox's, though the latter had said that he would not be included as agreeing for his reasons. That in any case he should not be for lodging power where there may be a temptation to prolong it." Fox replied again, "That a Regent could not be more dangerous than a King; and imagined that Pitt had meant that the Regent's speech should be intended to prevail on the Parliament to address her to alter the whole tenour of the Bill." The House grew tired of their altercations, and more of General Oglethorpe, who spoke after them; and divided between nine and ten at night, when the Council clause was voted by 278 to 90; and then they adjourned the further consideration of the Bill till next day.

17th.—The Committee on the Regency Bill was resumed. Lord Strange asked, if being nominated to the Council of Regency would vacate a seat in Parliament. T. Pitt proposed to leave out such words as precluded the Princess from disposing of offices. Old Horace Walpole ridiculed the Speaker, and was glad that with all his pomp and protestations he had no more influence. He was proceeding to preach up more regard to the King's Message, but was called to order by T. Pitt and Lord Strange, who objected to making such use of the King's name in a Debate. Prowse said, "he would appeal to that great treaty-maker, whether it was proper that fourteen persons should be entrusted with all the steps of a negotiation? That for the nomination of Bishops and Judges, he thought it a trifle; but disapproved extremely of the Council having any power to dispose of the Treasury, which with so great an army of revenue-men might be dangerous, if in the opposite scale to the Crown." Horace Walpole replied, "That some had carried it so much beyond him, as to be willing to trust the secret of treaties to seven hundred persons."

Horace Walpole[123] was still one of the busiest men in Parliament; generally bustling for the Ministry to get a Peerage, and even zealous for them when he could not get so much as their thanks. With the King he had long been in disgrace, on disputing a point of German genealogy with him (in which his Majesty's chief strength lay) whose the succession of some Principality would be, if eleven or twelve persons then living should die without issue. He knew something of everything but how to hold his tongue, or how to apply his knowledge. As interest was in all his actions, treaties were in all his speeches. Whatever the subject was, he never lost sight of the peace of Utrecht, Lord Bolingbroke, and the Norwich manufactures; but his language and oratory were only adapted to manufacturers. He was a dead weight on his brother's Ministry; the first to

---

[123] Brother to Sir Robert Walpole, had been secretary to Earl Stanhope in Spain, was afterwards made Secretary to the Treasury, and Auditor of the Plantations, and was several times Ambassador in Holland and France, then made Cofferer of the Household, and lastly one of the Tellers of the Exchequer, and was created a Baron in 1756, and died February 5, 1757, aged 79.

take off that load on his brother's fall;[124] yet nobody so intemperately abusive on all who connected with his brother's enemies; nobody so ready to connect with them for the least flattery,[125] which he loved next to money—indeed he never entirely forgave Lord Bath for being richer. His mind was a strange mixture of sense alloyed by absurdity, wit by mimicry, knowledge by buffoonery, bravery by meanness, honesty by selfishness, impertinence by nothing.

Sydenham, as an old Tory, spoke for the undiminished prerogative, quoted Greek, and said that subjects had never before attempted to make Peers; and that the commissions of Judges determine at the King's death. Robinson urged that the House can only be adjourned by itself; but Sir William Yonge gave him precedents to the contrary; particularly, that the two first sessions of the late King's first Parliament had been adjourned by the Crown; and that nobody is at liberty to speak after the Crown has sent a Message for adjournment. Sir John Cotton asked, if the Crown had the power of adjournment, seeing the method is to send to desire the House would adjourn itself? T. Pitt (who the last summer had held a tin Parliament in Cornwall, had been baffled by an opposition erected by the Boscawens, under the auspices of the Ministry) was obliged from his own case to argue for the prerogative, and said, "That during his holding that Parliament he had searched for precedents, and had found that the Crown could adjourn even by proclamation, or by a message from the Secretary of State." Robinson acquiesced, but observed, "That there is no possibility of suspending the power of the legislature; that if the Regent can repeal this Act, she may repeal the three that by this she is excepted from the power of repealing." The Solicitor-General answered, "That it is only a direction to

---

[124] He paid the greatest court immediately to Lord Wilmington, and the instant the secret committee was voted, he set out for his house in the country, to burn, as he said in the House of Commons, dangerous papers; after which he professed himself very easy for what might happen.

[125] This was so much his foible that, when W. Pitt wanted to reconcile himself to the Whigs, he used to flatter H. Walpole in his speeches in the grossest manner; and when he was ambitious of being Secretary of State, he proposed H. Walpole for it as the only proper person, knowing that would be impossible to be effected, and hoping it would then come by rebound to himself.

her not to give her consent to the repeal of the three Acts, though, if she should, it would be valid."

The clause for continuing the sitting Parliament to the end of the minority, was then read. Lord Limerick, with as much zeal as if he too had lately held a tin Parliament, made a panegyric on the two Georges, and on the blessings which the people had enjoyed under them without tasting them;[126] and hoped the nation would be in such profound tranquillity as not to need the prolongation of the Parliament; and that the Ministers then will not act by half measures, and by expedients from day to day; and in confidence that they will dissolve the Parliament as soon as they may with safety, he made a motion of amendment to the clause, that it may be the last dissolved Parliament that shall assemble on the King's death, if another, though chosen, shall not have met and sat. Lord Strange approved the Motion, except that he liked just the reverse of it; and would have established the newly elected Parliament. Dr. Lee answered, "That the act of Queen Anne on a parallel case, prefers the old Parliament:" and Gybbon assigned the reason, because there may arise Debates on the new Speaker and double returns.

Mr. Fox asked, "If the prolonged Parliament is not to dissolve of course as soon as the minor King comes of age?" The Attorney-General replied, "The general law of the land will then operate for its dissolution." But Henley said, "That, as the new elect might be composed of ignorant persons, he wished the prolonged Parliament were to last six months after the commencement of the majority, that the young King might have the same benefit from that act that an older Prince would have!" Sir William Yonge approved this opinion, and said, he remembered that on the late King's accession, instead of attending the business of the House, everybody ran out of town to secure their re-elections. The Solicitor-General replied, "That as the prolonging Parliaments was neither an eligible nor popular measure, he was glad the regulation extended no further; though it was more necessary now to continue their duration for

---

[126] The decency of this censure from Lord Limerick may be gathered from the long time he had been in Opposition himself, and from his being the person who made the famous motion for removing Sir Robert Walpole, as the supposed author of all the calamities of the present reign.

some time after a King's death than when Parliaments did not give the Revenue." George Townshend spoke against the Parliament's prolonging itself, and said, "There was nothing so dangerous as to inculcate into a young King, that he owes his safety to anything unconstitutional."

Fazakerley made a tedious calculation, which he seemed to intend for humour, of how long the Parliament might possibly continue if every one of the late Prince of Wales's children should happen to die just at a given time. The Solicitor replied, "That, if such melancholy accidents should happen, the reasons for the continuation would increase in proportion." Morton spoke for, Dowdswell and Sir John Cotton against the amendment; but it was voted. Lord Harley[127] then spoke prettily against the whole clause, and said, "That all the arguments that had been used would hold good upon all elections, and would tend to make any Parliament perpetual; and that such groundless apprehensions ought not to be appeased at the expense of the constitution; that the people will be cheated who will not have opportunities of changing such representatives as they dislike; and that upon the whole he observed, that Parliaments had originally been annual, then were stretched to triennial, then lengthened out to septennial, and now were going to be made perpetual."

Lord Hilsborough said, "That the arguments urged against the clause were reducible to those of power, right, and expedience. That the Parliament has power to prolong itself, is plain from the very debating upon it; that it has a right, appears from the Triennial and Septennial Acts, and from the Sixth of Queen Anne; and for the expedience, it is a known maxim, *salus populi suprema lex esto*. That in the case of a Rebellion, would a Parliament allow of its own dissolution, which would bring on the tumults of new elections? or in case of a plague, would any wise Government give occasion to great and populous assemblies, when it would even be unfit for the Parliament itself to meet? That the event in question might include all the others, and probably would some of them; and that the prolongation now in Debate would not be actual, but discretionary, while the circumstance of the manner in which it came

---

[127] Eldest son of the Earl of Oxford.

recommended must strike the breast of every man." Bowes, Vyner, and T. Pitt, spoke against the clause; Charles Yorke for it. Sir John Rushout observed that T. Pitt had made the King's Message the foundation of the Debate, and then had objected to its being pleaded. He was called to order, and so were some others; Gray and Dowdswell then spoke against, and Southwell for the clause, which was carried at half an hour after seven, by 258 to 81.

Then was read the clause to prevent the young King from marrying before the expiration of his minority, unless with consent of the Regent, and the major part of the Council; and to annul any such marriage, and to declare all the persons concerned guilty of high treason. This clause, which on the very face of it is a flat contradiction to the established opinion of the Church of England, which never heard of dissolution of marriage for political reasons, had passed uncontroverted through the House of Lords, undisputed by the Bench of Bishops. So obsequiously now did the sages of the Ecclesiastic Courts bow to temporal power! Fazakerley alone in the Commons remonstrated against it, and showed "the dangers that may arise from pronouncing the King's wife guilty of high treason, and her children illegitimate; and the mischiefs it may occasion, as he may marry her again after his majority—unless you will divest the Crown of the prerogative of pardon, and that in the dearest case, and will bind the Regency not only to prosecute a new species of treason, but to enforce the penalty. If this illegal Queen may be pardoned, and then espoused again, what confusions, what contests may not spring from the different children she may bear during her first and second marriage, when one son may plead his birthright under the new establishment, the other his seniority under all the known descriptions of legitimacy in the Church of England."

The Attorney-General made a slight answer, and this new kind of divorce passed without farther opposition.[128] Schisms and holy wars have

---

[128] A second instance of the same kind of complaisance from the Bishops appeared in May, 1753. Lord Bath had brought in a Bill to prevent clandestine marriages, which being very exceptionable, a new one was ordered to be brought in by the Judges, and was accordingly drawn up and warmly patronized by the Chancellor, and as warmly, though ineffectually, opposed by the Duke of Bedford; the whole Episcopal Bench consenting to the Act, though there were several clauses which enjoined dissolution of marriage for temporal reasons. In

sprung from smaller seeds! But religious animosities were out of date; the public had no turn for controversy; the Church had no writers to make them fond of it again. This had lately appeared; Dr. Middleton,[129] the best writer of the age, had overturned the Fathers, and exploded some visions of the Bishop of London, without a tolerable answer being made in defence of either. Of the prelates, the Archbishop[130] was a harmless good man, inclined to much moderation, and of little zeal for the tinsel of religion. Hutton, the other Archbishop, was well bred and devoted to the Ministry. Honest old Hoadley,[131] who, to the honour of his times, had, though the champion of Liberty, risen to the rich Bishopric of Winchester, was in a manner superannuated. Sherlock of London, almost as able a combatant for the power and doctrines of the Church, was past his strength, and still fonder of the politics of the Government than of the honour of the Keys. The Bishop of Durham[132] had been wafted to that See in a cloud of metaphysics, and remained absorbed in it. Gooch of Ely, the highest Churchman in his heart, had risen to his present greatness in the Church by shifting his politics. The rest were men neither of note nor temper to give the Ministry any disturbance.

---

the House of Commons it was opposed by Fox and Nugent; on the other hand, the Attorney-General, who had been bred a Presbyterian, supported it, and applauded the conduct of the Bishops, *who*, he said, *had at last reduced Christianity to common sense*. This sentence occasioning great astonishment, he softened it by adding, that he only meant that the Bishops had at last consented to remove a superstructure, raised on the foundation of the Gospel, which Christ and the Apostles had never projected, it being only intended by the New Testament that marriages contracted under the laws of the country should be indissoluble; and that it was nowhere said that even the intervention of a priest was essential to the validity of matrimony.

[129] Dr. Conyers Middleton, author of the Life of Cicero, of the Inquiry into the Miraculous Powers, of an Examination of the Bishop of London's Letters on the Use and Intent of Prophecy, and of several other celebrated works. Much was written against him—nothing well; yet the University of Oxford bestowed the degree of Doctor on two of his opponents. He died July 28, 1750; and it was obvious how much personal prejudice had influenced his antagonists, for after his death some tracts, which he had held too offensive for publication, and much stronger against Christianity than any of those he had published, were printed—and nobody wrote against them!

[130] Dr. Thomas Herring, Archbishop of Canterbury. He died March 13, 1757.

[131] He died, after an illness of two hours, at his palace in Chelsea, April 17, 1761. What is here said of his being superannuated relates to the infirmities of his body, not of his mind, he retaining his senses perfectly to the last.

[132] Dr. Butler, author of the Divine Analogy, &c. He died in June, 1752.

Then the præmunire clause was read. Mr. Fox said, "He was ready either to wait for the opinions of the lawyers, or to endeavour to amend the clause himself. That he had several objections to the wording of it; that *Acts passed* may be Acts of Parliament; that *in order to vary the Settlement* ought never to be words in a penal Act; by the same rule a person would be guilty of robbery who went to a gunsmith's with another to buy pistols *in order* to rob. That *null and void* must mean Acts of Parliament, not letters-patent, for they cannot supersede Acts of Parliament. That the crimes intended to be punished by this law should be certainly known, and not subject to constructions. That the door of the house where the plague was would be marked, and then whoever entered, let him die!" He then proposed to leave out the word *præmunire*, and to leave the pursuit of the crime to the common course of the law of the land; or to make it even high-treason, provided it was made clear to the subjects, what the crime was to be; as no man can suffer but for known crimes. That the maxim, *Misera est servitus ubi lex est inserta*, can only be meant of penal laws, for all other laws are undoubtedly much too uncertain. Fox frequently attacked the lawyers; he loved disputing as much as they do, but as he loved sense and argument, which they make a trade of perplexing, he could not bear a society who at once inverted the use of reason and the profession of justice.

He was answered by Murray, the Solicitor-General,[133] a frequent antagonist of his, who had quickness and eloquence enough to defend or not to want the knowledge of the Law, of which he was master. He said, "There could be no hurt in omitting the words that conveyed any doubtful meaning; that the Bill was calculated against unlawful acts, such as force and usurpation, upon the foundation of former examples, particularly the disposition made by Henry the Eighth; that it was only a clause *in terrorem*; that there must be an overt act; that the House had already passed a sanction of the same nature in the marriage clause: but if these words were disliked, you might insert *unlawfully and without consent of*

---

[133] William Murray, brother to Lord Stormont, and to the titular Earl of Dunbar, the Pretender's first Minister. Pope's Imitation of *Nil Admirari* is addressed to him. He was made Solicitor-General soon after Sir Robert Walpole's resignation.

Parliament; and that the Regent would certainly not be included within the words."

Fox accepted the proposed words, but would have omitted *in order*, which would still leave the necessity of the overt act in full force. He insisted "that the clause affects nobody but those who assist the Regent in endeavouring the repeal of this Act, and consequently that she is tied up from innovating, while her Council are at liberty to attempt what farther usurpations they please upon hers and the royal authority. It is difficult to ascertain what her accomplices must or must not will and know, to include them within the penalty; that if she takes out letters-patent to be sole Regent, are the clerks who draw them to be subject to the præmunire? That it must be right to omit the words *in order*, since in the Solicitor's opinion they were useless; in his, dangerous: but supposing they were still to remain, he could not help insisting on being told, what punishment there would be for him or any man who should attempt to cancel the Regency Bill without the connivance of the Regent?" The Solicitor replied, "That such act would be against the King, because he was in her hands; but that this provides against doing it *with* her consent. That the words *in order* were neither so unheard of, nor so formidable as was pretended; that the Coventry Act has the equivalent words *with intent*; and that the Mutiny Bill (brought in by Mr. Fox) has even the words *in order*. He owned that those words were inserted to prevent the connivance of the Regent from giving an air of legality to any attempts of innovation." The Master of the Rolls said, "He could not point out words to describe the crime, but he thought *with intent* preferable to *in order*."

Fox asked, "If whether, as it was allowed that it would be lawful to attempt the repeal of the Act by parliamentary methods, the attempters would be guilty of a præmunire, if the Parliament should not concur for the repeal? But that as it was confessed by great lawyers that the crime could not be described, he desired to have it considered, whether it would not be more proper, more humane, and more sensible, to leave the punishment to the Judges?" Sir Richard Loyd said "That the words *in order* were not dangerous, but that *advising* was too vague, as it may be proper to give the Regent such advice; that if the word *promoting* stood, he should wish to insert *unless to apply to Parliament*." Fazakerley approved the addition of *without the consent of Parliament*. The Attorney said, "That *intent* could only relate to the person, not to the concurrence; that he thought the words *Acts passed* might be omitted, but that the lowest persons concurring knowingly to defeat the Act, ought to incur equal punishment." Lord Strange said, "It must mean Acts of Parliament, for nothing else could set aside this:" and then he moved the amendments that had been proposed.

Pitt said, "He imagined they were already agreed to; that he would have *Acts passed* omitted, but liked *in order*: that he approved the addition of the word *unlawful*, but would omit *without consent of Parliament*, because it would be inviting applications to Parliament, and would make men turn their minds to get this Act repealed, though there was no doubt already, but that the Parliament could alter this settlement if it should please." He then moved to leave out *Acts*, and was seconded by Fox. Fazakerley asked whether it would not be necessary to have a Commission of Regency if the Princess should be ill. Pitt then moved to insert *unlawfully*, and Fox yielded not to mention *without consent of Parliament*, and to let *in order* stand. Lord Strange said, if he were to have the Princess's ear, he would advise her to get this Act repealed. Fox moved for leaving out *concurring*. Old Horace Walpole argued for its remaining; and Sir William Yonge defended it as meaning no more than the three other words that accompanied it. Fox ridiculed him on his reverence for the sacredness of tautology, and said, that if all those words had the same meaning, he would leave out three of them. Pitt was for retaining the word, because it had once been inserted, and to omit it now, would be telling the people that they might concur. Thus at half-an-hour after ten at night, this inquisition clause, having dwindled into a grammatical dispute, was voted, with corrections more worthy of grammarians than a House of Commons, by 126 to 40; a few of Mr. Fox's and the Duke of Bedford's friends insisting upon a division, though the former would himself have acquiesced.

20th—The Bill was reported, read a third time, and passed, with nothing material but a long bad speech of Mr. Beckford against it, and Mr. Pelham's, who was now got free from the chair, for it. He said, "He would not observe on what any particular person had said, but must express his surprise at so much Debate, after the message had been sent by the King, who had recommended restrictions, which had been approved by both Houses, and his Majesty had received Addresses of Thanks from both upon it." He said, that notwithstanding this, the Debates had not been upon any particular restrictions, but against any at all; yet he must ask, how appointing a Council for the Regent was a breach of the constitution? That as to precedents, for his part he had never heard one exactly stated and followed in observations; that in the present case, what was to be learnt from precedents, was, the danger of minorities; and that the remedy now to be applied, was not a breach, but a preservative of the constitution, against it could operate again. That his motive for approving the Council, was, that he would not lead the Princess into temptation; that he was willing to give her all the agreeable part of authority; and that the Council would be no check, where she was to exert grace and favour, but only where there should be weighty points that might introduce difficulties. That it was possible she might get favourites about her; that a Regent may be subject to them as well as a King; that it was for her security to have a Council responsible. That when the settlement of the Crown was made in favour of the House of Hanover, greater restrictions than those in question had been proposed, and somewhat stronger than temporary Regencies. That the Regent would only be limited in those great acts, where the Crown itself is limited, of peace and war.

Is there, continued he, any person here wise enough to tell me, who is answerable for the acts of the Regent? She herself is; and as this provision takes off that subjection from her, it is a respect to her. I hope I shall not be thought to want respect to her, if I, who have ventured to speak my mind under the King my master, am as freely spoken in what regards the Princess. He then mentioned the clause for prolonging the Parliament, and said, that ever since the Restoration, there has always been a dissolution or suspension of Government during general elections; that a contagion has constantly arisen, which has suspended all connections of friendship, all notions of right and wrong; and that many a man has given his vote for one man, who would leave the care of his children to that very man's antagonist. That our constitution gives sanctions to invasions, to that bad spirit of disaffection, which makes our enemies lie in wait till they see how elections turn out. He added, that he should say very little upon the clause of præmunire, which had been so fully explained and answered by the lawyers; though it was sufficient that Englishmen wanted no farther safety, who must be tried by juries, that are not likely to stretch constructions. One thing he would say, *that the Bill cannot be too strictly observed.* For the objections, they were not against the whole Bill; and the Committee had acquiesced in amending those parts that were most liable to exception. That indeed he could not but lament that the approbation of the House had not been more general, as he knew, when differences arise there, what constructions are made upon them without doors: but that he only lamented this, did not pretend to blame, as he spoke without prejudice, passion, or partiality, and that he was persuaded nobody would suspect him of any prospect to power for himself from this Bill, as he should be too great a wretch to build views of grandeur on what he must regard as the greatest misfortune, and what would shake the foundations of his country. It is observable, that of the two persons who had framed, and were to glut their own ambition the most by this Bill, the Chancellor and Mr. Pelham, the former pronounced any man a fool, the latter stamped him a villain, who expected or laid a plan of power from it. It passed without a division. The greater part of the late Prince's Court voted for the Bill. Lord Egmont for nothing but prolonging the Parliament.

21st.—The amendments were explained to the Lords by the Duke of Newcastle and the Chancellor, and agreed to.

Chapter 6

The day after the Committee in the House of Commons, the King said aloud in the drawing-room at Kensington, that the amendments to the præmunire clause were rightly made. The Chancellor answered, "the insertion of the word *unlawfully* was unnecessary." "That," replied the King, "is a distinction only for lawyers to make." Mr. Pelham would have explained it to him in a low voice, but he would talk upon it publicly.

About the same time, the King talking to Mr. Fox in his closet upon the Bill, asked him, whom he would have made Regent? "Sir," said Mr. Fox, "I never thought I should be asked, and therefore never thought—if it was impossible the Duke should!" The King replied, "My affection was there;" but avoided talking on the impossibility. He assumed to himself the chief direction of the Bill, and added, "I have a good opinion of the Princess, but I don't quite know her." He then spoke largely and sensibly on the restrictions, and gave reasons for them. "That a Council was necessary for her, even in cases of treason: women are apt to pardon; I myself am always inclined to mercy; it is better to have somebody to refuse for her. As to the power of peace and war, I never would declare either without consulting others. And as to the objection of the Council being irremoveable, who knows it will be composed of the present people? It will be the Ministers I shall leave: had you rather have those I shall leave, or have the Princess at liberty to go and put in Lord Cobham or Lord Egmont? What did you say against the Bill?—do you like it? tell me honestly." Fox answered, "If you ask me, sir—no. What I said against it was, because what was said for it was against the Duke." The King told him, "I thank you for that: my affection is with my son: I assure you, Mr. Fox, I like you the better for wishing well to him. The English nation is so changeable! I don't know why they dislike him. It is brought about by the Scotch, the Jacobites, and the English that don't love discipline; and by all this not being enough discouraged by the Ministry."

To complete the history of this memorable Bill, I shall subjoin some account of its author.

Sir Philip Yorke, Baron of Hardwick, and Lord Chancellor, was the son of an attorney at Dover. He was a creature of the Duke of Newcastle, and by him introduced to Sir Robert Walpole, who contributed to his grandeur and baseness, in giving him an opportunity of displaying the extent of the latter, by raising him to the height of the former. He had good parts, which he laid out so entirely upon the Law in the first part of his life, that they were of little use to him afterwards, when he would have applied them to more general views. He was Attorney-General, and when the Solicitor Talbot was, after a contest, preferred to him for the Chancellorship (the contest lay between their precedence, for Talbot was as able a man, and an honest one), Sir Robert Walpole made Yorke Chief-Justice for life, and greatly encreased the salary. Talbot dying in a short time after his advancement, to the great grief of all good men, Yorke[134] succeeded. In his Chief-Justiceship he had gained the reputation of humanity, by some solemn speeches made on the Circuit, at the condemnation of wretches for low crimes; a character he lost with some when he sat as Lord High Steward at the trials of the Scotch Lords, the meanness of his birth breaking out in insolent acrimony. On his promotion, he flung himself into politics; but as he had no knowledge of foreign affairs, but what were whispered to him by Newcastle, he made a very poor figure.

---

[134] A story is current, that Sir Robert, finding it difficult to prevail on Yorke to quit a place for life for the higher but more precarious dignity of Chancellor, worked upon his jealousy, and said, that if he persisted in refusing the Seals, he must offer them to Fazakerley. "Fazakerley!" exclaimed Yorke; "impossible! he is certainly a Tory, perhaps a Jacobite." "It's all very true," replied Sir Robert, taking out his watch, "but if by one o'clock you do not accept my offer, Fazakerley by two becomes Lord Keeper of the Great Seal, and one of the *staunchest Whigs in all England*." Yorke took the Seals and the Peerage.—E.

In the House of Lords, he was laughed at; in the Cabinet, despised.[135] On the Queen's death, he went deep into the Duke's shallow scheme of governing the King by the Princess Emily; for this cabal thought that he must necessarily be ruled by a woman, because the Queen was one, not considering it was because she was a wise one. This scheme was to be built on the ruin of Sir Robert Walpole, who had no other trouble to make it miscarry than in making the King say "*Pho!*" to the first advice this junto gave him. Their next plot was deeper laid, and had more effect: by a confederacy with the chiefs of the Opposition, they overturned Sir Robert Walpole; and in a little time, the few of their associates that they had admitted to share the spoils. When Yorke had left none but his friends in the Ministry, he was easily the most eminent for abilities. His exceeding parsimony was qualified by his severity to and discouragement of usurers and gamesters; at least, he endeavoured to suppress that species of avarice that exists by supplying and encouraging extravagance. The best thing that can be remembered of the Chancellor is his fidelity to his patron; for let the Duke of Newcastle betray whom he would, the Chancellor always stuck to him in his perfidy, and was only not false to the falsest of mankind.

The Pelhams having thus secured the duration of their power by Act of Parliament, determined at least to remove every object that gave any interruption or uneasiness to their enjoyment of it. It will not easily be understood how the Duke of Bedford and Lord Sandwich, who were the present objects of offence, could give them any uneasiness. The latter was willing to submit to any indignities to keep his place; and the former neither had, nor pretended to any power, though Secretary of State. No measure, foreign or domestic, but was transacted without his participation. So far from having had any share in the nomination of Officers and Governors to the young Prince of Wales, the Duke of Bedford was not even told he was to have any, nor acquainted when they were actually appointed. He was not consulted upon any one step of the Regency Bill;

---

[135] Yet, in the course of the work, the author laments Lord Hardwick's influence in Cabinets, where he would have us believe he was despised, and acknowledges that he exercised a dominion nearly absolute over that House of Parliament, which, he would persuade his readers, laughed at him. The truth is, that wherever that great magistrate is mentioned, Lord Orford's resentments blind his judgment, and disfigure his narrative.—E.

only when it was entirely resolved, and had been actually communicated to the Cabinet Council, at which Lord Sandwich, his friend, was present, the Chancellor went to impart it to him at his own house, where he was confined with the gout. Indeed, at first he was pleased with this farce of attention, till his friends pointed out the insult of it. Notwithstanding all this submission, the Duke of Newcastle had no peace till they were removed. As he had no cause from *their* characters, we must seek it in his own; and to show the force of his jealousy, it will be necessary to give a deduction of his several treacheries.

He succeeded young to an estate of about thirty thousand pounds a year, and to great influence and interest in several counties. This account in reality contains his whole character as a Minister; for to the weight of this fortune he solely owed his every-other-way most unwarrantable elevation. His being heir to his uncle, the old Duke of Newcastle, obtained from the Crown a new creation of the title in his person; and, though he was far from having parts to procure him a Peerage, his Peerage and vast income procured him the first posts in the Government. His person was not naturally despicable; his incapacity, his mean soul, and the general low opinion of him, grew to make it appear ridiculous. A constant hurry in his walk, a restlessness of place, a borrowed importance, and real insignificance, gave him the perpetual air of a solicitor, though he was perpetually solicited; for he never conferred a favour till it was wrested from him, but often omitted doing what he most wished done. This disquiet and habit of never finishing, which, too, proceeded frequently from his beginning everything twenty times over, gave rise to a famous *bon mot* of Lord Wilmington,—a man as unapt to attempt saying a good thing, as to say one. He said, "the Duke of Newcastle always loses half an hour in the morning, which he is running after the rest of the day without being able to overtake it."

He early distinguished himself for the House of Hanover, and in the last years of Queen Anne retained a great mob of people to halloo in that cause. He and his brother Harry raised a troop for King George on the Preston Rebellion, where the latter gave proofs of personal courage. The Duke was rewarded with the Garter, and sometime after made Lord

Chamberlain. The late King chose him for the honour of being Godfather to a new-born son of the Prince of Wales, which his Royal Highness much disapproving, was the immediate cause of that famous breach in the Royal Family, when the Prince and Princess left the palace very late at night. On Lord Carteret's being sent into honourable banishment as Lord Lieutenant of Ireland, by the power of Lord Townshend and Sir Robert Walpole, the latter proposed to make the Duke of Newcastle Secretary of State, having experienced how troublesome a man of parts was in that office. The Viscount's first wife having been the Duke's sister was another reason for their depending the more on his attachment to them; but that very relation had given Lord Townshend too many opportunities of discovering how little he was to be trusted, particularly from his having betrayed Lord Sunderland, his first patron, to Lord Townshend, who earnestly objected to the choice of him, and endeavoured to convince Sir Robert Walpole how much his falsehood would give an edge to his incapacity. As the disagreement increased between those two Ministers, the Duke in every instance betrayed his brother-in-law to Sir Robert. The Viscount was not of Walpole's forgiving temper, and was immediately for discarding the Duke. He pressed both King and Queen to it; exclaimed against his childishness and weakness, and insisted upon his dismission as the only terms of reconciliation with Sir Robert. The King, who always hated him, easily yielded to make Sir Paul Methuen Secretary of State in his room; but the greater power of Sir Robert with the Queen (whose policy had long been employed in keeping open the breach, in order to govern both), saved the Duke for future scenes of perfidy[136] and ingratitude.

Towards the decline of Sir Robert Walpole's Ministry, the Duke of Newcastle, who feared to fall with him, and hoped to rise upon his ruins, dealt largely with the Opposition, to compass both. The late Duke of Argyle, after that Minister's defeat, and his own disappointment in not succeeding to a greater portion of power, commissioned his brother, Lord Islay, to tell Sir Robert, that the Duke of Newcastle and the Chancellor had long been in league with himself and Lord Granville to effect his ruin.

---

[136] Sir R. Walpole often said of the Duke of Newcastle, "His name is Perfidy." (Vide Appendix.)

Lord Granville was scarce warm in power before Newcastle betrayed him to Lord Chesterfield; and the latter having introduced Lord Sandwich, who was sent Minister to the Hague, this young statesman and the Duke of Newcastle kept the secrets of his own office from Lord Harrington, who had been restored to the place of Secretary of State, for the assistance he had lent in overturning Lord Granville. On Lord Harrington's discovering and resenting this treachery, the Seals were given to Lord Chesterfield; but he being, like his predecessors, excluded from all trust the moment he had a right to be trusted, soon resigned them. The Duke of Newcastle, who had newly entered into connections with the Duke of Bedford, (as he and his brother did successively with every chief of a faction, till they had taken out their stings by dividing them from their party, and then discarded them) wished to give the Seals to Murray, who was, or to Pitt, who was canvassing to be, his creature; but the Duke of Bedford abruptly and positively insisted on having them—and had [them, together with] their constant perquisites,—the Duke of Newcastle's suspicions and treachery.

The Duke of Newcastle had no pride, though infinite self-love: jealousy was the great source of all his faults. He always caressed his enemies, to list them against his friends; there was no service he would not do for either, till either was above being served by him: then he would suspect they did not love him enough; for the moment they had every reason to love him, he took every method to obtain their hate, by exerting all his power for their ruin. There was no expense to which he was not addicted, but generosity. His houses, gardens, table, and equipage, swallowed immense treasures: the sums he owed were only exceeded by those he wasted. He loved business immoderately, yet was only always doing it, never did it. His speeches in Council and Parliament were flowing and copious of words, but empty and unmeaning: his professions extravagant, for he would profess intentions of doing more service to many men, than he even did hurt to others. Always inquisitive to know what was said of him, he wasted in curiosity the time in which he might have earned praise. He aimed at everything; endeavoured nothing. Fear,[137] a ridiculous

---

[137] He never lay in a room alone; when the Duchess was ill, his footman lay in a pallet by him.

fear, was predominant in him; he would venture the overthrow of the Government, and hazard his life and fortunes rather than dare to open a letter that might discover a plot. He was a Secretary of State without intelligence, a Duke without money, a man of infinite intrigue, without secrecy or policy, and a Minister despised and hated by his master, by all parties and Ministers, without being turned out by any!

It may appear extraordinary that Mr. Pelham, who had not so much levity in his character, should consent to be an accomplice in his brother's treacheries, especially as upon every interval of rivalship, the Duke grew jealous of him. The truth was, that Mr. Pelham, who had as much envy[138] in his temper, and still more fondness for power, was willing to take advantage of his brother's fickleness, and reaped all the emolument without incurring the odium of it. He had lived in friendship with Sir Robert Walpole, Lord Chesterfield, and the Duke of Bedford; while his brother was notoriously betraying them shrugged up his shoulders, condemned the Duke, tried to make peace, but never failed to profit of their ruin the moment it was accomplished. The falsehood and frivolousness of their behaviour can never appear in a stronger light than it did in the present instance, and in all the transactions that relate to Lord Granville. That Lord had hurried into power on Sir Robert Walpole's disgrace, and declared he would be a Page of the Back Stairs rather than ever quit the Court again. He had no sooner quitted his party, who had long suspected him, than he openly declared himself a protector of Sir Robert Walpole; and to give the finishing stroke to his interest with the King, drove deep into all his Majesty's Hanoverian politics, persuaded, in spite of the recent instance before his eyes, that whoever governed the King, must govern the kingdom.

His person[139] was handsome, open, and engaging; his eloquence at once rapid and pompous, and by the mixture, a little bombast.[140] He was an

---

[138] An instance of it: after Sir Robert Walpole was out, he often pressed Mr. Pelham to take care of Sturt, who had been employed in Spain, which he neglecting, Sir Robert said one day to Mr. Pelham, "Here has been poor Sturt with me." Mr. Pelham could not help interrupting him, and crying out, "G— d— the rascal! what does he come to *you* for?"

[139] John Carteret, Earl of Granville, was early distinguished in business, and sent Embassador to Denmark, and made Secretary of State when very young; but attempting to undermine Sir

extensive scholar, master of classic criticism, and of all modern politics. He was precipitate in his manner, and rash in his projects; but, though there was nothing he would not attempt, he scarce ever took any measures necessary to the accomplishment. He would profess amply, provoke indiscriminately, oblige seldom. It is difficult to say whether he was oftener intoxicated by wine or ambition: in fits of the former, he showed contempt for everybody; in rants of the latter, for truth. His genius was magnificent and lofty; his heart without gall or friendship, for he never tried to be revenged on his enemies, or to serve his friends. One of the latter, Lord Chief-Justice Willes, being complimented on Lord Granville's return to Court, replied, "He my friend! He is nobody's friend: I will give you a proof. Sir Robert Walpole had promised me to make my friend Clive one of the King's Council; but too late! I asked him to request it of Mr. Pelham, who promised, but did not perform. When Lord Granville was in the height of his power, I one day said to him, 'My Lord, you are going to the King; do ask him to make poor Clive one of his Council.' He replied, 'What is it to me who is a Judge, or who a Bishop? It is my business to make Kings and Emperors, and to maintain the balance of Europe.' Willes replied, 'Then they who want to be Bishops and Judges will apply to those who will submit to make it their business.'" I will mention one other short instance of his style. When, during his power, he had a mind to turn out the Chancellor, and prefer Willes, he said to Mr. Pelham, "I made Willes Chief Justice." "You may make him more if you please, and perhaps will," replied Mr. Pelham, "but I thought Sir Robert Walpole made him Chief Justice." "No, it was I: I will tell you how: I knew him at Oxford; Queen

---

Robert Walpole, he was removed to the Lieutenancy of Ireland, and afterwards entirely laid aside. He became the principal speaker against the Court in the House of Lords; but towards the end of that Opposition, he was compelled by his associates, who suspected that he was negotiating a peace for himself, to make the famous motion for removing Sir Robert Walpole, on whose fall he was again made Secretary of State.

[140] In one of his speeches upon the war with Spain, he said, "We were entering upon a war that would be stained with the blood of Kings, and washed with the tears of Queens!" It was in ridicule of this rant, that Sir Charles Williams, in an unfinished poem, called the "Pandemonium," where he introduced orations in the style of the chief speakers of the Opposition, concluded Lord Granville's with the following line, at the close of a prophetic view of the ravages of the war,

"And Visiers' heads came rolling down Constantinople's streets."

Anne's Ministry had caught him scribbling libels: I had even then an interest with men in power—I saved him from the pillory—now, you know, if he had stood in the pillory, Sir Robert Walpole could never have made him a Judge."

He carried this extravagance into his whole behaviour: divided Europe, portioned out the spoils of the King of Prussia, conquered France—and all these visionary victories, without deigning to cultivate the least interest in the House of Commons, where the Pelhams were undermining like moles, and thinking as little of Europe—as ever they did afterwards. Pitt, who was building fame by attacking this Quixote Minister, received profuse incense from Mr. Pelham; while Lord Granville kept no measures of decency with his new associates. He treated the Duke of Newcastle, the Chancellor, and Lord Harrington, with unmeasurable contempt, and would not suffer their patience to be, what their tempers inclined them to be, the humblest of his slaves. These men, who, if they had any talents, had the greatest art that ever I knew at decrying those they wanted to undo, soon kindled such a flame in the nation, that the King was forced to part with his favourite, and all his airy schemes of German glory. Lord Granville had endeavoured early, by the intervention of Lord Hervey, to unite with Sir Robert Walpole, but he absolutely declined it, being persuaded that Lord Granville had connections with the Pretender,[141] which, if he ever had, he now and long since had undoubtedly broken off. In their distress to get rid of their great antagonist, the Pelhams had recourse to Sir Robert Walpole. I don't know whether the Duke of Newcastle, like another King-making Warwick, would not even have offered to raise him again to the height from which he had tumbled him, had he stipulated for any terms. Lord Orford, who the year before had by his single interest prevented the rejection of the Hanover troops, now came again to town, and having been instructed by

---

[141] Sir Robert Walpole used to relate the following passage. When Lord Granville was Secretary of State the first time, the Ministry had made some discoveries into the schemes of the Jacobites, and at a meeting at the Cockpit, determined to take up the Lord North and Grey, who was deeply engaged. The instant the meeting broke up, which was very late at night, Lord Granville rode away post all alone to Epping Forest, where that Lord lived, to give him notice; and when the messengers arrived soon afterwards to apprehend him, he was fled.

John Selwyn, who was dispatched to meet him upon the road, wrote a letter to the King, which prevailed upon him to dismiss his Minister.

The Pelhams then entered into a coalition with the Duke of Bedford, Lord Chesterfield, Pitt, and that faction, which went on tolerably smooth, till Pitt's impatience to be Secretary at War opened the door to a new scene. Lord Bath and Lord Granville, who still preserved connections with the King, through the intervention of my Lady Yarmouth, persuaded him not to admit that incendiary into his closet. The Pelhams discovered from whence the rub came; and growing apprehensive that as soon as the session should be closed, and the Supplies completed, they should be discarded, not only determined to resign their own places, but engaged the whole body of the King's Ministers and servants, down to the lowest clerks in offices, in a league of throwing up their employments in order to distress their master: and the whole nation, which for four years together had seemed possessed with a madness of seizing places, now ran into the opposite phrensy of quitting them—and must not it be told:—or will it be credited, if it is told?—The period they chose for this unwarrantable insult, was the height of a Rebellion; the King was to be forced into compliance with their views, or their allegiance was in a manner ready to be offered to the competitor for his Crown, then actually wrestling for it in the heart of his kingdom! A flagrancy of ingratitude and treachery not to be paralleled, but by the behaviour of the Parliament at the beginning of the Civil War, who connived at the Irish Rebellion, in order to charge King Charles with fomenting it. What attention they had already exerted for suppressing the Rebellion, appears from Sir John Cope's trial, where, in answer to his repeated memorials for succours, and representations of the young Pretender being actually in Scotland and in arms, the Council tell him, "That they are unwilling to send him supplies, for fear of alarming people."

This general banding of the King's servants against him, joined to Lord Granville's neglect of all precaution to strengthen himself by a party, had the desired effect. He had offered the Seals to Willes but the very day of the execution of their scheme, who prudently declined them. Winnington, though far from being a friend to Mr. Pelham, and wishing well to Lord Granville, yet understood his own interest too well to undertake the management of the House of Commons, and was at last forced to mediate the parley between the King and the mutineers. Lord Granville took the Seals, which Lord Harrington had been the first to resign, and sent for Lord Cholmondeley from Chester to take the others. This was[142] a vain empty man, shoved up too high by his father-in-law, Sir Robert Walpole, and fallen into contempt and obscurity by his own extravagance and insufficiency. Lord Winchelsea,[143] who had been at the head of the Admiralty on the first change, and the only man who had raised his character (by his conduct at that Board) when the rest of his friends had sunk theirs, was again named to that dignity; and Lord Bath at last obtained that object of his every passion, the government of the Treasury. The other employments they had not time to fill up, for on the third day of this meteor-like Ministry, no volunteers coming in, business at a stand, the nation in astonishment, and the Parliament in indignation, the two Lords were forced to tell the King, that he must once more part with them, and submit to his old governors. Lord Granville left St. James's laughing; Lord Bath slipped down the back stairs, leaving Lord Carlisle in the outward room, expecting to be called in to kiss hands for the Privy Seal.

The King sent for Winnington, and commissioned him to invite the deserters to return to their posts. Winnington[144] had been bred a Tory, but had left them in the height of Sir Robert Walpole's power: when that Minister sunk, he had injudiciously, and to please my Lady Townshend, who had then the greatest influence over him, declined visiting him in a manner to offend the steady old Whigs; and his jolly way of laughing at his own want of principles had revolted all the graver sort, who thought deficiency of honesty too sacred and profitable a commodity to be profaned and turned into ridicule. He had infinitely more wit than any man

---

[142] George, Earl of Cholmondeley, married Mary, daughter to Sir Robert Walpole. He was Knight of the Bath, and Lord of the Admiralty, and then Master of the Horse to the Prince of Wales; but resigning that post on the rupture between the King and Prince, he was made Chancellor of the Duchy of Lancaster, Lord Privy Seal on the resignation of Lord Gower, which place he was forced to give back on the coalition, and was appointed joint Vice-Treasurer of Ireland.

[143] Daniel Finch, Earl of Winchelsea and Nottingham.

[144] Thomas Winnington was first made Lord of the Admiralty, then of the Treasury, then Cofferer, and lastly Paymaster of the Forces, when Mr. Pelham was raised to the head of the Treasury.

I ever knew, and it was as ready and quick as it was constant and unmeditated. His style was a little brutal; his courage not at all so; his good-humour inexhaustible: it was impossible to hate or to trust him. He died soon after by the ignorance of a quack,[145] when he stood in the fairest point of rising, to the great satisfaction of Mr. Pelham, whom he rivalled and despised.

The *ligue*, who had retired for no other end, did not make the King expect them long. Lord Harrington alone, when Mr. Pelham announced to him the summons for their return, said, "Go back!—yes, but not without conditions." One was, that Lord Granville should give up the promise of the Garter; which he did—but got while out of place, and saw Lord Harrington sacrificed to the King's resentments.

The King had fewer sensations of revenge, or at least knew how to hoard them better than any man who ever sat upon a Throne. The insults he experienced from his own, and those obliged servants, never provoked him enough to make him venture the repose of his people, or his own. If any object of his hate fell in his way, he did not pique himself upon heroic forgiveness, but would indulge it at the expence of his integrity, though not of his safety. He was reckoned strictly honest; but the burning his father's will[146] must be an indelible blot upon his memory; as a much later instance of his refusing to pardon a young man[147] who had been condemned at Oxford for a most trifling forgery, contrary to all example when recommended to mercy by the Judge; merely because Willes, who was attached to the Prince of Wales, had tried him, and assured him his pardon, will stamp his name with cruelty, though in general his disposition was merciful, if the offence was not murder. His avarice was much less

---

[145] Dr. Thompson, who blooded and purged him to death in a very few days, for a very slight rheumatism. Several pamphlets were published on this case.

[146] [For an account of this curious transaction, see the author's Reminiscences in the fourth volume of his printed works.]—E.
It is said that there was a large legacy to his sister, the Queen of Prussia, which was the original cause of the inveteracy between the King and his nephew, the present King of Prussia.

[147] Paul Wells, executed at Oxford, Sept. 1, 1749, for the following, scarce to be called forgery:— Being sued by a Mrs. Crooke for a debt of only nine pounds odd money, he altered the date of the year in the bond to the ensuing year, to evade the suit for twelve months.—Vide an authentic account of his life, by a gentleman of C. C. C. Oxon.

equivocal than his courage: he had distinguished the latter early;[148] it grew more doubtful afterwards: the former he distinguished very near as soon,[149] and never deviated from it. His understanding was not near so deficient, as it was imagined; but though his character changed extremely in the world, it was without foundation; for [whether] he deserved to be so much ridiculed as he had been in the former part of his reign, or so respected as in the latter, he was consistent in himself, and uniformly meritorious or absurd.

His other passions were, Germany, the Army,[150] and women. Both the latter had a mixture of parade in them: he [treated] my Lady Suffolk, and afterwards Lady Yarmouth, as his mistresses, while he admired only the Queen; and never described what he thought a handsome woman, but he drew her picture. Lady Suffolk[151] was sensible, artful, and agreeable, but had neither sense nor art enough to make him think her so agreeable as his wife. When she had left him, tired of acting the mistress, while she had in reality all the slights of a wife, and no interest with him, the Opposition affected to cry up her virtue, and the obligations the King had to her for consenting to seem his mistress, while in reality she had confined him to mere friendship—a ridiculous pretence, as he was the last man in the world to have taste for talking sentiments, and that with a woman who was deaf![152] Lady Yarmouth[153] was inoffensive, and attentive only to pleasing

---

[148] At the battle of Oudenarde.

[149] Soon after his first arrival in England, Mrs. ****, one of the bedchamber women, with whom he was in love, seeing him count his money over very often, said to him, "Sir, I can bear it no longer; if you count your money once more, I will leave the room."

[150] He was nicknamed by the Jacobites, *the Captain*.

[151] Henrietta, daughter of Sir Henry Hobart, and sister of John, the first Earl of Buckinghamshire, of that family.—(Vide Appendix.)

[152] A relation of Cheselden the surgeon was condemned to be hanged; Cheselden proposed, if the King would pardon him, to take out the drum of his ear, in order to try what effect it would have; and if it succeeded, the experiment was to be repeated on my Lady Suffolk. The man was pardoned—the operation never tried!

[153] Amelia Sophia, wife of the Baron of Walmoden, created Countess of Yarmouth. She had a son by the King, who went by the name of Monsieur Louis, but he was not owned. The day Lord Chesterfield kissed hands on his being appointed Secretary of State, after so long an absence from Court, he met Sir William Russel, one of the Pages, in the antechamber of St. James's, and began to make him a thousand compliments and excuses for not having been yet to wait on him and his mamma; the boy heard him with great tranquillity. When the speech was at an end, he said, "My Lord, I believe you scarce designed all these honours for me. I suppose you took me for Monsieur Louis!"

him, and to selling Peerages whenever she had an opportunity. The Queen had been admired and happy for governing him by address; it was not then known how easily he was to be governed by fear.

Indeed there were few arts by which he was not governed at some time or other of his life; for not to mention the late Duke of Argyle, who grew a favourite by imposing himself upon him for brave; nor Lord Wilmington,[154] who imposed himself upon him for the Lord knows what; the Queen governed him by dissimulation, by affected tenderness and deference:[155] Sir Robert Walpole by abilities and influence in the House of Commons; Lord Granville by flattering him in his German politics; the Duke of Newcastle by teazing and betraying him; Mr. Pelham by bullying him,—the only man by whom Mr. Pelham was not bullied himself. Who

---

[154] Sir Spencer Compton, son of the Earl of Northampton, was Speaker of the House of Commons and Knight of the Bath in the reign of King George the First. On the accession of the present King, when Sir Robert Walpole went to receive his orders, he bad him go for them to Sir Spencer Compton. This was a plain declaration! The first business was to prepare the new King's speech to his Privy Council, which the new Minister was so little able to draw, that he was forced to apply for it to the old one, who drew it—willingly, it may be believed; and the Queen knew how to make the request and condescension have their effects. He was then created Baron, and afterwards Earl of Wilmington and Knight of the Garter, and made President of the Council. On the resignation of Sir Robert Walpole, he succeeded him as First Lord of the Treasury, with the new Commissioners, but had so little influence even at that Board, that Sandys, Rushout, and Gybbon, used to put the disposal of places to the vote, and carry them against him and his nephew Compton. He died in about a year and a half after he had been raised to this uneasy situation. He was the most formal solemn man in the world, but a great lover of private debauchery: after missing the first Ministership, he entered into a secret league with Mr. Pulteney, which Sir R. Walpole discovered by the means of Mr. Pulteney's gentleman, who betrayed to him the letter he was carrying from his master to Lord Wilmington. As this was soon after a treaty between them, Lord Wilmington was much shocked when Sir Robert reproached him with it, and continued so steady for the future, that when the famous motion was made against that Minister, he went to vote in the House of Lords with a blister on his head, after having been confined to his bed for some days with a fever.

[155] She always affected, if anybody was present, to act (and he liked she should) the humble ignorant wife, that never meddled with politics. Even if Sir Robert Walpole came in to talk of business, which she had previously settled with him, she would rise up, curtsey, and offer to retire; the King generally bad her stay, sometimes not. She and Sir Robert played him into one another's hands. He would refuse to take the advice of the one, and then when the other talked to him again upon the same point, he would give the reasons for it which had been suggested to him: nay, he would sometimes produce as his own, at another conversation to the same person, the reasons which he had refused to listen to when given him. He has said to Sir Robert, on the curtseys of the Queen, "There, you see how much I am governed by my wife, as they say I am! Hoh! hoh! it is a fine thing indeed to be governed by one's wife!" "Oh! sir," replied the Queen, "I must be vain indeed to pretend to govern your Majesty!"

indeed had not sometimes weight with the King, except his children and his mistresses? With them he maintained all the reserve and majesty of his rank. He had the haughtiness of Henry the Eighth, without his spirit; the avarice of Henry the Seventh, without his exactions; the indignities of Charles the First, without his bigotry for his prerogative; the vexations of King William, with as little skill in the management of parties; and the gross gallantry of his father, without his goodnature or his honesty:—he might, perhaps, have been honest, if he had never hated his father, or had ever loved his son.

Of all the resigners, the Duke of Grafton had treated his master with the greatest decency: he had retired to hunt, according to his custom, on the first scent of a storm; and it was with the greatest reluctance that he was forced to declare himself for any Ministry that was in a disputable situation: nothing could have forced him to it but the inequality of the dispute. When he went into the closet, he told the King, as if laughing at those he sided with, "Sir, I am come to direct you who shall be your Minister."

The Duke of Grafton[156] was a very extraordinary man; with very good common sense and knowledge of mankind, he contrived to be generally thought a fool, and by being thought so, contrived to be always well at Court, and to have it not remarked that he was so: yet he would sometimes boast of having been a short time in Opposition, and of having early resolved never to be so again. He had a lofty person, with great dignity; great slowness in his delivery, which he managed with humour. He had the greatest penetration in finding out the foibles of men that ever I knew, and wit in teazing them. He was insensible to misfortunes of his own[157] or of his friends: understood the Court perfectly, and looking upon himself as of the Blood Royal, he thought nothing ought to affect him, but what touched them: as he had no opportunity of forsaking them for a family to which he was more nearly related, one must not say he would have forsaken them: betraying was never his talent; he was content to be ungrateful, when his

---

[156] Charles Fitzroy, the second Duke of Grafton, Lord Chamberlain and Knight of the Garter, grandson to Charles the Second. He died May 6, 1757, aged 78.
[157] All his three sons died before him.

benefactors were grown unhappy. He was careless of his fortune, and provided against nothing but a storm that might remove him from his station. An instance once broke out of his having ambition to something more than barely adorning the Court. On the Queen's death, whom he always hated, teazed, yet praised to the King, he was imprudent enough in a private conversation with Sir Robert Walpole and the Duke of Newcastle, to dispute with the latter, whose the power should be, both silently agreeing, fools as they were, in his very presence, that it was no longer to be Sir Robert's. Grafton thinking to honour him enough by letting him act under him, said at last in a great passion to t'other Duke, "My Lord, sole Minister I am not capable of being; first Minister, by G—, I will be." The foundation of either's hopes lay in their credit with Princess Emily, who was suspected of having been as kind to Grafton's love, as she would have been unkind in yielding to Newcastle's, who made exceeding bustle about her, but was always bad at executing all business. The Queen had in reality a thorough aversion to the Duke of Grafton for the liberties he took with one of her great blood; and if she had not been prevented by Sir Robert Walpole, would one night have complained to the King, when the Princess and the Duke, who hunted two or three times a week together, had staid out unusually late, lost their attendants, and gone together to a private house in Windsor Forest. The Queen hated him too for letting her see he knew her. He always teazed her, and insisted that she loved nobody. He had got a story of some Prince in Germany,[158] that she had been in love with before her marriage: "G—, madam," he used to say, "I wish I could have seen that man that you *could* love!" "Why," replied she, "do you think I don't love the King?" "G—, I wish I was King of France, and I would be sure whether you do or not!"

    Princess Emily detached herself from that cabal, and united with her brother the Duke and the Bedfords. She was meanly inquisitive into what did not relate to her, and foolishly communicative of what was below her to know: false without trying to please, mischievous with more design, impertinent even where she had no resentment; and insolent, though she

---

[158] It was the Duke of Saxe Gotha, father of the Princess of Wales.

had lost her beauty, and acquired no power. After her father's death, she lived with great dignity; but being entirely slighted by her nephew, who was afraid of her frankness, she soon forbore going to Court or to keep a Drawing-room herself, on pretence of her increased deafness. She was extremely deaf, and very short-sighted; yet had so much quickness and conception, that she seemed to hear and see more readily than others. She was an excellent mistress to her servants, steady to her favourites, and nobly generous and charitable.

When the Pelhams were returned to Court, they for some time sat but loose in the King's affections. The Duke of Newcastle had long been used to be called names by his master; and of whatever breach of duty he was guilty, he took care to submit with patience to abuse from his Sovereign. Mr. Pelham having more pride, was more resty under ill treatment, and soon threatened again to resign. The King, who would not venture again suddenly to be making Ministers upon his own authority, asked him who he wished should succeed him? He said peevishly, "Winnington." "No," said the King; "you know he is too much your friend." "I had rather," replied Mr. Pelham, "you would give my place to Lord Granville than keep it." "That is better still!" said the King; "you make it impossible for him to have it, and then want me to give it to him!"

If that three-days' Ministry had lasted, Lord Hartington, as errant a bigot to the Pelham faction as ever Jacques Clement was to the Jesuits, had offered to impeach Lord Granville—so soon had Sir Robert Walpole's friends forgot the abhorrence they had expressed for the motion to remove him without a cause; and so little do the silly bravos of a party foresee how soon they may be brought to adopt and refine upon the most unjustifiable excesses of their antagonists! This new violence was the more odious than its precedent, as here was a man to be impeached only because he was going to be an unpopular Minister! In four years, Lord Granville and Lord Hartington came into place together!

The Duke of Newcastle, who had conquered every obstacle to power, but the aversion of his master, began to think he might as well add his favour to the other attributes of a Minister; and having overturned Lord Granville for his German adulation, was so equitable as to make the King amends by giving into all excess of it himself. There was one impediment; he had never been out of England, and dreaded the sea. After having consulted his numerous band of physicians[159] and apothecaries, he at last ventured; and himself and his gold plate,[160] and his mad Duchess, under a thousand various convoys, treated Europe with a more ridiculous spectacle than any it had seen since Caligula's cockle-shell triumph.

He was now at the height of his wishes, but was still unsatisfied. The connection of the Duke with Lord Sandwich, and through him with the Duke of Bedford, had given him the uneasiness that was mentioned at the beginning of these Memoirs; and the Prince's death having smoothed all opposition, it was determined by the brothers in their Cabinet Council, to dismiss their rivals, whose interest in the House of Commons could now turn no scale into which it might be thrown. The measure was taken to remove Lord Sandwich, and thereby provoke the Duke of Bedford to resign; or to give the latter some more insignificant post, as Master of the Horse, President of the Council, or Master of the Ordnance. Mr. Fox, who saw the insult that was aimed at the Duke, endeavoured as much as possible to save his honour, by persuading the Duke of Bedford to acquiesce in the latter plan, as he would have more opportunities of crossing his enemies while he staid at Court, than probability of returning thither if once totally removed. Lord Sandwich laboured the same point, and even hoped to be overlooked if he could persuade the Duke of Bedford to accept one of the other less obnoxious employments; but the Duke was swayed to the contrary opinion.

He was a man of inflexible honesty, and good-will to his country: his great economy was called avarice; if it was so, it was blended with more generosity and goodness than that passion will commonly unite with. His parts were certainly far from shining, and yet he spoke readily, and upon trade, well: his foible was speaking upon every subject, and imagining he

---

[159] It is scarce credible what sums he spent on doctors and apothecaries, besides other emoluments bestowed on them. Mr. Graham's foreman was taken into the family, with the grant of an ample place in the revenue; Dr. Shaw had an annuity of £400 per annum, till another place of £700 per annum should fall in, with the reversion of the latter for his son.
[160] It was generally in pawn, and only fetched out on festival occasions. On its return from this journey to Hanover, it was landed in Yorkshire, whither a party of Dragoons were sent to convoy it to London.

understood it, as he must have done, by inspiration. He was always governed; generally by the Duchess,[161] though immeasurably obstinate, when once he had formed or had an opinion instilled into him. His manner was impetuous, of which he was so little sensible, that being told Lord Halifax was to succeed him, he said, "He is too warm and overbearing; the King will never endure him." If the Duke of Bedford could have thought less well of himself, the world would probably have thought better of him.

His friend Lord Sandwich[162] was of a very different character; in nothing more than in the inflexibility of his honesty. The Duke of Bedford loved money, to use it sensibly and with kindness to others; Lord Sandwich was rapacious, but extravagant when it was to promote his own designs. His industry to carry any point he had in view was so remarkable, that for a long time the world mistook it for abilities; but as his manner was most awkward and unpolished, so his talents were but slight, when it was necessary to exert them in any higher light than in art and intrigue. The King had never forgiven his indecent reflections[163] upon the Electorate when he was in Opposition, and as soon as ever he found his Ministers would permit him to show his resentment, he took all occasions to pay his court to them by treating Lord Sandwich ill, particularly by talking to Lord Anson before him on all matters relating to the fleet. An incident (one should have thought quite foreign to the Administration) contributed to give the King a new handle to use Lord Sandwich with indignity: the Bedfords had transacted a marriage between one of the Duchess's sisters[164] and Colonel Waldegrave, against the consent of her father, Lord Gower;

---

[161] Gertrude Leveson Gower, eldest daughter of Earl Gower, second wife of this John Duke of Bedford.

[162] John Montagu, Earl of Sandwich, made a Lord of the Admiralty on the coalition, and First Lord, on the Duke of Bedford's being appointed Secretary of State. He signed the peace of Aix-la-Chapelle. [He was First Lord during Lord North's administration, and died 1792. Our author disparages his abilities. He was a lively, sensible man, attentive to business, and not a bad speaker in Parliament.]—E.

[163] On the Debate in the House of Lords on the Hanover troops, he made a comparison between taking the Hanoverians into the pay of England, and the French taking the troops of the Duke John Frederic into their pay in 1672; and used these words,—"That *little* Prince would have duped Lewis Fourteenth; but he treated him like a *little* Prince, and would not accept his troops but upon his own terms."

[164] Lady Elizabeth Leveson Gower, Lady of the Bedchamber to Princess Emily, married to John Waldegrave, brother to Earl Waldegrave, and Groom of the Bedchamber to the King.

and Lord Sandwich had been so imprudent as to let the ceremony be performed at his apartments at the Admiralty. The Pelhams, who always inoculated private quarrels on affairs of state, dispatched my Lord Gower to ask a formal audience of the King, and complain of Lord Sandwich's contributing to steal his daughter. Lord Gower[165] was a comely man of form, had never had any sense, and was now superannuated. He had been educated a stiff Jacobite, elected their chief on his first coming into the King's service, and had twice taken the Privy Seal before he could determine to change his principles. The King entered into his quarrel; and the Pelhams by this artifice detached him from his family, and persuaded him that to resign with them would be sacrificing himself in the cause of Lord Sandwich, who had offered him such an indignity.

When Lord Sandwich found his disgrace unavoidable, and even had got intelligence of the day on which he was to be dismissed, he endeavoured by his own solicitations, and by the interposition of the Duke, to prevail on the Duke of Bedford to throw up the Seals first. This finesse, which did not succeed, was calculated to prevent the appearance of the Duke of Bedford's resigning upon his account, and consequently the new obligations to be laid upon him by that measure: governing that Duke no longer, he chose to be no longer connected with him; but Bedford now would neither stay in, nor go out by his advice.

---

[165] John Leveson Gower, Baron Gower, was elected President of the Board (the Jacobite meeting) in 1742, on the death of the Earl of Lichfield, while he was Lord Privy Seal, which he resigned soon after; but came into the same place again on the coalition, and was some time after created an Earl.

Chapter 7

June 13th.—The Duke of Newcastle wrote to Lord Sandwich, that the King had no farther occasion for his service; and in the evening sent Mr. Legge to acquaint the Duke of Bedford with the dismission of his friend. Legge was a younger son of Lord Dartmouth, who had early turned him into the world to make his fortune, which he pursued with an uncommon assiduity of duty. Avarice or flattery, application or ingratitude, nothing came amiss that might raise him on the ruins of either friends or enemies; indeed, neither were so to him, but by the proportion of their power. He had been introduced to Sir Robert Walpole by his second son, and soon grew an immeasurable favourite, till endeavouring to steal his patron's daughter,[166] at which in truth Sir Robert's partiality for him had seemed to connive, he was discarded entirely; yet taken care[167] of in the very last hours of that Minister's power; and though removed from the Secretaryship of the Treasury, being particularly obnoxious to Lord Bath, he obtained a profitable employment[168] by the grossest supplications[169] to the Duke of Bedford; and was soon after admitted into the Admiralty by as gross court paid to Lord Winchelsea, whom he used ill the moment he found it necessary to worship that less intense but more surely-rising sun, Mr. Pelham. He had a peculiarity of wit and very shrewd parts, but was a dry and generally an indifferent speaker. On a chosen embassy to the King

---

[166] Lady Maria Walpole, since married to Charles Churchill.
[167] He and Mr. Benjamin Keene had the reversion of a place in the Revenue between them, after the death of the then Earl of Scarborough.
[168] Surveyor of the King's Woods and Forests.
[169] They are contained in two letters still preserved by the Duke of Bedford.

of Prussia, Legge was duped and ill-treated by him. Having shuffled for some time between Mr. Pelham, Pitt, the Duke of Bedford, and Lord Sandwich, and wriggled through the interest of all into the Treasury, and then to the Treasurership of the Navy, he submitted to break his connections with the two latter by being the indecent messenger of Lord Sandwich's disgrace. The Duke met him on the steps of Bedford-house (as he was going to Lord Gower to know what part he would take on this crisis) and would scarce give him audience; but even that short interview could not save Legge from the confusion he felt at his own policy; and with the awkwardness that conscience will give even to an ambassador, he said, he had happened, as he was just going out of town, to visit the Duke of Newcastle, where he had not been in two months before, and had been requested by him to be the bearer of this notification.

The Duke of Bedford, who carried Lord Trentham with him, found Lord Gower in no humour to resign with him; on the contrary, enraged at his son, who told him he could not serve under Lord Anson, the new head of the Admiralty. "Sir," said his father, "he is your superior; he is a Peer." "Who made him so?" replied Lord Trentham. Lord Gower told the Duke of Bedford that he had listed all his children against him; and threatened Lord Trentham to disinherit him of all that was in his power; who told him in pretty plain terms, how much he was a dupe to the Pelhams; and after many high words, they both left him.

When the Duke of Bedford arrived at Kensington, he found none of the opposite faction but Lord Lincoln, whom he desired to acquaint the Duke of Newcastle with what he was going to say to the King. "Tell him, my Lord, because perhaps he would not like to come in and hear it; I shall neither say more or less for his presence or absence. If he comes into the closet and begins to dispute, I will not altercate with him there; I will afterwards wherever he pleases." When he went in to the King, he spoke above an hour warmly and sensibly on his own grievances, particularly on the Duke of Dorset being designed Lord Lieutenant for six months before he was made acquainted with it; on his relation, Lord Hartington, being named in the same manner for the Master of the Horse, and called up to the House of Peers, for which he had that very morning kissed hands; on the dismission of his friend Lord Sandwich; and on all the treacheries of the Duke of Newcastle, which he recapitulated, and the scenes of mischief which Mr. Pelham had been acting in Lord Gower's family: and he concluded with telling the King, that their persecution of him and Lord Sandwich arose solely from their attachment to his son the Duke; and then desired leave to resign the Seals. The King was struck and pleased with this remonstrance; agreed to all he had said of the Duke of Newcastle; doubted of the facts charged on Mr. Pelham; and with regard to Lord Sandwich, only said, "I don't know how it is, but he has very few friends." He told the Duke of Bedford, that if he was uneasy in his present post, he would give him that of President; but the Duke said it was impossible for him to act with the two brothers. He begged three reversions in the Secretary's office for his two secretaries, Mr. Leveson and Mr. Aldworth, and his steward Butcher; to which the King deferred giving an answer till next day, but then granted them; and parted with him with particular marks of favour and approbation.

As soon as the Duke of Bedford had resigned, Lord Trentham sent his resignation in a very explicit letter to Mr. Pelham, in which he spoke warmly on malicious people who had prejudiced his father against him. Mr. Pelham, who could neither avoid doing wrong nor bear to be told of it, was inconceivably stung with this reproach; and as if shifting off the consequence would clear him from being the cause, he would have waved accepting the resignation, sending Lord Trentham word that he was misinstructed in sending it to him, who had no authority to receive it, but yet was sorry for what he was doing.

17th.—Lord Granville was appointed President of the Council, Lord Hartington Master of the Horse, Lord Albemarle Groom of the Stole, Lord Anson First Lord, and the Admirals Boscawen and Rowley Commissioners of the Admiralty; the latter attached to Lord Granville, the other to nothing but his own opinion. He was on the worst terms with Anson, who had carried off all the glory of the victory at Cape Finisterre, though Boscawen had done the service, and whom he suspected of having sent him on the impracticable expedition to Pondicherry on purpose to ruin him. Lord Anson was reserved and proud, and so ignorant of the world, that Sir

Charles Williams said he had been round it, but never in it. He had been strictly united with the Duke of Bedford and Lord Sandwich, but not having the same command of his ambition that he had of his other passions, he had not been able to refuse the offer of the Chancellor's daughter, nor the direction of the Admiralty.

Lord Hartington, and his father, the Duke of Devonshire,[170] were the fashionable models of goodness, though their chief merit was a habit of caution. The Duke's outside was unpolished, his inside unpolishable. The Marquis was more fashioned, but with an impatience to do everything, and a fear to do nothing. Sir Robert Walpole had set up the father as the standard of Whiggism; in gratitude, he was constantly bigoted to whoever passed for head of the Whigs: but the dexterity of raising his son to so eminent a post as Master of the Horse during his own life, and obtaining a Peerage for his own son-in-law,[171] by retiring from power himself, extremely lessened the value of the rough diamond[172] that he had hitherto contrived to be thought.[173]

---

[170] October 11, 1764.—Tuesday noon, an express arrived from the Duke of Devonshire (Lord Hartington in the text), at the Spa in Germany, which brought advice that his Grace was much better, and that there were great hopes of his recovery; but these agreeable hopes were soon damped by the arrival of Lord John Cavendish, the Duke's youngest brother, at seven o'clock the same night, at Devonshire House, who brought the melancholy news, that his Grace had relapsed, and departed this life the 3rd instant, at half an hour past nine o'clock at night, at the above place.

His Grace was eldest son of William, late Duke of Devonshire, by his Duchess Catherine, daughter and sole heir of John Hoskins, Esq. In March, 1748, he married the Lady Charlotte Boyle, youngest daughter and heiress of Richard, late Earl of Burlington, which lady died in December, 1754, by whom he had issue,—1, William, Marquis of Hartington, born in December, 1748, who is now the fifth Duke of Devonshire, a minor, at Harrow school; 2, Lord Richard, born June 19, 1752; 3, Lord George Henry, born in March, 1754; and 4, Lady Dorothy, born August 27, 1750.

His Grace, at the time of his decease, was Lord High Treasurer, and a Privy Counsellor of Ireland, Governor of the county of Cork in that kingdom; a Governor of the Charter-house, Fellow of the Royal Society, and Knight of the Garter; but some time since had resigned all his places on the British establishment. The many amiable and truly excellent public and private virtues, and the very shining accomplishments which his Grace possessed, added a lustre to his high rank, and render his death a public loss.—(Public Journals.)

[171] Lord Duncannon, eldest son of the Earl of Besborough, who was created an English Baron, was one of the Lords of the Admiralty.

[172] So Sir Robert Walpole called him.

[173] The above sarcastic remarks may be ascribed to a recent family quarrel, in which the Duke of Devonshire and Lord Hartington had sided with Horace Walpole, the uncle, against the nephew, the author of these Memoirs. The injustice of them is sufficiently proved by the estimation in which both these noblemen (especially Lord Hartington) appear to have been

However, the Whigs were so satisfied with the promotion of Lord Hartington, that they overlooked the conjunction of Lord Granville, though so little time had passed since they had been enrolled in a crusade against him; and it would have been difficult for the Pelhams to have told what they had done to give Lord Granville a higher opinion of them, or what he had done to give them a lower opinion of him: what had happened to make him feel less contempt for them; or they to see less danger in him. So little reason had they to expect better union with him, that when he was wished joy on their reconciliation, he replied, "I am the King's President; I know nothing of the Pelhams; I have nothing to do with them." The very day he kissed hands, he told Lord D, one of the dirtiest of their creatures, "Well, my Lord, here is the common enemy returned!" Nugent, the Sancho Pança of this Quixote, began to beat up for volunteers for him; and himself made large overtures to Fox, desired to have some private conversation with him at Holland House, and told him he would reconcile himself to the Duke. Fox replied, "They have paved your way." Lord Granville the next day repeated this conversation to Mr. Pelham, with the only difference of inverting the persons of the speakers, and ascribing to Fox all the overtures that had come from himself. Two or three of his inferior dependents were promoted, but no mention made of his fellow martyrs.

On the 18th appeared the last and greatest phenomenon, Lord Holderness,[174] who had been fetched from his Embassy in Holland to be Secretary of State. In reality, he did justice to himself and his patrons, for he seemed ashamed of being made so considerable, for no reason but because he was so inconsiderable. He had a formality in his manner that would have given an air of truth to what he said, if he would but have assisted it with the least regard to probability; but this made his narrations harmless, for they were totally incredible. His passion for directing operas and masquerades was rather thought a contradiction to his gravity, than below his understanding, which was so very moderate, that no relation of

---

held by their contemporaries, and by the conduct of the latter even in delicate and difficult times, as related by the author himself.—E.

[174] Robert Darcy, Earl of Holderness, Lord of the Bedchamber, had been Embassador at Venice and the Hague, where he married the Greffier Fagel's niece. His mother was a daughter of Duke Schomberg, and married a second time to the Earl of Fitzwalter.

his own exploits would, not a little time before, have been sooner credited, than his being made Secretary of State. What contributed a little to make the King consent to this wonderful promotion was his mother, Lady Fitzwalter, being distantly related to the Royal Family. The Queen and Princesses always talked to her in French, though she had never been out of England, because her ancestors came originally from Germany.

When the King delivered the Seals to Lord Holderness in the presence of the Duke of Newcastle, he charged him to mind only the business of his province; telling him that of late the Secretary's office had been turned into a mere office of faction. The Duke of Newcastle, who understood the reprimand, and Lord Holderness, who did not, complained equally of the lecture. The former could not well complain of any direct chiding; for the King, who had parted with the Duke of Bedford, to quiet his wayward humour, to revenge the Duke of Bedford would not speak to the Duke of Newcastle for some weeks; an excuse he made advantage of pleading to the Duke of Marlborough, who had solicited for a Prebend of Windsor; and to Lord Halifax, who was pushing to get the West Indies entirely subjected to the Board of Trade, and to be nominated a third Secretary of State for that quarter of the world. As Lord Halifax persisted in this demand, and the Duke of Newcastle did not care to push the King any further, especially in the tender article of new appointments, Lord Holderness was made to taste of the servile uses for which he was introduced, and ordered to solicit the King to take so fair a feather from his own command as the direction of the West Indies; but for this time the Monarch would not, and Lord Halifax, after many vain threats, was forced to yield. He was[175] a man of moderate sense, and of great application to raise the credit of his employment; but warm, overbearing, and ignorant of the world.[176]

---

[175] George Montagu, third Earl of Halifax, of that house, and First Lord of Trade. He had set out in Opposition with Lord Sandwich, and came into place at the same time.
[176] Monday, June 10, 1771.—On Saturday morning, at four o'clock, died George Montagu Dunk, Earl of Halifax, Viscount Sunbury, Secretary of State for the northern department, Ranger and Warden of Salcey Forest and Bushy Park, Lord Lieutenant and Custos Rotulorum of Northamptonshire, and one of his Majesty's Most Hon. Privy Council, Knight of the Garter, a Governor of the Charter-house, and ranked as Lieutenant-General of his Majesty's Forces. His Lordship was born October 5, 1716, succeeded George, his father, the preceding Earl, May 9, 1739, and married in 1741, Miss Anne Dunk, daughter and heir of —— Dunk, of

25th.—The King put an end to the Session. The Speaker touched but gently and artfully on the Regency Bill; enough to show his disapprobation, and not enough to reflect on the decision of the House; praying for the King's life, because of the difficulties in which the Princess would be involved in a Regency without Sovereignty.

The instant the Parliament was prorogued, the two Sheriffs of London—I forget their names—accompanied by Lord Carpenter and Sir George Vandeput, went to Newgate, released Murray, and conducted him in paltry triumph to his own house. On the 28th, his case, scurrilously written by one Whitehead,[177] a factious poet, was published, for which the printer was taken into custody.

In July, the posthumous child of which the Princess was delivered was christened. The Prince had affected to baptize all his children by popular names; but his wife being more prolific than the English history, in heroes and heroines, the Edwards and Elizabeths were exhausted, and he had been forced to go back as far as the Conqueror's daughter. The King would not suffer the last Princess to be called Matilda,[178] but now, out of regard to his son's memory, indulged it.

Soon after the Prince died, an unlucky discovery had been made. George Lyttelton had written a lamentation, on that occasion, to his father,[179] an antiquated Baronet in Worcestershire, telling him that he and his friends had just renewed their connections with the Prince of Wales, by the mediation of Dr. Ayscough, which, though not ripe for discovery, was the true secret of their oblique behaviour this session in Parliament. This letter he had delivered to a gentleman's servant, who was going into that

---

Hawkhurst, in Kent, Esq., which lady dying in 1753, left three daughters,—viz., Lady Anne, who died in 1761; Lady Frances, who died in 1764; and Lady Elizabeth, married on March 1, 1766, to Lord Viscount Hinchinbroke, son and heir of the Earl of Sandwich. His Lordship, on the breaking out of the Rebellion in 1745, raised a regiment of Foot for his late Majesty. On March 20, 1761, his Lordship was nominated Lord Lieutenant of Ireland, and his administration of the government of that kingdom did him great honour.—(Public Journals.)

[177] Paul Whitehead, author, among other satiric writings, of the State Dunces, and Manners; for the last of which he was ordered by the House of Lords to be taken into custody. He was a man of most infamous character.

[178] She was christened Caroline Matilda.

[179] Sir Thomas Lyttelton had been a Lord of the Admiralty, but retired with a pension on his son's going so warmly into Opposition.

county; but the fellow having some other letters for the post, had by mistake given in the private negotiation, which was only subscribed *To Sir Thomas Lyttelton*. It was opened at the Post-office, and carried to Mr. Pelham. Had it been seen by no other person, the secret had been safe, and the treachery concealed, as carefully as if he had been in the conspiracy himself, instead of being the object of it; but it was talked of from the Post-office, though obscurely for some time, till at last it was nursed up somehow or other, and arrived at the King's ears, who grew outrageous, and could not be hindered from examining Shelvocke, the Secretary of the Post-office, himself. Here he got very little further light; for Shelvocke had been instructed to affirm that the letter was sent back to Mr. Lyttelton, unopened; but Lyttelton, who had not been so well instructed in his own secret, avowed it; and as if there were nothing to be ashamed of but the discovery, he took pains to palliate no other part of the story.

Absurdity was predominant in Lyttelton's composition: it entered equally into his politics, his apologies, his public pretences, his private conversations. With the figure of a spectre, and the gesticulations of a puppet, he talked heroics through his nose, made declamations at a visit, and played at cards with scraps of history, or sentences of Pindar. He had set out on a poetical love plan, though with nothing of a lover but absence of mind, and nothing of poet but absence of meaning; yet he was far from wanting parts; spoke well when he had studied his speeches; and loved to reward and promote merit in others. His political apostasy was as flagrant as Pitt's: the latter gloried in it: but Lyttelton, when he had been forced to quit virtue, took up religion, and endeavoured to persuade mankind that he had just fixed his views on heaven, when he had gone the greatest lengths to promote his earthly interest; and so finished was his absurdity, that he was capable of believing himself honest and agreeable.

In the beginning of September came news of the birth of a Duke of Burgundy; an event of the greatest moment to France, but not received with their usual transports. The Court had disgusted the clergy, by demanding an account of their revenues. The priests, equally ready at contriving or imputing an imposture, persuaded half the nation that the child was spurious; and to drive off the war from their own quarters, endeavoured to light up or to lay the foundation of a general war in the kingdom. The English Prelates sent Harry the Fifth to the conquest of France, to prevent a scrutiny of the same nature.

The same courier brought the Marquis de Mirepoix a patent of Duke. He was much esteemed in England, having little of the manners of his country, where he had seldom lived; and except a passion which he retained for dancing, and for the gracefulness of his own figure, there was nothing in his character that did not fall in naturally enough with the seriousness of the English and German Courts,[180] where he had been Ambassador; nor any quickness of parts that could have made him offensive, if our Ministry had been inclined to take exceptions. Their suspicions seldom ascended to enemies really formidable. They bore with General Wall,[181] an artful Irishman, Ambassador from Spain, and who but last year had clandestinely sent thither several of our woollen manufacturers. Greater insults were shown to us at Paris and Berlin, where Marshal Keith and Lord Tyrconnel, two outlawed Jacobites, were reciprocally Ambassadors. Indeed, it was a constant war of piques and affronts between the King and his nephew of Prussia. The latter had insisted upon the recall of Sir Charles Hanbury Williams, who had sacrificed to the ruling passion of the uncle, by treating the character of the Prussian King, in his public dispatches and private letters, in the strongest terms of satire.[182] He returned to Dresden, where, about this time, he concluded a subsidiary treaty with the King of Poland, to engage his vote for the Archduke Joseph to be King of the Romans—the darling object of the ambition of the Court of Vienna, and the common gulph of our profuse politics. The King of Prussia openly, the French underhand, opposed the election. The very opposition of the latter had a politic effect, as the longer it remained in suspense, the longer would be the duration of our extravagance. In one of the King of Prussia's rescripts, he taxed the King, whom he called the last and youngest of the Electors, with violating both his oath and the Golden Bull.

---

[180] Vienna.
[181] He came over very privately during the war, and negotiated the first overtures of peace.— Vide Lord Chesterfield's Apology.
[182] Vide Appendix, F. G. and H.

Sir Charles Hanbury Williams had been attached to Mr. Winnington, and was the particular friend of Fox. Towards the end of Sir Robert Walpole's power, they, Lord Hervey and Lord Ilchester, had forced the last into the Secretaryship of the Treasury, against the inclination of the Minister; an instance at that time unparalleled; much copied since, as the Government has fallen into weaker hands. Sir Charles remained a steady friend to Walpole, and persecuted his rival, Lord Bath, in a succession of satiric odes, that did more execution in six months, than the Craftsman had done in twice the number of years; for the Minister only lost his power, but the patriot his character. If Sir Charles had many superiors in poetry, he had none in the wit of his poetry. In conversation he was less natural, and overbearing: hated with the greatest good-nature, and the most disinterested generosity; for fools dreaded his satire—few forgave his vanity. He had thrown up his place on some disgusts; the loss of Mr. Winnington, and a quarrel with the Irish, occasioned by an ode[183] he wrote on the marriage of the Duchess of Manchester and Mr. Hussey, fomented by Lord Bath and his enemies, and supported with too little spirit, had driven him to shelter his discontents in a Foreign Embassy, where he displayed great talents for negotiation, and pleased as much by his letters, as he had formerly by his poetry.[184]

On the 13th of the following month, an express arrived of the death of the Prince of Orange, who, having been at Aix la Chapelle, caught a fever on his return, and died in five days.

He had long been kept out of all share in the government, like his predecessor, King William; like him, lifted to it in a tumultuous manner, on his country being overrun by the French; and the Stad-holdership made hereditary in his family before they had time to experience how little he was qualified to re-establish their affairs. Not that he wanted genius, but he was vain and positive, a trifling lover of show, and not master of the great lights in which he stood. The Princess Royal was more positive, and, though passionately imperious, had dashed all opportunities that presented

---

[183] The title of it was, "The Conquered Duchess." [It has been frequently printed, and is probably familiar to the reader.]—E.
[184] He died, [after much bodily and mental illness] November 2nd, 1759.

Chapter 7

for the Prince's distinguishing himself, from immoderate jealousy and fondness for his person. Yet the Mars who was locked in the arms of this Venus, was a monster so deformed, that when the King had chosen him for his son-in-law, he could not help, in the honesty of his heart, and the coarseness of his expression, telling the Princess how hideous a bridegroom she was to expect, and even gave her permission to refuse. She replied, she would marry him if he was a baboon. Well then, said the King, there is baboon enough for you!

The Princess immediately took the oaths as *Gouvernante* to her son, and all orders of men submitted to her as quietly as in a monarchy of the most established duration; though the opposite faction was numerous, and she herself lethargic and in a very precarious state of health. Lord Holderness was sent to condole and advise her. She, who had long been on ill terms with, and now dreaded the appearance of being governed by her father, received the Ambassador and three letters written with the King's own hand, in the haughtiest and most slighting manner. Lord Holderness was recalled in anger. The Princess, equally unfit to govern, or to be governed, threw herself into the arms of France, by the management of one Dubacq, a little Secretary, who had long been instilling advice into her, to draw her husband from the influence of Monsieur Bentinck and the Greffier, the known partizans of England; the former of whom, immediately after the death of the Prince, refused to admit Dubacq to a Council, to which she had called him, with the chiefs of the Republic, at the House in the Wood.

The Princess Royal was accomplished in languages, painting, and particularly music; the Queen, and the King too, before their rupture, had great opinion of her understanding; but the pride of her race, and the violence of her passions[185] had left but a scanty sphere for her judgment to exert itself.

---

[185] The Princess Royal was so proud and ambitious, that one day, when very young, telling the Queen how much she wished that she had no brothers, that she herself might succeed to the Crown, and the Queen reproving her, she said, "I would die to-morrow to be Queen to-day!" On the Queen's death, the Princess Royal, like others, imagining the King must be governed by a woman, pretended ill-health, and that her physicians had ordered her to Bath, and came over; but having been so indiscreet as to let her motive be known, the King would

November 14.—The Parliament met. Lord Coventry, and Lord Willoughby, of Parham, moved the Address in the House of Lords; Lord Downe and Sir William Beauchamp Proctor in the Commons. Sir John Cotton objected to the words *our flourishing condition*; but that was the only breath of opposition.

On the 18th, there was a meeting at the Speaker's, to consult on punishing the Sheriffs for their insolent behaviour on the delivery of Murray; but they came to no resolution, except on remanding Murray to his imprisonment. Accordingly, on the 20th, Lord Coke moved to have the former votes on him read, and then to revive them. He spoke well, and treated Murray and the Sheriffs with great contempt. Lord Coke[186] had ready parts, a great memory, great Whig zeal. There was too much pomp in his turn, and vehemence in the expression of his dislikes, which were chiefly now directed against the Scotch, who had persecuted him bitterly, on a quarrel with his wife, a daughter of the late Duke of Argyle. He was on ill terms too with Mr. Pelham, and had intended to have opened on the neglect shown to the old Whigs; but his friend, Lord Hartington, the officious tool to Mr. Pelham's ingratitude, had been with him that morning, and persuaded him to drop so general an attack. Lord Duplin seconded him. Sydenham opposed, and Lord Egmont,[187] who spoke with great caution, and apologized for undertaking the cause, was against unnecessary asperity; [he] said, "This man had demonstrated the insufficiency of the power of the House; that his imprisonment would not put a stop to pamphlets; that the public, who cannot judge as the House of Commons does, would think the whole an election matter—a point in which they are most jealous; that Murray had already suffered greatly; that to revive the sentence would be inflicting banishment, which will be no further voluntary, than as he will prefer it to imprisonment. That the sentence must

---

not sutler her to stop in London, but sent her directly to Bath, and, on her return, back to Holland; nor ever forgave her.

[186] Edward Coke, only son of Thomas, Earl of Leicester.

[187] Lord Chesterfield told Mr. Pelham from Lord Bolingbroke, that Lord Egmont being sent by the Prince to Lord Bolingbroke to consult on measures for opening his approaching reign, Lord Bolingbroke desired him to open his plan; Lord Egmont said it would be necessary for the Prince to begin with some popular act, and proposed for that end, immediately to restore feudal tenures! Lord Bolingbroke dissenting, they parted in heat.

be renewed every session; and that the Commons, though but a third part of the Legislature, would be exerting the power of banishment, which is unknown to the Crown itself. That such a stretch of authority would be doubly unpopular, after enacting a continuation of the Parliament by the Regency Bill last session. That in one point you had set yourselves a precedent of moderation by slighting the second set of Queries, after censuring the first, though the second attacked both King and Parliament; the first only the Duke. That contempt had stopped the progress of those libels; that contempt such as Lord Coke's would be the properest treatment of Murray. That this prosecution can't be pursued without some injustice, as it must be stopped somewhere, and it will be unjust not to proceed as far hereafter on any election complaint:" and then after a definition of true and false honour, he moved to adjourn.

Lord Coke replied in few but masterly words; defined true and false moderation, and said, "That true moderation is becoming when the culprit submits, but that it is *parvi animique pusilli* not to persecute a criminal who plumes himself on his defiance, and is the patron of a lost, fallen, unanimated cause!" Mr. Pelham commended both speeches, and added, "If the House has not all the authority it wishes, it ought at least to exert all it has." The Motion for adjournment was rejected, and the resumption of the sentence agreed to without a division. Lord Coke then moved, that Murray should receive the sentence on his knees; and that the pamphlet called *his Case* might be read, which was unanimously voted a false, scandalous, and seditious libel; and then Lord Coke moved to address the King to order the Attorney-General to prosecute the author, printer, and publishers; adding, that he would not move any censure on the Sheriffs, but hoped it would be a warning to the City what Magistrates they choose. Sir John Barnard was to have made their submission, if any vote had been proposed against them.

The 22nd, Lord Barrington moved that the number of seamen for the ensuing year should be increased to ten thousand, and said archly, "That he did not intend to defend the change of his own opinion, but of those who ought to preserve a political steadiness in their conduct; that he did not think so large a number always necessary, but circumstances made them so now." The Bedfords and Sandwichs were removed; the Pitts and the Lytteltons were to be cajoled, and so ten thousand became necessary. They were voted.

The 25th, Lord Coke moved to call the Serjeant-at-Arms, who reported that Murray was absconded. Lord Coke moved for a proclamation and reward for apprehending him, which Vyner and Sydenham opposed, and the latter made a speech worthy the ages of fanaticism, comparing Murray to Prophet Daniel, who would not kneel to Nebuchadnezzar's Idol, and alleged the example of the Dissenters, who do not kneel at the Sacrament. Alderman Jansen defended the City, on which Lord Coke had reflected, and said, "That to have touched the Sheriffs would have raised a tumult." A reward of five hundred pounds for apprehending Murray was voted on a division of 98 to 26.

The Duke had a fall as he was hunting at Windsor, was taken up speechless, and refusing to be blooded, grew dangerously ill with a pain in his side, and was given over by the physicians; but recovered. The King was inexpressibly alarmed, wept over him, and told everybody that was in his confidence, that the nation would be undone, left to nothing but a woman and children! He said to Mr. Fox of the Duke, "He has a head to guide, to rule, and to direct;" and always talked as if the Duke was to be sole Regent. Mr. Fox repeated this to him, who said, the King had talked to him himself in the same strain. "Why then, sir," replied Mr. Fox, "don't you just put him in mind, in those fits of tenderness, of what he has done to prevent your being so?" He replied, "That it was now too late to remedy; that the Regency Bill could not be repealed, and that even if it could, he had rather bear the ignominy that had been laid upon him, than venture giving the King the uneasiness of reflecting, if it were but for two hours in his own room, on the injury he had done him."

Mr. Pelham was uneasy at Mr. Fox's being admitted to the Duke in his illness, when he was excluded. The Duke asked Fox afterwards how the brothers had behaved during that crisis. He replied, "Both cried: the Duke of Newcastle over-acted it, but Mr. Pelham seemed really concerned."—"Ay," said the Duke, "I know they both cried; for the Duke of Newcastle, he cried, because he had not been in the morning to know how I did—but for Mr. Pelham, he is such a fellow, that I can believe he was in earnest!"

The 27th, Mr. Fox in the committee proposed the same army as last year, *as there was no alteration of circumstances*; Sir John Cotton to reduce it to fifteen thousand; and was seconded by Northey, Beckford, Prowse, Thornton, Norris, Bertie, and Robinson. Cotton was answered by William Lyttelton; as Beckford (who had wished that the Army had committed outrages, in order to have the nation sensible of the dangers from it) was by Dr. Lee, who, to palliate the change of his style, was so injudicious as to insist that the situation of affairs was highly altered by the deaths of the Prince and the Prince of Orange, and the birth of the Duke of Burgundy. Lord Egmont, who found himself almost alone in opposition, made a very artful speech; said, "He had hoped to have heard some answer from the Ministry to Sir John Cotton's arguments; that for his own part, he should be very gentle, as it was not a time to provoke a power that nothing could resist, but should coolly ask for an answer. He ridiculed Dr. Lee with great delicacy and compliments; knew that he had *reason* for what he did; and that he had *great views*, and overlooked small ones, and that such principles would justify little deviations. Yet if the dreaded event of a possible minority should come to pass, it would always be easy to call troops from Ireland, where, and by the number of officers, you always have the root of an Army. That to facilitate the assembly of one, the Parliament will be sitting: that the Ministry ought to affect to show the good disposition of Government, now everything is so quiet; and that such a display of tenderness to the subject would produce real security. He made a strong panegyric on the King, but said those good principles of his Majesty were prevented from being exerted by his Ministers, who govern by force in a reign that has given no pretence for it. That if any one of them would act constitutionally, he would support that man in spite of little reflections; and would extend his hand in defence, where he had never extended it, if once the Government would quit this road of rigour. That the death of the Prince of Orange could be no argument for maintaining so large an Army; we cannot govern Holland; that indeed were the Dutch strong, and in a more flourishing situation, it might be a reason, when we might give and receive mutual assistance. But for the pretence of the birth of a Duke of Burgundy, nothing could be more ridiculous; no argument more absurd than the birth of Foreign Princes; or than our increasing our Army whenever there is an heir to the Crown of France."

He asked, "in what period of our history the Crown had so much power? That in 1646, when the Army had conquered King and Parliament, they voted but 6000 men necessary. Yet, treble as the present Army is desired, he would offer a composition, which, if accepted, he would vote for the present plan within 900 men: he would offer it to one (Mr. Pelham) not used to negotiate in public; would make a treaty, without one secret article; and would promise peace for one year,—a term as long as any modern treaty is likely to last. The condition was, that the Ministry should consent to reduce the Cavalry, and omit the Staff, which would create a saving of 143,000*l.* He urged that the King had shown by a former reduction, that, though he ought not to be without Guards and marks of sovereignty, he despises show. That the Grenadiers may still be kept up to attend on the King's person; but he wished to break the Guards and the regiment of Blues. And he concluded with saying, that though he had no hopes of delivering the nation from the danger, yet he wished to rescue it from the expense of the Army, which cost very near as much as that immense one of the King of Prussia."

Mr. Pelham replied in a very dull speech, "That he had seen no force exerted by the Administration; and attempted to defend Dr. Lee: that if the King dies, you have already provided for the strength of the Government: will you now weaken it? that, whenever the Army has been much reduced, tumults have immediately arisen. France may be tempted to disturb you, without meaning to fix the Pretender here: that she might even mean that; and that some who heard him knew that there had been Jacobite meetings within the last six months. That his fears from that quarter made him always more earnest on the question of the Army, than upon any other; and that he desired no overt act to convince him of the still real existence of Jacobitism. That the reduction proposed was a poor pittance if meant for economy. That, indeed, if it were worth while, the Blues might be changed; he had not much objection to it, though they had always had the title of

Guards. That seventy men are as much as one officer can command; that the Army had already been reformed; a further reduction would be useless or dangerous, and will be a heavier burthen where quartered, from want of more officers." The House divided at five, and voted the same Army by 180 to 43. Only Lord Middlesex and Martyn, of the late Prince's faction, voting with Lord Egmont and the Speaker.

About this time, France seemed threatened with a cloud of intestine troubles. Louis the *well-beloved* had outlived the flattery of even French subjects. Verses,[188] recommending the assassination of him, were pasted up on the Louvre and the Pont-Neuf. Yet, though marked for destruction by his priests, it was with great difficulty that Madame de Pompadour, his mistress, could divert the melancholy cast of his mind from sinking into a habit of devotion. She perpetually varied his pleasures, and carried him from one palace and hunting seat to another,—journeys which cost immense sums, and made the people join in the clamour which the Clergy had conjured up. Gunpowder and some treasonable papers were found in the cradle of the Duke of Burgundy. The Dauphin, a dull, bigoted Prince, was zealously attached to his mother, and had hazarded brutalities to the mistress, which the King bore with great indulgence. It did not break out into factions, as the domestic quarrels of the Royal Family had done for two generations here in England, but appeared in little marks and distinctions, such as different manners of wearing the Cordon, &c. among the creatures of either Court. In the midst of these uneasinesses, a new flame broke out. The Archbishop of Paris was a favourite, having made his court even at the expense of his brethren the clergy. The hospitals had always been managed with so much integrity as to become the most creditable fund for charity; the Parliament directed them. The Archbishop endeavoured to arrogate the sole command of them to himself: the King supported his pretensions. The Parliament having in vain remonstrated, concurred to throw up their employments; and though they submitted to resume their functions, it was not without having inspired the Court with a temper of moderation, which is as seldom learnt by despotic Kings, as such

---

[188] Vide the Appendix, I.

firmness is seldom practised by Parliaments renowned for far greater liberties.

December 4th.—Mr. Pelham opened the Land Tax of three shillings in the pound; and recommended as his maxim *to preserve and improve our situation, seldom to gain, and then our enemies will not be offended.* Lord Harley and Beckford, with Vyner, Oglethorpe, Robinson, Admiral Vernon, Sydenham, Thornton, and Cooke, (the sad refuse of all the last Oppositions,) opposed it. So did Sir John Barnard, who said, "He had declared two years ago, that, if the peace continued, he would vote no more for three shillings; that the peace was made because our Allies had not contributed equally to the expense of the war; and he proposed a wild scheme of tying down 600,000*l.* a year, out of the Sinking Fund, to pay the National Debt, by which means, in fifty years, we should be able to carry on as extensive a war as ever we ought to wage." A scheme by which, if strictly pursued, and a new war should intervene, we should be paying off money borrowed at three per cent., while obliged to borrow other money at five, six, or whatever interest extortion should find it a proper season to demand. Lord Strange spoke for the question. Sir John Cotton answered, "That country gentlemen would indeed have very *little ease*,[189] if three shillings land tax was thought necessary till our debts were paid, as Lord Strange had said, and nobody had contradicted." Mr. Pelham said, "Lands sell better now than ever they had done, and that luxury and election contests between neighbouring gentlemen occasion the change of property." Cotton replied, "The country gentlemen had learnt from the report of the Secret Committee, that the Court supports one side, and therefore they would grow more wary." They divided for two shillings, but it was carried for three, by 176 to 50.

The next day, on the report, Sydenham made a lamentable speech, affected to cry, and asked pardon for quoting a ludicrous epitaph on so melancholy an occasion, but which he could not help thinking applicable to the great Minister of these times, who has so burthened land:—

---

[189] This alludes to the proposal in the foregoing session, of confining Murray in the dungeon called *Little Ease*.

Lie heavy on him, Land; for he
Laid many a heavy load on thee.

The 10th, the Mutiny Bill was read in the Committee. Lord Egmont made some faint opposition on the old points; but not finding himself supported, went away before the division, which was but 19 to 118. Sir Harry Erskine voted for the Bill, without mentioning the clauses he had last year promised to bring in.

Lord Halifax had stayed in the country out of humour, having in vain demanded to be made a Cabinet-Counsellor, as an introduction to the Regency, and the Secretaryship for the West Indies. His friend, Lord Barrington, was now sent to acquaint him that the King persisted in a refusal, but might be brought to acquiesce in more moderate demands. Lord Halifax came to town, protesting he would resign, but was pacified with a promise of the West Indies being in a great measure subjected to the Board of Trade.

The 12th died Lord Bolingbroke;[190] a man who will not be seen in less extraordinary lights by posterity than he was by his contemporaries, though for very different reasons. His own age regarded him either as the greatest statesman, oppressed by faction, and the greatest genius persecuted by envy; or as the most consummate villain, preserved by clemency, and the most treacherous politician, abandoned by all parties whom he had

---

[190] Henry St. John, Lord Viscount Bolingbroke, Secretary of State to Queen Anne, had, on the accession of George the First, been impeached for his share in the treaty of Utrecht, and fled. Sir Robert Walpole (strongly against the inclination of his brother Horace, Lord Townshend, and others of his friends) obtained his pardon, though Lord Bolingbroke and his advocates afterwards pretended that the Minister had no hand in it. The day after his return he dined at Chelsea, to thank Sir Robert; but his confusion and uneasiness were so great, that he had like to have been choked with the first bit he ate, and was forced to rise from table. He soon endeavoured to supplant Sir Robert, by the assistance of his enemy the Duchess of Kendal, who obtained an audience for him in the late King's closet, where he presented a representation against Sir Robert, which the King immediately afterwards delivered to Sir Robert, and repeated the conversation to him. A parallel case happened afterwards to the same Minister. Lord Stair endeavoured to supplant him with Queen Caroline, and even was so hardy as to make love to her, which not succeeding, he wrote a long letter to her, and went the next morning for an answer. She sent him out word by her Chamberlain, Lord Grantham, that she had given his letter to Sir Robert Walpole, and had ordered him to deliver her answer. Lord Stair saw his situation, and set out next morning for Scotland.

successively betrayed. Posterity will look on him as the greatest philosopher from Pope's writings; or as an author of a bounded genius from his own. To see him in a true light, they must neither regard all the incense offered to him by Tories, nor credit all the opprobrium cast on him by Whigs. They must see him compounded of all those vices and virtues that so often enter into the nature of a great genius, who is not one of the greatest.

Was it being master of no talents to have acted the second part, when little more than a youth, in overturning such a Ministry, and stemming such a tide of glory, as Lord Godolphin's and the Duke of Marlborough's? Were there no abilities, after his return from banishment, in holding such a power as Sir Robert Walpole's at bay for so many years, even when excluded from the favourable opportunity of exerting his eloquence in either House of Parliament? Was there no triumph in having chiefly contributed to the fall of that Minister? Was there no glory in directing the councils and operations of such men as Sir William Windham, Lord Bath, and Lord Granville? And was there no art in persuading the self-fondest and greatest of poets, that the writer of the Craftsman was a more exalted genius than the author of the Dunciad? Has he shown no address in palliating the exploded treaty of Utrecht? Has he not, in his letters[191] on that event, contrived to make assertions and hypothesis almost balance stubborn facts?[192] To cover his own guilt, has he not diverted our attention towards pity for the great enemy, in whose service he betrayed his own country?

On the other hand, what infamy to have sold the conqueror to the conquered! What ingratitude in labouring the ruin of a Minister, who had repealed his sentence of banishment! What repeated treasons to the Queen, whom he served; to the Pretender,[193] who had received and countenanced him; to the late King, who had recalled him! What ineffectual arts to acquire the confidence of the late King, by means of the Duchess of Kendal, and of the present King, by Lady Suffolk! What unwearied

---

[191] On history, published since his death.
[192] See Lord Walpole's answer to these letters. All Lord Bolingbroke's art, all his beauties of style, vanish before these plain, unadorned, argumentative, demonstrative replies.
[193] In a late apology for Lord Bolingbroke, the author (supposed to be Campbell) has endeavoured to deny this known fact, but without the least proof.

ambition, even at seventy years of age, in laying a plan of future power[194] in the favour of the Prince of Wales! What deficiency in the very parts that had given success to the Opposition, to have left him alone excluded from reaping the harvest of so many labours! What blackness in disclosing the dirtiness of Pope,[195] who had deified him! And what philosophy was that which had been initiated in the ruin of the Catalans; had employed its meridian in labouring the restoration of Popery and arbitrary power; and busied the end of its career, first in planning factions in the Pretender's Court, by the scheme of the father's resigning his claim to the son; and then in sowing the seeds of division between a King and a Prince, who had pardoned all his treasons!

---

[194] Lord Egmont gave me the following instances. Lord Bolingbroke gave the Prince a scheme for vesting the Revenue in the Crown for every six years, without a Civil List, and for having Parliaments holden every five or six years. The Court he paid to the Prince was to a degree of adoration. One day that he dined with Lord Egmont, the Prince came in as they were drinking coffee, and bad them not mind him. Lord Egmont, who knew that to obey was to respect, gave Lord Bolingbroke a dish; but he, who thought that to disobey from respect was more respectful (and who perhaps knew, that though the Prince seemed to encourage familiarity, he never forgave it), started and cried, "Good God! my Lord, what are you doing? Do you consider who is present?" One of his views was to be an Earl; and, knowing that the Prince had had an inclination for his sister, Lady St. John, he took her son into his own house, under pretence of educating him and making him his heir, as an inducement to the Prince to promise him the Earldom. The Prince often sent his first Minister, Dr. Lee, to him; and one day said to Lord Egmont of Lord Bolingbroke, "That man is at fourscore just what he was at forty! I know how he flatters Lee to his face, and yet he is always teasing me to discard him, and telling him that he is not fit to hold a candle to an Administration."

A few years after this note was written, I met with the following words in the eleventh letter of the Dissertation on Parties, p. 151, of the quarto edition: "Should a King obtain, for many years at once, the supplies and powers which used to be granted annually to him, this would be deemed, I presume, even in the present age, an unjustifiable measure, and an *intolerable grievance*; for this plain reason, because it would alter our constitution in the fundamental article, that requires frequent assemblies of the whole legislature, in order to assist, and control too, the executive power, which is entrusted with one part of it." What must be the heart of that man, who, merely to load an envied Minister, could suppose instances of wicked administration, which had not entered into the head of any other man; and who could afterwards adopt those suppositions himself, and try to recommend himself to a Prince by those individual bad measures, the creatures of his own brain: and this at past seventy years old! hazarding, for a very few years of unenjoyable power, to entail so calamitous a system on his country!

[195] Lord Bolingbroke had trusted him to get six copies printed off of his Letters on Patriotism; after Pope's death, it was discovered that he had secured a vast number of copies for his own benefit. Vide the Preface to the Idea of a Patriot King, where this story is exposed. What aggravated Lord Bolingbroke's exposing his friend was, that after his own death it was discovered that he had secretly preserved a copy of Dr. Middleton's Essay on Prayer, which his lordship had persuaded the doctor's executors to burn.

Sir Robert Walpole and Lord Bolingbroke had set out rivals at school, lived a life of competition,[196] and died much in the same manner, provoked at being killed by empirics;[197] but with the same difference in their manner of dying as had appeared in the temper of their lives: the first with a calmness that was habitual philosophy; the other with a rage that his affected philosophy could not disguise. The one had seen his early ambition dashed with imprisonment, from which he had shot into the sphere of his rival, who was exiled, sentenced, recalled; while Walpole rose gradually to the height of temperate power, maintained it by the force of his single talents against Bolingbroke, assisted by all the considerable geniuses of England; and when driven from it at last, resigned it without a stain or a censure, and retired to a private life, without an attempt to re-establish himself—almost without a regret for what he had lost. The other, unquiet, unsteady, shocked to owe his return to his enemy, more shocked to find his return was not to power, incapable of tasting the retirement which he made delightful to all who partook it, died at last with the mortification of owing his greatest reputation to the studies he had cultivated to distress his antagonist. Both were beloved in private life; Sir Robert from the humanity and frankness of his nature; Bolingbroke from his politeness of turn and elegance of understanding. Both were fond of women; Walpole with little delicacy; Bolingbroke to enjoy the delicacy of pleasure. Both were extravagant; and the Patriot who accused, and the Minister who had been accused of rapine, died poor or in debt. Walpole was more amiable in his virtues; Bolingbroke more agreeable in his vices.[198]

Cresset was made Treasurer to the Prince of Wales, in the room of Mr. Selwyn, who died. Nich. Herbert succeeded him as Treasurer, and Mr. Harding as Auditor to Princess Emily, who had wished to give those places to William Leveson, Lord Gower's brother, but attached to the Duke of Bedford. Mr. Leveson applied to Mr. Pelham, who insisted on his asking Lord Gower's interest, which he refused to do. Oswald, who, by the

---

[196] Vide Appendix, K.
[197] Sir Robert Walpole was killed by Jurin's medicine for the stone; Lord Bolingbroke by a man who had pretended to cure him of a cancer in his face.
[198] In quibusdam virtutes non habent gratiam, in quibusdam vitia ipsa delectant.—*Quintil.*

consent of Pitt, and the faction of cousins, was to have kissed hands for Clerk of the Green Cloth to the Prince of Wales, but two days before the Prince's death, was now made a Lord of Trade.

About the middle of this month, died his Majesty's youngest daughter, the Queen of Denmark, a Princess of great spirit and sense, and in the flower of her age. Her death, which was terrible, and after an operation which lasted an hour, resembled her mother's—a slight rupture which she concealed, and had been occasioned by stooping when she was seven months gone with her first child. The Queen had in a manner prophesied to her when she was expiring herself: "Louisa, remember I die by being giddy, and obstinate in having kept my disorder a secret!" Her fate, too, had borne a resemblance to her mother's; for the King of Denmark, though passionately fond of her, to prevent the appearance of being governed, had kept a mistress, and given her great uneasiness: yet she never mentioned it in her confidential letters to her own family. The Duke said, she had always told them, that if she was unhappy, they should never know it. In her last moments, she wrote a moving letter to the King, the Duke, and her sisters, to take leave of them. This letter, and the similitude of hers and her mother's death, struck the King in the sharpest manner, and made him break out into warm expressions of passion and tenderness. He said, "This has been a fatal year to my family! I lost my eldest son—but I am glad of it;—then the Prince of Orange died, and left everything in confusion. Poor little Edward has been cut open (for an imposthume in his side), and now the Queen of Denmark is gone! I know I did not love my children when they were young; I hated to have them running into my room; but now I love them as well as most fathers."

The 19th.—The Parliament adjourned; an era for ever remarkable in English annals! Opposition, which had lasted from the days of Queen Elizabeth, and even the distinctions of parties having in a manner ceased at this period! Popery, which had harassed the reign of that heroine; the spirit of liberty which had struggled against four Stuarts; the spirit of slavery which had wrestled to restore their descendants; all the factions which had distracted King William, possessed Queen Anne, and ridiculed the House of Hanover; and the Babel of parties that had united to demolish Walpole, and separated again to pursue their private interests; all were now sunk into a dull mercenary subjection to two brothers, whose administration resembled that of King James for timidity, of King William for change of Ministers, and of Queen Anne for an ignominious peace! Buckingham had been attacked in the arms of King James; Laud and Strafford beheaded; Hyde banished, though allied to the Crown; the virtuous Somers impeached; the victorious Marlborough disgraced; the favourite Walpole removed. Pelham alone could teach servility to a Parliament, whose privileges were yet untouched!

In Sweden there seems the same indifference for liberty. Count Tessin, the pattern of the British Minister, always affecting to resign, always entreated by his creatures to retain his power, is known to be meditating the restoration of absolute power. In France, where the Crown is despotic, and the people bigoted to whatever phantom is their King, there is a set of men, whose remonstrances, steadiness, and patriotism would figure with any senate, that Greece, Rome, or former Britain knew. But it is time to conclude the history of this extraordinary year, all the chief events of which having terminated in confirming the power of Mr. Pelham, it will be proper, before I take leave of the reader, to add this person's portrait to those of the under-actors; and the better to illustrate it, I shall take the liberty of examining his and his master Sir Robert Walpole's characters together, though it is difficult to compare two Ministers, when on one side genius must be entirely left out of the question: nor could anything draw on a parallel between a man of genius and a man of none, but the singular case of the latter having affected what the former could not—I mean power without unpopularity.

When Elijah was hurried to heaven, he left his cloak to Elisha with a *double* portion of his spirit: but that legacy[199] in no sense happened to Mr.

---

[199] This allusion is manifestly borrowed from Sir Charles Hanbury Williams, who, in an epistle written in 1745, but not printed till many years afterwards, thus draws the character of Mr. Pelham, and contrasts him with Sir Robert Walpole. Apostrophizing the Goddess of Prudence, he says—
    Turn to your altars, on your votaries shine,
    See Pelham ever kneeling at thy shrine;
    By you at first by slow degrees he rose,
    To you the zenith of his power he owes;

Pelham, who was as much inferior to Sir Robert Walpole in political courage as in abilities. Sir Robert Walpole was bold, open, steady, never dejected; he would attempt for honest ends where strict morality did not countenance his opinion; he always disclosed his arts after they had effected his purpose; and sometimes defeated them by too early discovery. He never gave up his party to serve himself, though he has departed from his own opinion to please his friends, who were serving themselves; nor did he ever lose his cheerfulness, though he had hurt himself against his opinion.

Mr. Pelham was timorous, reserved, fickle, apt to despair. He would often not attempt when he was convinced it would be right; would sooner hurt himself by not telling his mind, than attain his aim by being communicative; and often gave up his party, indeed not to serve himself, but his enemies, and frequently disappointed himself of success, by never expecting to succeed. Presumption made Sir Robert Walpole many enemies; want of confidence in himself kept from Mr. Pelham many friends. Sir Robert Walpole was content to have one great honest view, and would overlook or trample upon the intermediate degrees. Mr. Pelham could never reach a great view, by stumbling at little ones; he would scruple to give an hundred pound to one opponent, and to buy off another would give up a question[200] that might endanger the nation. Sir Robert Walpole loved power so much, that he would not endure a rival; Mr. Pelham loved it so well, that he would endure anything. The one would

---

> You taught him in your middle course to steer,
> Impartial, moderate, candid to appear;
> Fearful of enmity, to friendship cold,
> Cautiously frank, and timorously bold,
> And so observant, never to offend
> A foe, he quite forgets to fix a friend.
> Long versed in politics, but poor in parts,
> The courtier's tricks, but not the statesman's arts;
> His smile obedient to his purpose still,
> Some dirty compromise his utmost skill;
> In vain his own penurious soil he till'd;
> In vain he glean'd from Walpole's plenteous field;
> In vain th' exchequer robes about him flow,
> The *mantle* does not make the *prophet* now.—E.

[200] As he gave up the Hanover troops, to pave the way for Mr. Pitt's coming to Court—and voting for them himself next year!

risk his administration, by driving every considerable man from Court, rather than venture their being well there; the other would employ any means to take able men out of the Opposition, though he ventured their engrossing his authority and outshining his capacity; but he dreaded abuse more than competition, and always bought off his enemies to avoid their satire, rather than to acquire their support: whereas, Sir Robert Walpole never trading but for members, and despising invectives, and dreading rivals, gained but weak, uncertain assistance, and always kept up a formidable Opposition. His apprehension of competitors was founded on prudence, because great part of his authority depended upon the King's favour: Mr. Pelham owing nothing to that, had the less reason to fear losing it; as he maintained himself in the Ministry in spite of the King's partiality to abler men, he had no reason to be jealous of their getting interest at Court.

Sir Robert Walpole raised himself to the head of the Administration, without interest, without fortune, without alliances, and in defiance of the chiefs of his own party:[201] he rose by the House of Commons—he fell by it. Mr. Pelham found himself next upon the list, and was recommended to a strong party by their leader. He would never have risen, had he had no other foundation than the House of Commons, and would fall to-morrow if he had no other support; for he must be undone whenever his safety depends upon himself. Sir Robert Walpole's eloquence was made for use, and he never could shine but when it was necessary[202] he should. He wanted art when he had no occasion for it; and never pleased, but when he did more than please. I am not going to contrast this part of their characters, nor to say that Mr. Pelham only shone upon trifling and unnecessary occasions, for he did not do even that; he was obscure upon the most trivial occurrences, perplexed even when he had but one idea, and whenever he spoke well, it was owing to his being heated; he must lose his temper before he could exert his reason. Sir Robert Walpole palliated too little, Mr. Pelham too much. The one would defend his errors by a

---

[201] As Lord Sunderland, Lord Stanhope, Craggs, and Lord Townshend.
[202] How little he shone in formal ornamental eloquence appeared from his speech at Sacheverell's trial, which was the only written one, and perhaps the worst he ever made.

majority; the other with a greater majority would excuse his merit, and would sooner obscure and depreciate his meaning when right and clear of itself, than not apologize for it. Sir Robert Walpole could not deviate but with openness and sincerity; the other degraded truth by timidity, sense by mystery, and right by asking pardon for it.

The one was honoured by his enemies, the other at best pitied by his friends. His most prejudiced opponents[203] often grew convinced that the former was in the right: the heartiest friends of the latter knew he meant to be so, but never found stronger reasons to confirm them in their opinion. The one durst do right and durst do wrong too; the other dared either so little, that it generally ended in his doing the latter. Sir Robert Walpole never professed honesty, but followed it; Mr. Pelham always professed it, and kept his word, when nothing happened to make him break it; and then he broke it for some other honest end, though perhaps far from being equally cogent.

Sir Robert Walpole's mastery was understanding his own country, and his foible, inattention to every other country, by which it was impossible he could thoroughly understand his own. Mr. Pelham understood more of his own country than of others, though he would have made a better Minister for any other nation; for as he would not have met with opposition or contradiction, two things his nature could not bear, and as he meant exceedingly well, he would have served the country that employed him to the best of his understanding, and that might have cleared up as well as his temper, when he had nothing to perplex it. In the knowledge of the Revenue, he and all other men must yield to Sir R. Walpole, though he and all other men make the same use of that knowledge, which is to find new funds for the necessities of the Government, and for the occasions of the Administration: by those occasions, I mean corruption, in which I believe Mr. Pelham would never have wet his finger, if Sir Robert Walpole had not dipped up to the elbow; but as he did dip, and as Mr. Pelham was persuaded that it was as necessary for him to be Minister as it was for Sir

---

[203] That Lord Granville, Pitt, and Lyttelton, recanted all their invectives, must not be produced as unbiassed evidence; but the Duke of Bedford and Lord Cornbury will be allowed too honest to have acted from any motives but conviction.

Robert Walpole, he plunged as deep. The difference was, that Mr. Pelham always bribed more largely as he had more power; for whenever it tottered, he the less ventured to prop it by those means, as he was the more afraid of being called to account for putting them in practice.

Sir Robert Walpole, with the greatest confidence of himself, had no pride; Mr. Pelham had the most, with the least self-sufficience. Both were loved in private life. Sir Robert Walpole loved magnificence, and was generous to a fault: the other had neither ostentation nor avarice, and yet had little generosity. The one was profuse to his family and his friends, liberal indiscriminately, unbounded to his tools and spies: the other loved his family and his friends, and enriched them as often as he could steal an opportunity from his extravagant bounty to his enemies and antagonists. Indifferent people were too indifferent to him; and for intelligence, it was one of the greatest blemishes of his Administration, he wanted it so entirely—not resolution more! Sir Robert Walpole's friendships were chiefly confined to persons much below him; Mr. Pelham's were almost all founded on birth and rank: the one was too familiar, the other never so. Sir Robert Walpole was forgiving to a fault, if forgiveness can be faulty; Mr. Pelham never forgave, but when he durst not resent. Sir Robert Walpole met with much ingratitude; Mr. Pelham was guilty of much. Both were frequently betrayed: Sir Robert Walpole without being deceived; Mr. Pelham not half so often as he suspected it. The one was most depreciated while he was Minister; the other will be most when he ceases to be Minister. All men thought Mr. Pelham honest till he was in power; the other never was thought so till he was out.

Both were fortunate in themselves, unhappy in their brothers. With unbounded thirst for politics, the Duke of Newcastle and Horace Walpole were wretched politicians: each inferior to their brothers in everything laudable; each assuming and jealous of their own credit, though [neither] the Duke nor Horace could ever have been considerable, but by the fortune of their brothers. The one childish and extravagant, the other a buffoon and avaricious; Horace sunk into contempt when his brother fell with honour; the Duke was often on the point of dragging his brother down, and was the object of all contempt, even where his brother had still power and honour.

Mr. Pelham maintained his inferiority to Sir Robert Walpole even in the worthlessness of his brother.

> "J'aye dict le mot, pour ne frustrer la postérité."
> *H. Etienne, Apologie d'Herodote.*

Chapter 8

1752.

Pour être bon historien, il ne faudroit être d'aucune religion, d'aucun pais, d'aucune profession, d'aucun parti.

I sit down to resume a task, for which I fear posterity will condemn the author, at the same time that they feel their curiosity gratified. On reviewing the first part of these Memoirs, I find the truth rigidly told. And even since they were written, I have often been struck with the censures which are passed on such historians as have fairly displayed the faulty sides of the characters they exhibit. Theopompus is called a satirist: Timæus was so severe,[204] as to be nicknamed Epitimæus, the Blamer. Some of our own annalists, as Wilson, Weldon, Osborn, (though frequently quoted,) are seldom mentioned without reproach. I defend them not: if their representations are exaggerated, they not only deserve reproach, but discredit.

On the other hand, I examined the candid authors. Two of our own, who deal wonderfully in panegyric, Clarendon and Echard, I find to have dispensed invectives with a liberal hand on men of parties opposite to their own—does then the province of praise and censure depend on the felicity of choosing one's party? *That* shall never influence me—I would as soon wish to be rejected for flattering one party, as for blaming another. Nor can I, on the strictest consideration, determine to write like biographers and

---

[204] One of the reasons for reckoning him severe was, his laughing at those who wrote on Phalaris's bull.

authors of Peerages and Compendiums, who sink all executions in a family, all blots in a 'scutcheon, and lay out their personages as fair as if they wrote epitaphs, not history. Does any noble family extinguish? One should grieve, on reading their genealogies, that such a succession of heroes, statesmen, patriots, should ever fail; if a little knowledge of mankind did not call forth the blemishes, which these varnishers have slubbered over. If I write, I must write facts. The times I describe have neither been glorious nor fortunate. Have our affairs gone ill, and yet were our Governors wise? Have Parliaments been venal, servile, and yet individuals upright? If I paint the battle of Dettingen in prosperous colours, am I an admired historian? If I mention hostages sent to France, am I an abusive one? Are there no shades, no degrees of vices and misconduct? Must no Princes be blamed, till they are Neros? Must Vespasian's avarice pass unnoticed, because he did not set fire to the city—because he did not burn the means of gratifying his exactions?

Suppose I were to comply with this indulgent taste, and write thus:— George the Second was the most glorious Monarch that ever sat on the English Throne; his victories over the united arms of Spain and France[205] will illustrate our annals till time is no more; and his condescension and generosity will conspire to raise his private character to a level with his public. The Duke of Newcastle was a prodigy of sincerity, steadiness, and abilities. Mr. Pelham was the humblest man, the bravest Minister, the heartiest friend, the openest enemy. The Earl of Holderness the most graceful dancer that ever trod the stage of business since the days of Chancellor Hatton—avaunt, Flattery! tell the truth, my pen!

The miscarriage of the Rebellion had silenced Jacobitism; the death of the Prince of Wales had quashed opposition; and the removal of the Duke of Bedford and Lord Sandwich had put an end to factions in the Ministry. The ascendant of the Pelhams drew the attention of the disaffected, who began to see a prospect of the restoration, if not of the Stuarts, at least of absolute power; and this union was not a little cemented by the harmony of hatred, in which both the Pelhams and the Jacobites concurred against the

---

[205] This was written before the last war in the reign of George the Second, in which, he really triumphed over both France and Spain, but it was by the Ministry of Mr. Pitt.

Duke and the Duke of Bedford; neither the one nor the other were disposed at this juncture to stem the torrent. The Duke was determined not to give the Pelhams so fair an opportunity of mischief, as by setting up the standard of opposition during his father's life; and the treasures which he expected at the King's death, and would not risk losing,[206] he knew would indemnify the delay of his revenge. The Duke of Bedford, who had been driven into contention, not sought it himself, did not feel resentment enough for the loss of power, which he had never much coveted, to make him eager in returning ill-usage; and as he thought himself distinguished by the King's esteem, he affected gratitude to the Master, more than revenge to the Ministers. Pitt and his little faction were rather unsatisfied, than in possession of any title to complaint; and yet from that quarter seemed to lower the first small cloud that might at all obscure the present halcyon season.

A new subsidiary treaty with Saxony (a strange codicil to a general peace!) had been lately concluded; the pretence, the purchase of another Electoral vote for the Archduke Joseph, whom we persisted in making a candidate for the succession of the Empire, though his father and his mother were equally averse to see him King of the Romans. As he was immediate heir to his mother's vast dominions, the Emperor could not but foresee, that, if the estates of the House of Austria fell to his son, it might even become difficult for himself to retain the empty diadem, when the means of grandeur should be devolved on his child; and the Empress-queen, who had not ceded a jot of power to a husband whose person she loved, was not desirous of calling her son Emperor, who might be less tractable, and more impatient to reign in earnest. Yet the dread the King felt of a new war in Germany, his jealousy of his nephew of Prussia, and even the favourite impulse of acting in contradiction to him, made his Majesty eager to hurry on the election, and profuse of subsidies, which were not to be issued from his own coffers. Lord Cobham, who, having no place to forfeit, was always used by Pitt as the trumpet of their discontents,

---

[206] The Duke of Cumberland's subsequent patience on his father's unjust ill-treatment of him after the battle of Hastenbeck, and his Royal Highness's total indifference to money, fully vindicate him from this suspicion.

openly sounded his disapprobation of the Treaty: and old Horace Walpole, who had waded through, and transacted so many treaties, without attaining a Peerage, was at last determined to try if he could not traverse negotiations to better purpose than he had negotiated.

On January 7th, the Parliament met again after the adjournment; and on the 16th, Mr. Pelham laid the Treaty before the House. The Duke of Bedford came to town on the 15th; so far from meditating opposition, that he was resolved to make use of the remains of the King's favour, to ask a pension for the Duchess's sister, Lady Elizabeth Waldegrave. The Duchess, who could not bear to be out of favour as well as out of power, and who always kept a reconciliation in view, had planned this suit, with at least as much prospect to tie down the Duke by an obligation to the King, from reverting to Opposition, as from kindness to her sister; and there was no doubt but the Pelhams would have pressed the King to grant so trifling a boon; for what could they wish more, when they had driven the Duke of Bedford to resign the power of serving all his friends, than to silence his murmurs, by serving the first friend of his for whom he should submit to solicit?

The prospect of allies in Opposition was immediately hung out to the Duke of Bedford, by some[207] who wished to fix him against the Court, and who wanted to engage him to speak against the Treaty, which they knew would either prevent him from soliciting the pension, or by touching so tender a point as a German subsidy, would provoke the King to refuse his request. This train caught effectually; and though the Duchess was alarmed, yet not having time to work back her husband, whose warmth was most impetuous, the Duke determined at once to oppose the Saxon Treaty.

22nd, Mr. Pelham opened the Treaty in the Committee. Old Horace Walpole spoke against it in a manner that showed how well he knew where the weakness of such treaties lay; and however astonishing such arguments were when coming from him, they were pressed with such force and weight as stilled their ridicule, had he not himself done justice upon himself, and concluded his oration with professing such duty to the King,

---

[207] Particularly by the Author of these Memoirs.

that, though so averse to the Treaty, he should yet vote for it. The House burst into laughter at such absurd pretence for zeal, which could conquer its own conscience, but had not prevented him from exposing the measures of a Prince, for whom he expressed such veneration! Murray, Potter, Sir Harry Erskine, Sir Thomas Robinson, Sir William Yonge, Lord Hilsborough, Mr. Fox, Sir Peter Warren, Mr. Legge, and Charles Townshend, spoke for; Sir Walter Blacket, Beckford, Lord Strange, and Lord Cobham against it; but it was agreed to by 236 to 54.

On the 23rd it was reported to the House. Northey and George Haldane opposed it again. Nugent was zealous for it. Sydenham, reflecting on Nugent's former religion, said, that he seemed not content with a majority of electors, but would have an Emperor chosen, *like a Pope*, by two-thirds. Vyner reflected on the King for bringing such expenses on the nation, after such obligations to it, and such noble provision made for his children. This Mr. Pelham answered finely, seriously, and pathetically; a manner in which he particularly shone. There was no division.

On the 28th the Treaty was debated in the House of Lords. The Duke of Bedford opened the opposition to it, with professing, that his greatest difficulty lay in its having been the act of the King, so good a King, whom he had served seven years, and to whom he was agitated with the fear of being misrepresented: yet, that he could neither in conscience acquiesce, nor be content with silently opposing subsidiary treaties in time of peace; and the dangerous measures of wasting, when we ought to be saving. That if you treat after a war, you may obtain conditions certain; but what advantages can you make, where there is nothing to be given up or restored? That by paying for votes for the Archduke, we are purchasing advantages for our Allies, instead of for ourselves; and at the same time instruct those Princes who take our money, never to unite with us but for money. That with the people it must be a measure most unpopular, to tax them for money to be sent abroad, when they cannot possibly discern how it touches their own interest. And that in no shape the measure can be right, but when a war is approaching; whereas, we are but just emerged out of one. That the preamble is most injurious to the dignity of our Crown; it speaks us suppliants to that inconsiderable Prince, the King of Poland, who is most incapable to serve us, not only from the situation of his country, but from his bad administration. Besides, he might have been obliged to join us by the two Imperial Courts, as his ruling passion is to make Poland hereditary in his family—how great then is his condescension, if he will not take part against you! If he did, it would be of little consequence: it is only giving so much for levy-money. If England were attacked, of what use would Saxons be? That he did not think this country or Holland should always have such preparatory connections on the Continent; and yet that this Treaty did not even stipulate that his Polish Majesty shall increase his forces. That the fifth Article was wretchedly drawn! and for that King's vote—had it been secured, when it might have been—that Cologne had been lost for want of proper words to tie him down: a fit example to have made us more wary! and yet how many evasions open, if this Saxon Prince is disposed to elude his engagements! That we are not likely to bring about this election; and that we even keep off two of the electors, by showing them that they may ask a price for their votes. That Prussia's protesting against the election is a new doctrine—and as new is this opportunity for Lords who love subsidizing! Notify your intentions, you may have thirty or forty of the College of Princes, who will take your money. Yet, while we are thus bounteous, Russia takes no steps, Austria few. But he supposed he should be told, that Holland is to pay part; he was sorry for it; Holland is still less able than we to be thus extravagant. But if Holland should not pay, who is to make good the deficiencies? If this is done with the consent of France, she only will have the merit: if without her consent, it will bring on a war.

He then turned to home considerations, and (as this was supposed to be a sacrifice offered by the Duke of Newcastle to the King's German passions, contrary to the inclination of Mr. Pelham), he said it was extravagant imbecility, if this measure was yielded to by the Minister against his will. That the tenour was throughout the same, and parsimony or profusion took their turns, as individuals took prepossessions. That to please individuals,[208] the material service, the Navy, had been reduced to

---

[208] Pitt and the Grenvilles. See the preceding year.

8000 seamen: that to please individuals,[209] Nova Scotia had been profusely suckled, and its deficiences always supplied. That the land-tax, the malt-tax, the reduction of interest, had been carried on with spirit: yet for what have the public creditors been taxed, if the savings made at their expense are scandalously lavished? If measures are not changed, if men are not changed, we must go on *de mal en pire*. That when we pretend to economy, how judiciously is it exerted! It is displayed in contracting the rewards for removing the mortality of the cattle, or for discovering highwaymen! That our youngest daughter, Nova Scotia, is favoured, while Jamaica is neglected, by an Administration who neither grant protection to commerce, nor endeavour at any reformation of morals. The Duke concluded with a Motion for an Address, to represent that subsidiary treaties ought never to be concluded in time of peace, especially after a long war, and that they are neither necessary at present, nor likely to procure any real advantage.

The Duke of Newcastle replied in a wild, incoherent, incomprehensible speech of an hour and a quarter, in which he set out with saying, that he would not answer general heads, because the Duke of Bedford had descended to particulars; and yet the greatest deduction of his defence was an account of the three last wars. That for this, it was a measure of peace and economy, and that *it is little as it is, because it is so great*. That he remembered the argument used to blacken the great war was, that we have no interest on the Continent; and that the Dutch were reproached then, and are now. That he that is not for us, is against us: that there are those who would gladly accept the union of the Dutch. That if he thought this a greater burthen than England could bear, in proportion to the objections, he should be against it; but that if it prevents a war, the sooner England concludes this Treaty the better. That if we do not connect with the Continent, we shall be obliged to enter into the next, as we were into the last war. What was the occasion of the three last wars? Of the first, the succession to the Crown of Spain—*but that can never happen again*. Everybody knows the zeal of the present King of Spain. In the second, the

---

[209] Lord Halifax.

war occasioned by the vacancy of the Throne of Poland, England took no part: if we had, it would have prevented the last; at least, it would have been better carried on. The last war was occasioned by the ambition of Bavaria. *It cost us much, yet glad he was, for we should have been in a worse condition, if we had not entered into it.* From the Treaty of Utrecht to that of Aix-la-Chapelle, there have been no four years without greater expenses than these four last. If the last war was occasioned by the vacancy of the Imperial Throne, the treaty in question is calculated to prevent such a vacancy and such consequences. That Holland, he hoped, would emerge out of her difficulties *by the prudence of the present conjuncture*—that his meaning was sufficiently explained, though it might be more elegantly; that more plainly, would be improper. That we have received the strongest assurances—what they are: if there should be any Motion for laying them before the House, he would be the first to oppose it. Have we never seen Saxony act against its interest? If any means had been omitted for engaging that Power in the common cause, the Ministry would have much to answer for. That the question of the necessity of the unanimity of the electors had been fully considered, *though there was a time when no elector would have opposed.* That the election had not hitherto proceeded, because Cologne did not understand itself obliged to concur. That we must get six votes, and therefore, whatever is demanded, must be granted, though Cologne did ask more, and it was not granted. All arts were tried to engage that elector without a subsidy. He then proved that the election might have been carried and been valid with a majority, and yet that we waited till we could secure two-thirds. That he was told we meddled everywhere; an accusation he was sometimes surprised to hear from some people. That the Fleet had repaired the miscarriages of the Army—was it not the duty of economic Ministers to supply the Sea Service? That for what had been hinted of the provocation we should give to France, *the wisdom of that Power will admire us, not be angry, if we do nothing to hurt her.*

    This, and some few preceding harangues of this extraordinary person, I give merely as a specimen of the rhetoric of a man, who certainly did not govern his country by his oratoric abilities. The reader must excuse me, if for the future I omit them, unless on very particular occasions; for though I have generally given myself the trouble to minute them down at the delivery, it were too impertinent to commit them to history. And I must beg so much indulgence, as when argument, or connection, or grammar is observably wanting, that it may be remarked that at least in all other speeches I have taken care to write true English: in those of the Duke of Newcastle, the original has been faithfully copied.

Lord Sandwich then, with most ungraceful delivery, which yet was as powerful as the matter of his speech, lamented his misfortune of differing with his friend the Duke of Bedford, which he must do, though he found the reasons preponderate very little on the side of the Treaty, and though he agreed with his Grace in near half he had said: that he considered how little regard was paid to economy, and that nobody was less prepossessed in favour of the Ministry, whom he should gladly oppose, but where the exigencies of the public required his concurrence. That he knew their sentiments were to silence opposition at any rate; that influenced by that motive, they had last year reduced the Navy: however, he must own that the event had justified the reduction; that he should not concur now, if he did not hope that granting this subsidy would stop greater profusion. And, that the public might at least have this security even from the badness of the present Ministers, that they will even wave their own bad purposes, rather than hear disagreeable truths; which, for his part, he should always be ready to utter, though he did not approve being actuated by private connections in public affairs.

The secret of this speech was, that the Duke of Bedford having acquainted Lord Sandwich with his intention of opposing the Treaty, and having desired him to consult the Duke, the latter had approved the opposition, but would not openly concur, for fear of offending the King; and as Lord Sandwich was the known creature of the Duke, it was thought proper that he should act this middle part, of voting for the Treaty, and censuring the Pelhams. The Duke went so far as to tell the King, that the Duke of Bedford spoke just better than the Duke of Newcastle, but that Lord Sandwich alone shone. The truth was, Lord Sandwich ruined his little remains of character for abilities; the Duke of Bedford was seen in a new light. The method with which he went through the Treaty, the great variety of matter of which through the whole Debate he showed himself master, and the coolness with which he mastered his own temper too, made him considered as a very formidable and able speaker.

Lord Halifax then rose and said, "They who disapprove all treaties, cannot like this: they who are for no connection with the Continent—" the Duke of Bedford interrupted him, and said, "That is not my opinion." Lord Halifax replied, "But very like it." The Duke again interposed, but the Duke of Argyle called him to order, and with acrimony said, that he had never seen such interruption given twice in one Debate. Lord Halifax then continued, that if the peace was not strengthened, it would only be a cessation of arms: that we must not be parsimonious, while France was dealing out a million in subsidies (this had been a most exaggerated calculation of the Solicitor-General[210] in the House of Commons), that she had offered more to Saxony, who had preferred our alliance with the lesser sum. That the money granted for Nova Scotia had been given to establish the settlement, not to carry on a war: that if the ships had been sent out too late last year, it was the fault of the Admiralty; and that of all men he least expected opposition from those two Lords, who had so lately approved these treaties.

This was the accusation for which the Duke of Bedford had waited; and he embraced it artfully. He said, that this was so far from a preventive measure, that it was more likely to raise a war; that he had indeed said nothing hitherto to explain the consistence of his own conduct, foreseeing that he might be attacked on it. That he had always wished to detach Bavaria from France, and thought it a great point gained, though not with a view to engage that vote for a King of the Romans; but that, while he had acted in the Ministry, he had disapproved this profusion of subsidies; and that, having made the most earnest representations against that to Bavaria, he had received the strongest assurances from *one*,[211] who had inclination to prevent, and power to hinder, that the subsidy then granted to the Elector of Bavaria should be the last we would give. He had then in his pocket a letter from Mr. Pelham, with a solemn promise of this.

---

[210] Mr. Murray.
[211] Mr. Pelham.

Lord Granville put an end to the debate by a speech of spirit and humour; that the Motion was full of inflammatory matter, and that it was drawing the House into declaring against subsidiary treaties in general: that France can be attacked by no single Power; that leagues must humble her, subsidies cement leagues. France has no Pretender to be set up against her. She might say, "I will give no subsidies,"—and yet she does. That formerly during his Embassies, he had been asked by a great Prince[212] (the King of Denmark) what we meant by that magnificent bravado in the Preamble to our Mutiny Bill, where we say, that we keep up eighteen thousand men to preserve the balance of Europe. "I told him, my Lords, 'One day can make those eighteen fifty thousand.' If you say you will pay no more electors, you have erected a bridge without complete arches—and what kind of policy is that, if this House rejects a treaty already ratified by King and Commons! The Court of France does not regard guarantees—or indeed what Powers do? Would Prussia retain Silesia long, if he had nothing to defend it with but the guarantee? for, my Lords," concluded he, laughing, "I must bring out some of my secrets too." The Motion was rejected without a division. The next time the Duke of Bedford went to Court, the King took no notice of him; nor for some time.

29th.—Lord Harley, seconded by Northey, made a Motion for declaring against subsidiary treaties in time of peace. It occasioned a warm Debate; and Prowse, escaping from his usual plausibility, said, that he could discover no symptoms of economy in the Administration, though indeed they had enforced it, for by lowering interest, and by the land-tax of three shillings, both landed and monied men were reduced to be economists. Beckford, Fazakerley, Sir Roger Newdigate, Morton, Sydenham, Cooke, Delaval, and Sir Walter Blacket, spoke for the Motion: Hampden against it, but with a sneer, said, that he approved *bribing electors*, as he saw *by other instances* how it had contributed to quash opposition. Mitchell taxed old Horace Walpole with his unparliamentary behaviour, in speaking on one side and voting on the other. The Solicitor-General, Sir Henry Erskine, Nugent, Ellis, Tracy, and Sir William Yonge,

---

[212] Very probable that a King of Denmark should have seen a Preamble to a Mutiny Bill!—but there was no hyperbole too extravagant for Lord Granville to use.

all opposed the Motion; and lastly, Mr. Pelham, who seized the opportunity of venting the anguish he had felt the day before in the House of Lords (which from that day he never attended more), and of abusing with much bitterness and ability the Duke of Bedford and Lord Sandwich. The Motion was rejected by 180 to 52. After the Debate, Mr. Pelham asked Fox, if he had gone too far in invectives. "No," answered Fox, "as they began; though you originally gave the provocation." "Oh! Fox," replied he, "you did not feel for me, as I should for you in the same circumstances!"

In the beginning of February, Lord Cardigan was appointed Governor of Windsor Castle, and was succeeded as Chief Justice in Eyre by the Duke of Somerset.

4th.—Died Sir John Cotton; the last Jacobite of any sensible activity.

21st.—Sir John Barnard, whose popularity had suffered by the share he had had in reducing the interest of the public debt to three per cent., made a proposal to tie down six hundred thousand pounds a year of the Sinking Fund, from the year 1758, towards discharging the whole national incumbrance. Beckford supported him; but Mr. Pelham and the Solicitor-General opposing it, his scheme was rejected without a division. We shall see him afterwards addressing himself to his lost popularity with more success, and as it often happens, on a worse foundation.

25th.—Lord Winchelsea had summoned the Lords to consider an Admiralty Bill, which had passed the Commons without opposition, and which was designed to commute the punishment of transportation into working in the Dockyards. Bills of less invidious appearance had often raised a flame in combustible seasons: this seemed to introduce a kind of galley slavery, yet was really converting a species of disgraceful criminals, who only corrupt our Plantations, into useful members of society. Could the monthly shambles at Tyburn (that scene that shocks humanity, and reproaches our Police!) be exchanged for severe labour in the same way, it would reflect honour on a Legislature, which ought not to wanton in such punishment of its members as death and banishment, but to extract public utility, even from crimes. The Duke of Newcastle, fearing to be attacked himself, and the Chancellor, as apprehensive for his silent son-in-law, Lord Anson, the head of the Admiralty and patron of the Bill, prevailed on Lord

Northumberland to rise, commend the Bill, and then move to have it put off for six weeks. The Duke of Bedford called him to order for entering upon the Bill before it was read.

28th.—Lord Tyrawley was sent to Lisbon, to accommodate some differences which had been occasioned by our Captains openly running Portugal pieces, which used to be brought on board our ships by the *decent* intervention of the Monks.

The same day was read for the first time a Bill to empower the Government to purchase, at the rate of about an hundred thousand pounds, the estates in Scotland forfeited by the late Rebellion, and which the King was to cede to the public, in order to have colonies settled on them, especially of Foreign Protestants. The necessity of the purchase was pretended to arise from mortgages on them, and which would even consume the property in a few years, and pass them from the King's hands into those of the mortgagees. Grants of money to Scotland have ever been suspicious: the influence of the Duke of Argyle over the ductility of the Ministry was most notorious; the claims now erected on these forfeitures most incredible; and the establishment of Colonies in parts so barren, so uninviting, of such unpleasant neighbourhood, most improbable and impracticable. One circumstance alone, of public notoriety, staggered all credit in the sum demanded. Lord Lovat, at the bar of the House of Lords, had declared that his was the best estate in Scotland, for there were no debts upon it—it now appeared charged with a mortgage of thirty thousand pounds! Vyner, Northey, Beckford, Sydenham, Fazakerley, Prowse, and the Whig-General Mordaunt, opposed the Bill. The Scotch Lord Advocate, Mr. Pelham, Sir William Yonge, and Oswald, with fine warmth supported it, and it passed that day without a division; and again on the second reading, March 2d, when it was faintly opposed by the same people, and defended by the same, and by the Attorney-General.[213]

March 4th.—The Bill was reported: Vyner observed that no retribution had been made to any parts of England that had suffered by the Rebels, though ten thousand pounds had been given to Glasgow alone, to

---

[213] Sir Dudley Rider.

compensate their damages. Sir John Mordaunt asked with spirit, whether Englishmen would go to these intended settlements for twenty pounds a year, only to have land a fifth cheaper? Whether the English Ministry meant to send 28,000 men only to starve? or whether they would suffer themselves to be sent? He said, the Scotch were so attached to the individual spots of their tribes, that when Glenbucket had wanted to transplant his M'Donalds to the site of the M'Phersons, the colonists had been murdered, their houses burnt, and Glenbucket himself received several wounds. That this scheme would set the whole Highlands in a flame—"when that is done," said he, "I will congratulate the gentlemen who brought in the Bill—in the meantime, let me tell them, that so impotent or so supine is the Government in that part of the island, that there is now a person, a man of five hundred pounds a year, who forced three or four hundred Drummonds into the Rebellion, and has sons in Lord John Drummond's regiment in France, who lives tranquilly, securely, on his own estate in Scotland, and triumphs over the well-affected and loyal."

General Campbell maintained the probability of establishing the Colony in question, and instanced in one at Strontean, where mines are carried on by a company from hence, who are well received there, who have polished the country, and where three to one are well-affected. Legge said, that this system will have more effect than all that had been done about dress and jurisdictions, because those regulations were imposed by force; but this was to be purchased: that the economy of the measure could not be questioned, as, by buying mortgaged estates, you may prevent future Rebellions, and consequently avoid the heavy charges which Rebellion occasions. That the Colony must be sent armed; and that for some time the Army must be used as a succedaneum to this measure, though force produces only artificial loyalty in breasts, that will still be waiting for opportunities of revenge; but that nest-egg of Rebellion must be crushed in time of peace; that if this measure is not adopted, the remaining alternatives were, to acquiesce under incidental Rebellions, or to exterminate the disaffected by fire and sword; that what is loyalty or disloyalty here, is there food or starving. Feed the clans, they will obey; starve them they must rebel: that the means, therefore, of eradicating this spirit in the common people are obvious; polish them, introduce the arts of peace amongst them—the disloyalty of the gentlemen is with more difficulty to be subdued.

Lord Coke spoke with animosity[214] against the measure, as being a Scotch measure; Lord Hilsborough with approbation of it, as resembling what, he said, he had experienced in Ireland, where he had seen mountains of Papists settled at last by Protestants, after two or three colonies had been successively driven off; and he said sensibly, "have we 6000 men who keep all Scotland in order, and will they not be able to protect this little colony?"

Northey objected to the economy of a measure which was pretended [to be] calculated to save the expense of an Army, and yet must be put in execution by an Army! and he stated the collusive manner in which the calculation was drawn up, and observed that the claims erected were 270,000*l.*; that the estates to be purchased are 16,000*l.* a year; that it is allowed, that there is personal estate sequestered to the amount of 19,000*l.*; and yet that that sum was not allotted towards the purchase. The Report was agreed to by 171 to 34. Lord Gower's sons[215] were in the minority: none of the Duke's servants were present but Felton Hervey, and he too was against the Bill.

7th.—Prince Edward, the young Prince of Orange, and the Earls of Lincoln, Winchelsea, and Cardigan, were declared Knights of the Garter: the Scotch Earl of Dumfries had the Green Ribband, and Lord Onslow the Red.

Some differences happened upon a ship of ours taking sailors out of an Embden vessel; and a Bill was brought in to prevent insuring Embden ships.

9th.—The Scotch Bill was passed in the Commons, on a division of 134 to 39.

---

[214] He was much hated by the Scotch, since his quarrel with and separation from his wife, Lady Mary, youngest daughter of John, Duke of Argyle.

[215] Earl Gower stuck to the Pelhams: his sons, Lord Trentham and Richard Leveson, acted with their brother-in-law, the Duke of Bedford.

Chapter 9

March 10.—Lord Bath moved for an account of the produce of the Window-tax in Scotland. It had not, since first laid, brought in one shilling.

The Scotch Bill had hitherto only raised some warmth in particular men, who either did not love that nation from prejudice, or from resentments contracted against them during the late Rebellion. It now took a more serious turn. The Duke, who had conquered the Scotch like an able General, who had punished them like an offended Prince, and whose resentments were not softened by the implacability of their hatred to him, was not a little disgusted at seeing measures of favour to them adopted, and himself totally unconsulted upon those measures. Yet he could not, as they were concerted by the King's Ministers, openly oppose them. It was almost as difficult for him to blow up any opposition against them underhand. The discontented in the House of Commons were either the refuse of the late Prince's party, or the Jacobites; and even these latter could not be supposed heartily eager against favours being showered on their never-failing allies, the Scotch. In the other House, the only phantom of opposition consisted in half a dozen Jacobite Lords, and in the person of the Duke of Bedford, between whom and his Royal Highness a coldness had arisen, as has been mentioned. In this dilemma the Duke lighted upon a measure, which had ample effect. Lord Sandwich was too much connected with him, and too much detached from the Duke of Bedford, to make it expedient to offer any overtures directly through him: but the Duke sent him to a person[216]

---

[216] The Author of these Memoirs.

who had private connections with the Duke of Bedford, and who he knew would not be sorry to traverse Mr. Pelham's measures, to offer him very extraordinary anecdotes on the Scotch affairs, which he might impart to the Duke of Bedford. It is strange how this train caught! That person persuaded the Duke of Bedford to accept and make use of the information, without knowing from whom it came; and it must appear amazing, that a man who could make so distinguished a figure as his Grace did, by the management of the materials, should have submitted to be put in motion so blindly!—but that was his character; when he shone in public with most energy, he perhaps acted the least upon his own motives—but it is proper to enter into a deduction of the Debate.

17th.—The Bill was read in the House of Lords. The Duke of Bedford began with showing the impracticability of the measure, from the difficulties both of maintaining a colony on the forfeited estates, and of procuring people to settle on them. Troops can be of no service to support them in winter, unless forts are built; an expense that would far exceed the views of this Bill. English would not go thither; Irish cannot be spared, for you must not weaken the Protestant interest in that island; Scotch Highlanders will not remove thither from their own fastnesses; *Germans* indeed will migrate—but not to *worse* countries. But, he asked, had the Ministry permitted the disloyal inhabitants to remain upon these estates for six years since the Rebellion, and did they now propose to banish them? Would they engraft cruelty upon their negligence? and that in a case which decides the inhumanity, as it would punish the oppressed, yet not derive any benefit to the public,—the only justifiable pretence for national severities: for what benefit will the public reap from the change of Lords, under whom these Highlanders are to be placed by this Bill? Indeed, he said, he feared such encouragement was given to that country, by this and some other Bills, as would, even in our time, produce a new Rebellion— Glasgow—the great Lords, have received such sums, such means of new commotions, as they could have obtained no other way—and though particular towns and persons are pretended to be relieved, money is, through their channels, circulated over the whole country, and we deprive ourselves of the advantages that might accrue even from treason, when the disaffected have contributed to despoil and impoverish their own country. He feared Rebellion would grow a national malady! Danger is even to be apprehended from the method of putting this Bill in execution: should the Commissioners not act, it is a needless, an useless Bill—if they do, what is to encourage them? power and interest? and into what hands are you going to trust those formidable enemies? Are you not taking the same method you took with Lord Lovat? Will you empower more Lord Lovats to nurse up more Rebellions? He was a single instance, and the subsidy to him a trifle in comparison: this is a plan for the most formidable power ever attempted hitherto to be established in that country.

He then told the House, that he was but too well founded in his apprehensions of new commotions, both from the countenance showed to the disaffected, and the discouragement given to the loyal. He told them that he had in his hands a long and crying catalogue of facts, which would prove both his assertions, and which facts he was ready to prove. As a sample, he mentioned two cases; the first of one John Cummings, who at the time of the late Rebellion, being Collector at Montrose, assisted the Rebels in seizing the Hazard sloop, for which service the titular Duke of Perth appointed him Collector for the Pretender. This Cummings, on the Duke's arrival in Scotland, was imprisoned by his Royal Highness's command, and carried into Inverness; from thence he escaped, was again imprisoned, but at the desire of Lord Milton was released by Mr. Bruce, who had a power at that time to continue or to release prisoners. This Mr. Cummings is now Collector of Excise at Aberdeen; a place worth almost double of what he formerly enjoyed at Montrose!

The other was the case of Hume of Munderson, a man engaged in the former Rebellion, or, as the Scotch call it, in the *fifteen*. His brother was executed for the last Rebellion; but he himself has been made a General Supervisor of Excise. "My Lords," continued the Duke, "these are among many flagrant instances of the favour, I may truly say, of the rewards conferred on Rebels. I can, if I am called upon, produce many more equally striking, and of what perhaps is still more alarming, of punishments inflicted, or permitted to be inflicted on the well-affected to his Majesty's government and person. I will not now recapitulate them, nor dwell even on the fate of Mr. Davidson, Minister of Navar, above Brechin in the Braes of Angus, who with sixty of his parishioners was persecuted after the Rebellion, for making bonfires on the Duke's birth-day, under the pretence of wilful fire-raising!"

After a pause, he said: "My Lords, these, and facts like these, call for inquiry: what I have more to say, strikes directly at the Bill itself, which various circumstances concur to evince, is but a more extensive job. Such is the impropriety of the time, the end of a session, to offer a Bill of this nature, when, so far from having leisure to examine it, we have barely time to pass it; and that this must have been the effect of design is evident, since the Report of the Barons of the Exchequer, who were to examine into the nature and state of these forfeitures, was given in so long ago as December, 1749. The money to be raised is a most unjust burthen upon England: the Commissioners at least, who ought to see this Act put in execution, ought to be English. If they are not, we are grounded to suspect that this money will be as much perverted as other taxes have been fallaciously collected. Let us cast our eyes but on the produce of the coach-tax in that part of the United Kingdom; to what does it amount? for the first year to one thousand pounds!—for the second, to what? to nothing. Must we suppose that this burthen was so heavily felt, that the whole Nobility and Gentry of Scotland at once concurred to lay down their equipages? In those years England paid on the same account 60,000*l.*, 58,000*l.* If such are their partialities, is it not allowable for Englishmen to have some? Be that as it may, my Lords, let us know what grounds there are for these complaints, for these accusations. I move your Lordships to put off the farther consideration of this Bill, till we have had time to inquire into facts."

It required more art than the Chancellor possessed, to efface the impression made by this speech. To dispute the facts would be admitting that they ought to be examined. He thought the most prudent method was to admit their authenticity, but to endeavour to show that the previous examination of them was not necessary, either in that place, or before the conclusion of the Bill. This method he followed; it served to palliate the resolutions of a majority of which he was secure; but had that bad effect for the Ministry, that the Duke of Bedford's assertion of the facts, and the

Chancellor's admission of them, or at least his not disputing them, left the world persuaded of their reality, and of the timidity, indolence, or wickedness of the Administration.

The Chancellor, therefore, in a very long and elaborate speech, said, that if what had been advanced against the Bill was true, it was one of the worst Bills on the best plan that ever was formed. That indeed the Bill was only a part of the plan formerly concerted of buying the jurisdictions of the great Lords into the hands of the Crown; and that it fell in naturally enough to that plan, as these estates must necessarily be sold. That the only blame he should have expected was that this Bill had not been brought in sooner. Formerly the complaint had been that forfeited estates were restored and given back from the Crown. That indeed he did believe many of the claims upon these estates were fictitious: however, they must be determined in Scotland; here is the last place where they must be examined. That this Bill alone can enable you to have fair purchasers; and that if the claims are fraudulent, it is an additional reason for passing such a Bill; otherwise, the original proprietors might re-acquire their estates for nothing. That the great view of the Government was to destroy clanships; his own great wish, to see the King a great Highland landlord: that one of the chief benefits to arise from this scheme, secondarily to the extension of loyalty, is the improvement of the linen manufactures, an establishment at once so useful to our trade, and so inconsistent with arbitrary principles, that there had been but three single men of those manufacturers engaged in the last Rebellion. That with regard to the difficulty of finding colonists, he did not doubt but some English might be prevailed on to settle there, probably some Lowlanders too, nay, some Irish, if they can be spared. He believed, indeed, that the greater part of the old inhabitants must remain at first; but that some of the well-affected clans might be induced to transmigrate to those settlements; and that he did not despair of reclaiming even the present tenants, at least in the next generation of them, if they were once emancipated from dependence on their chiefs. That the danger from distributing money among the disaffected, formerly so impolitic a measure of King William, must not be considered here in that light; this is not money to bribe traitors, but to pay lawful creditors; and that he had rather even fraudulent creditors should enjoy this money than have the estates revert to their old proprietors. That even the position laid down of encouragement given to Rebellions by largesses to that country, was not true; it was the restitution of forfeited estates which had hardened them to attempt new commotions; but that if we were still to see repeated insurrections, every Rebellion cuts off so much strength from the faction. That indeed, as to the article of the Commissioners, he wished those words, *without fee or reward*, were not in the Bill; that he must own he saw many just grounds of complaint, but could not approve national reflections. That to the honour of that country he must say, the linen manufactures were carried on by Directors who received no salary. If these Commissioners should prove less meritorious, or more blameable, they are not for life; they are removable. That now he must take a little notice of the heavy accusations enforced by the noble Duke; but previously he must observe, that it is not proper in a Debate, to raise objections from particular facts, which people cannot be prepared to answer. That Cummings's case was so flagrant, that if it was inquired into, he did not doubt but it would be remedied. But what did this and the other instances prove, but the want of the Bill? That another view of the Bill was, to raise towns and villages and stations *for* troops; not that it would take away the want *of* troops: that the money, supposing it a large sum, was but little in comparison of the benefits it was calculated to purchase: is it not a little sum, if it prevents only one Rebellion?

If it was true, as the Duke of Bedford had asserted, and as he believed it was, that the Lowland share of the forfeited estates was not mortgaged to the full value, and that therefore they ought to be sold altogether, and the overplus go towards the purchase, for his part he believed nobody would advise his Majesty to sell those estates. That he did not believe the claims would be allowed to the extent given in; that the King, of his grace, may give the overplus towards the purchase, but that he should not advise it: he should rather advise that the distribution should be made to reward loyalty; for instance, could a nobler use be made of it, than in rewarding Sir Harry Monroe, who and whose family had done and had suffered so much for the service of the Crown? That the last thing of which he should take notice, was the insufficient manner in which the taxes had been collected in that northern quarter of the Kingdom: some method, to be sure, should be taken to make Scotland pay her taxes; but could any Ministry ever hit upon that method? it is not *vitium temporis* that the Ministers have not done the impossible thing. One good effect the very proposal of this will have, if it points out, or leads to a remedy for the nonpayment of these taxes.

The young Marquis of Rockingham entered into a Debate so much above his force, and pertly applied the trite old apologue of Menenius Agrippa, and the sillier old story of the Fellow of a College, who asked why we should do anything for Posterity, who had never done anything for us!

Lord Bath then joined the Duke of Bedford's opposition, after first reflecting on that Duke himself, who he said had entered his complaint both ways, that the Bill had not been brought in soon enough, and had been brought in too late. That for himself, he could not but think the proposal of examining the claims first very material. Should he, would any man, purchase an estate, before he had examined the nature and validity of the incumbrances? That on the first face of the account, he could descry false claims and misprision. On one little estate of thirty pounds a year he observed a mortgage of four thousand pounds. Who, he asked, had been in possession of these 16,000*l.* per annum since they had been forfeited? If the Government, where is the receipt? who accounts for it? If the creditors, why is not so much struck off from their claims? What must England say, if Scotland pays nothing towards four million of taxes? What must she say, when the weight of these taxes has been increased by Rebellions raised in Scotland? But who is it, must he ask, who takes upon them to remit taxes? Kings had been driven out for arrogating a dispensing power! where will these partialities end? He concluded with proposing a Bill to be enacted for punishing any frauds relative to forfeitures.

The Chancellor replied, that the Bill had been prepared as soon as possible, and had been brought in soon after Christmas. That the time for sale would lapse, and the estates fall to the mortgagees, if the Bill should now be postponed. That the mortgages, though real, could not extend beyond the value of the estates, which, he said, was a case frequent enough in Chancery.

Then rose a man, on whom all eyes had turned during the Debate—the Duke of Argyle. How was every expectation disappointed! As his power was uncontrolled in Scotland; as partialities could only be exercised under his influence, or connived at by his intrigues; as the Bill was known to be a sacrifice made to his ascendant; as its practicability had been questioned; who but himself was answerable, for favour to Jacobites, for tyranny to the loyal, for the necessity, for the utility, or for the feasibility of the regulation in question? He looked down, seemed abashed, spoke low and but a few words, then contemptuously, and at last said nothing to refute the charge of partialities, or in defence of the Bill. He only said, "What would have happened if any Scotch Lord had spoken against it? it would have been said, they are for keeping up their old barbarity and power. Whereas, the clans are to transfer their allegiance to Commissioners appointed by the King during his pleasure. If any man suspected him to be so low, as to have private views in this, God forgive him! That with regard to taxes, such difficulties there had been on the old tax on houses, that it had never been paid: few counties had even named their Collectors. That the window tax, if paid, would raise but 6000*l.*, and ninety-nine Collectors would have but fifteen shillings a piece. That on the coach tax there was no deficience. For himself, he despised reports."

Lord Tweedale spoke after him, and with passion; but as nobody expected any great lights from him, so he disappointed nobody.

The Duke of Newcastle, *flustered* by the Duke of Bedford's attack, and confounded by the Duke of Argyle's no defence, seemed to speak only to mark his own confusion, and to enforce what the Duke of Bedford had urged. He said he had taken minutes of the names mentioned by his Grace, and hoped such recommendations would be taken no more. That he had already sent the King's orders to apprehend some Rebels still resident in Scotland; but as yet they could not be taken.

Thus much effect followed: Cummings and some others in the Duke of Bedford's list were removed. The Bill passed; but though one great argument for driving it on had been the danger of the estates lapsing, neither English nor Scotch Ministers chose to have it discussed any further in Parliament. The Duke of Cumberland, who was present, did not vote. The Court Lords were fourscore; the minority only twelve: the Dukes of Bedford and Kingston; the Earls of Bath, Chesterfield, Sandwich, and Macclesfield; with six Tory Lords, the Duke of Beaufort, the Earls of Lichfield and Oxford, and the Lords Wentworth, Ward, and Maynard. Mr. Pelham was enraged beyond measure at the Duke of Argyle; the King charmed with the Duke of Bedford; and both these sensations were heightened by the Duke giving his father a list of sixty Jacobites, who had been preferred in Scotland since the Rebellion.

26th.—The King put an end to the session; and the Speaker, in his speech to him, launched out in invectives against the management in Scotland.

I shall conclude the history of this Bill with the character of its patron, not its defender, the Duke of Argyle.

Archibald Campbell, Earl of Isla, was younger brother of the admired John, Duke of Argyle, whom he succeeded in the title, and with whom he had little in common, but the love of command. The elder brother was graceful in his figure, ostentatious in his behaviour, impetuous in his passions; prompt to insult, even where he had wit to wound and eloquence to confound; and what is seldomer seen, a miser as early as a hero. Lord Isla was slovenly in his person, mysterious, not to say with an air of guilt in his deportment, slow, steady where suppleness did not better answer his purpose, revengeful, and if artful, at least not ingratiating. He loved power too well to hazard it by ostentation, and money so little, that he neither spared it to gain friends or to serve them. He attained the sole authority in Scotland, by making himself useful to Sir Robert Walpole, and preserved it by being formidable to the Pelhams. The former had disgusted the zealous Whigs in Scotland by throwing himself into the arms of a man of such equivocal principles: the Earl pretended to return it, by breaking with his brother when that Duke quarrelled with Sir Robert: yet one chief cause of Walpole's fall was attributed to Lord Isla's betraying to his brother the Scotch boroughs entrusted to his management in 1741. It must be told, that Sir Robert Walpole always said, he did not accuse him. Lord Isla's power received a little shock by Lord Tweedale's and Lord Stair's return to Court on that Minister's retreat; but like other of Lord Orford's chief associates, Lord Isla soon recovered his share of the spoils of that Administration. He had been ill with the Queen (of whom he knew he was sure while he was sure of Sir Robert Walpole) from his attachment to Lady Suffolk: he connected with Lord Granville, while Lord Granville had any sway; and as easily united with the Pelhams, when power was their common pursuit, and the humiliation of the Duke and the Duke of Bedford the object of their common resentment; for common it was, though the very cause that naturally presented them to the Duke of Argyle's hatred, their zeal and services, ought at least to have endeared them to the brothers.

By a succession of these intrigues, the Duke of Argyle had risen to supreme authority in Scotland: the only instance wherein he declined the full exertion of it was, when it might have been of service to the master who delegated it; in the time of the Rebellion: at that juncture he posted to London: the King was to see that he was not in Rebellion; the Rebels, that he was not in arms. But when this double conduct was too gross not to be censured, he urged a Scotch law in force against taking up arms without legal authority; so scrupulously attached did he pretend to be to the constitution of his country, that he would not arm in defence of the essence of its laws against the letter of them. In his private life, he had more merit, except in the case of his wife, whom having been deluded into marrying without a fortune, he punished by rigorous and unrelaxed confinement in Scotland. He had a great thirst for books; a head admirably turned to mechanics; was a patron of ingenious men, a promoter of discoveries, and one of the first great encouragers of planting in England; most of the curious exotics which have been familiarized to this climate being introduced by him. But perhaps too much has been said on the subject of a man, who, though at the head of his country for several years, had so little great either in himself or in his views, and consequently contributed so little to any great events, that posterity will probably interest themselves very slightly in the history of his fortunes.[217]

---

[217] Archibald Campbell, [Earl of Isla, and, on the death of his brother,] Duke of Argyle, died suddenly in his chair after dinner, at his house in Argyle Buildings, London, April 15, 1761.

31st.—The King set out for Hanover: the Duke of Newcastle, who attended him, would not venture himself in any yacht but the one in which Lord Cardigan had lately escaped a great storm.

While the King was absent, a scene was opened in a remote part of his dominions, which had not been accustomed to figure on the theatre of politics. Ireland had for many years been profoundly obedient to the Government. The Roman Catholics were too much overbalanced by the power of the Protestants to be formidable: the latter were too certain on any change of Government, to meet with no quarter from the professors of a religion, by whose plunder they were enriched, not to be inflexibly attached to the Prince on the Throne. Yet the insolence or wantonness of two men, new to power, contrived in a minute to throw that kingdom into a flame, and to create factions, who soon imbibed all the inveteracy of party, except disaffection. The internal councils of Ireland were chiefly guided by Mr. Boyle, the Speaker of the House of Commons, and Chancellor of the Exchequer, and during the absence of the Lord-Lieutenants, one of the Lords Justices. He was vain and popular, and as the idols of the people and of themselves generally are, a man of moderate capacity. It had been the unvaried practice of the Lord-Lieutenants to court this man, and to govern the House of Commons by his interest: the steadiness of his principles was unquestionable. Lord Harrington, the last Governor, had been much disliked, but conforming himself to this maxim, some discontented persons[218] had in vain attempted to give disturbance to the King's affairs.

He was succeeded by the Duke of Dorset, who was a man of dignity, caution, and plausibility, and who had formerly ruled Ireland to their universal satisfaction. But he then acted from himself; he was now in the hands of two men most unlike himself, his youngest son, Lord George Sackville, and Dr. George Stone, the Primate of Ireland. The former, a man of very sound parts, of distinguished bravery, and of as honourable eloquence, but hot, haughty, ambitious, obstinate. The Primate, a man of fair appearance, of not inferior parts, more insinuating, but by no means less ambitious, had with no pretensions in the world, but by being attached

---

[218] Headed by one Lucas, an apothecary, who was soon after banished from that kingdom, and turned physician in London, where he wrote controversy in his own profession.

to the house of Dorset, and by being brother of Mr. Stone, been hurried through two or three Irish Bishopricks up to the very Primacy of the kingdom, not only unwarrantably young, but without even the graver excuses of learning or sanctimony. Instead of attempting to conciliate the affections of a nation offended at his promotion, he thought of nothing but governing by the same influence by which he had been raised. Lord George, as little disposed to be controlled, would not stoop to the usual management for Mr. Boyle; and he was not likely to be persuaded to observe any attentions by the Primate, who had shaken them off himself. The Speaker, who had not lost his taste for power by being accustomed to it, was soon alarmed, and had an opportunity of revenge offered to him almost as soon as the offence.

The Duke of Dorset had recommended to the Parliament to provide more barracks for the soldiers, and to inquire into the late abuses of the money destined to that service. This was obliquely aimed at Lord Harrington, and intended, by casting odium on his Administration, to heighten the popularity of the new Lord-Lieutenant; but it had different and much further consequences than the junto had foreseen. The money was voted; but the Parliament, in prosecution of abuses, fell upon one Neville Jones, a creature of the Primate, and determined to express their aversion to that Prelate, by sacrificing his tool. When it is told that, till the era in question, no Opposition had been able to unite above eight-and-twenty voices in the Irish House of Commons against the Government, it will appear surprising that the contagion of new discontents should in a few weeks have infected even the majority there. Faction is as capricious as Fortune: wrongs, oppression, the zeal of real patriots, or the genius of false ones, may sometimes be employed for years in kindling substantial opposition to authority; in other seasons, the impulse of a moment, a ballad, a nickname, a fashion can throw a city into a tumult, and shake the foundations of a state. Spain, which surely must sometimes produce some heroic, some patriot natures, has groaned for centuries under tyranny and the Inquisition: the poor fisherboy of Naples, Massaniello, could, in the space of two days, set at defiance, overturn, a haughty, an armed, an established Government. It is certain that no innovation, no unwonted exertion of power, had provoked the Irish: but they thought themselves contemned: they saw the channel of power totally diverted from the natives: the indiscretion of the rulers presented a colour to the keenest invectives that a faction could wish to employ.

The Speaker furnished himself as chief to the faction; but they had wiser heads to direct both them and their chief. Of these were, Carter, the Master of the Rolls, Sir Richard Cox, and Malone. Carter had always been a Whig, but had as constantly fomented every discontent against the Lord-Lieutenants, in order to be bought off: an able, intriguing man, of slender reputation for integrity. Sir Richard Cox was a patriot, and the first deviser of the linen manufactures, which have been of such essential service to his country. He and Malone were distinguished orators, and had both been gained by Lord Harrington, but were neglected by the new Court at the Castle. Malone's family were Popish, and his own conversion suspected. But the Speaker was for some time the only ostensible idol of the party's adoration: to a confessed integrity and loyalty he united a romantic readiness for single combat, so much to the taste of his countrymen. The Castle were desirous of raising Mr. Ponsonby, a son of Lord Besborough, and son-in-law of the Duke of Devonshire, to the chair. The Parliament of Ireland, unless specially dissolved, sits during a whole reign, and the Speaker's dignity is of the same duration. Lord George's measures were apt to be abrupt: he directly offered the Speaker a Peerage and a pension of 1500*l.* a year. The Speaker replied, "If I had a Peerage, I should not think myself greater than now that I am Mr. Boyle: for t'other thing, I despise it as much as the person who offers it." This, and some indirect threats equally miscarrying, and the Castle finding that their creature Jones must be the first victim, endeavoured to defer what they could not prevent. The Speaker's party moved for a call of the House for that day three weeks; Lord George Sackville moved to have it that day six weeks—and was beat! Whoever[219] has seen the tide first turn in favour of an Opposition, may judge of the riotous triumphs occasioned by this victory. The ladies made balls, the mob bonfires, the poets pasquinades—if Pasquin has seen wittier,

---

[219] The Author could judge a little of this, by what he had seen himself at the conclusion of his father's Ministry.

he himself never saw more severe or less delicate lampoons. The Address that was soon after sent over to the King, applied directly to him, and not as was usual to the Lord-Lieutenant; and they told his Majesty, in plain terms, that it was from apprehension of being misrepresented. This was an unpleasant potion for the Duke of Dorset to swallow—but we must adjourn the further account of these dissensions to their proper place in order of time, and proceed to open a new scene of division at home, in which one of the principal actors was intimately connected with the Court-faction in Ireland.

In the former part of these Memoirs, it has been mentioned, that the young Prince of Wales, on the death of his father, was placed by the King under the care of the Earl of Harcourt, as Governor; of Dr. Hayter, Bishop of Norwich, as Preceptor; and of Mr. Stone and Mr. Scott, as Sub-governor and Sub-preceptor. The two former were favourites of Lord Lincoln, the ministerial nephew: Stone was the bosom-confidant of the Duke of Newcastle: Scott, as well as the Solicitor-General, Murray, and Cresset, the favourite of the Princess, were disciples of Lord Bolingbroke, and his bequest to the late Prince. Stone, in general a cold, mysterious man, of little plausibility, had always confined his arts, his application, and probably his views, to one or two great objects. The Princess could answer to all these lights: with her, he soon ingratiated himself deeply. Lord Harcourt was minute and strict in trifles; and thinking that he discharged his trust conscientiously, if on no account he neglected to make the Prince turn out his toes, he gave himself little trouble to respect the Princess, or to condescend to the Sub-governor. The Bishop, thinking himself already Minister to the future King, expected dependence from, never once thought of depending upon, the inferior Governors. In the education of the two Princes, he was sincerely honest and zealous; and soon grew to thwart the Princess, whenever, as an indulgent, or perhaps a little as an ambitious mother, (and this happened but too frequently), she was willing to relax the application of her sons. These jars appeared soon after the King's going to Hanover: and by the season of his return, they were ripe for his interposition.

Chapter 9

The English Court at Rome was as little free from intestine divisions as the Hanoverian Court at London. The Cardinal of York, whose devotion preserved him from disobedience to his father as little as his Princely character had preserved him from devotion, had entirely abandoned himself to the government of an Abbé, who soon grew displeasing to the old Pretender. Commands, remonstrances, requests, had no effect on the obstinacy of the young Cardinal. The father, whose genius never veered towards compliance, insisted on the dismission of the Abbé. Instead of parting with his favourite, the young Cardinal with his minion left Rome abruptly, and with little regard to the dignity of his Purple. The Holy See, which was sunk to having few more important negotiations to manage, interested itself in the reconciliation, and the haughty young Eminence of York was induced to return to his father, but without being obliged to sacrifice his Abbé. As I shall not often have occasion to mention this imaginary Court, I will here give a cursory picture of it.

The Chevalier de St. George is tall, meagre, melancholy in his aspect. Enthusiasm and disappointment have stamped a solemnity on his person, which rather creates pity than respect: he seems the phantom, which good-nature, divested of reflection, conjures up, when we think on the misfortunes, without the demerits, of Charles the First. Without the particular features of any Stuart, the Chevalier has the strong lines and fatality of air peculiar to them all. From the first moment I saw him, I never doubted the legitimacy of his birth—a belief not likely to occasion any scruples in one whose principles directly tend to approve dethroning the most genuine Prince, whose religion, and whose maxims of government are incompatible with the liberty of his country.

He never gave the world very favourable impressions of him: in Scotland, his behaviour was far from heroic. At Rome, where, to be a good Roman-catholic, it is by no means necessary to be very religious, they have little esteem for him: it is not at home that they are fond of martyrs and confessors. But it was his ill-treatment of the Princess Sobieski, his wife, that originally disgusted the Papal Court. She, who to zeal for Popery, had united all its policy, who was lively, insinuating, agreeable, and enterprising, was fervently supported by that Court, when she could no longer endure the mortifications that were offered to her by Hay and his wife, the titular Counts of Inverness, to whom the Chevalier had entirely resigned himself. The Pretender retired to Bologna, but was obliged to sacrifice his favourites, before he could re-establish himself at Rome. His next Prime Minister was Murray, nominal Earl of Dunbar, brother of the Viscount Stormont, and of the celebrated Solicitor-General. He was a man of artful abilities, graceful in his person and manner, and very attentive to please. He had distinguished himself before he was of age, in the last Parliament of Queen Anne, and chose to attach himself to the unsuccessful party abroad, and for whose re-establishment he had co-operated. He was, when still very young, appointed Governor to the young Princes, but growing suspected by the warm Jacobites of some correspondence with Sir Robert Walpole, and not entering into the favourite project of Prince Charles's expedition to Scotland, he thought fit to leave that Court, and retire to Avignon, where, while he was regarded as lukewarm to the cause, from his connection with the Solicitor-General here, the latter was not at all less suspected of devotion to a Court where his brother had so long been First Minister.

The characters of the Pretender's sons are hitherto imperfectly known; yet both have sufficiently worn the characteristics of the house of Stuart— bigotry and obstinacy and want of judgment. The eldest set out with a resolution of being very resolute, but it soon terminated in his being only wrong-headed.

The most apparent merit of the Chevalier's Court is the great regularity of his finances, and the economy of his exchequer. His income before the Rebellion was about 23,000*l.* a year, arising chiefly from pensions from the Pope and from Spain, from contributions from England, and some irregular donations from other Courts. Yet his payments were not only most exact, but he had saved a large sum of money, which was squandered on the unfortunate attempt in Scotland. Besides the loss of a Crown, to which he thought he had a just title, besides a series of disappointments from his birth, besides that mortifying rotation of friends, to which his situation has constantly exposed him, as often as faction and piques and baffled ambition have driven the great men of England to apply to or desert his forlorn hopes, he has, in the latter part of his life, seen his own little Court and his parental affections torn to pieces, and tortured by the seeds of faction, sown by that master-hand of sedition, the famous Bolingbroke, who insinuated into their councils a project for the Chevalier's resigning his pretensions to his eldest son, as more likely to conciliate the affections of the English to his family. The father, and the ancient Jacobites, never could be induced to relish this scheme. The boy and his adherents embraced it as eagerly as if the father had really a Crown to resign. Slender as their Cabinet was, these parties divided it; and when I was at Rome, Lord Winton was a patriot at that Court, and the ragged type of a minority, which was comprehended in his single person.

In September, the Margrave of Anspach, nephew of the late Queen, and to whom on that relation the King had given the Order of the Garter, wrote a circular letter to the Princes of the Empire, to dissuade them from holding a Diet of Election, till it was declared necessary to have a King of the Romans. The King was unlucky in his German alliances. The Landgrave of Hesse, and the Duke of Saxe Gotha, the one father-in-law of the Princess Mary, the other, brother of the Princess of Wales, declared themselves against the election.

With these disappointments, the King returned to England, and arrived at St. James's, November 18th. The Princess appeared again in public, and the King gave her the same honours and place as the Queen used to have. He was not in the same gracious mood with others of the Court. The calamity of Lord Holderness, the Secretary of State, was singular; he was for some days in disgrace, for having played at blindman's-buff in the summer at Tunbridge. To Lord Harcourt, the King said not a word. In the beginning of December, the Chancellor and the Archbishop sent to Lord Harcourt that they would wait on him by the King's command: he prevented them, and went to the Chancellor, who told him that they had orders to hear his complaints. He replied, "They were not proper to be told but to the King himself," which did not make it a little suspicious, that even the Princess was included in his disgusts. The first incident that had directly amounted to a quarrel, was, the Bishop of Norwich finding the Prince of Wales reading Père d'Orleans's *Revolutions d'Angleterre*; a book professedly written by the direction, and even by the communication, of James the Second, to justify his measures.

Stone at first peremptorily denied having seen that book in thirty years, and offered to rest his whole justification upon the truth or falsehood of that accusation. At last it was confessed that the Prince had the book, but it was qualified with Prince Edward's borrowing it of his sister Augusta. Stone acted mildness, and professed being willing to continue to act with Lord Harcourt and the Bishop: but the sore had penetrated too deep, and they, who had given the wounds, had aggravated them with harsh provocations. The Bishop was accused of having turned Scott one day out of the Prince's chamber, by an imposition of hands, that had at least as much of the flesh as the spirit in the force of the action. Cresset, the link of the connection, had dealt out very ungracious epithets both on the Governor and Preceptor; and Murray, by an officious strain of strange imprudence, had, early in the quarrel, waited on the Bishop, and informed him, that Mr. Stone ought to have more consideration in the Prince's family: and repeating the visit and opinion, the Bishop said, "He believed that Mr. Stone found all proper regard, but that Lord Harcourt, the chief of the trust, was generally present."—Murray interrupted him, and cried, "Lord Harcourt! pho! he is a cipher, and must be a cipher, and was put in to be a cipher." A notification, however understood before by the world, that could not be agreeable to the person destined to a situation so insignificant! Accordingly, December 6th, Lord Harcourt had a private audience in the King's closet, and resigned. The Archbishop waited on his Majesty, desiring to know if he would see the Bishop of Norwich, or accept his resignation from his (the Archbishop's) hands. The King chose the latter.

The Junto did not find it so easy to fix new ciphers as to displace the old. Dr. Johnson, the new Bishop of Gloucester, was the object of their wishes for Preceptor; but his education with Murray and Stone, and his principles, which were undoubtedly the same as theirs (whatever theirs were), proved obstacles they could not surmount. The Whigs were violently against his promotion; the Archbishop strongly objected to him. It was still more difficult to accommodate themselves with a Governor: the post was at once too exalted, and they had declared it too unsubstantial, to leave it easy to find a man, who could fill the honour and digest the dishonour of it. Many were named; some refused it. At last, after long waving it, Lord Waldegrave, at the earnest request of the King, accepted it, and after repeated assurances of the submission and tractability of Stone. The Earl was very averse to it; he was a man of pleasure, understood the Court, was firm in the King's favour, easy in his circumstances, and at once undesirous of rising, and afraid to fall. He said to a friend, "If I dared, I would make this excuse to the King; Sir, I am too young to govern, and too old to be governed."—But he was forced to submit. A man of stricter honour, or of more reasonable sense, could not have been selected for the employment; yet as the Whig zeal had caught flame, even this choice was severely criticized. Lord Waldegrave's grandmother was daughter of King James; his family were all Papists, and his father had been but the first convert.

The Preceptor was not fixed till the beginning of the new year, but I shall include his promotion here, not to interrupt the thread of the narration: it was Dr. Thomas, who during the first civil war of Leicester-house, had read prayers to the present King: it was not till within two years of this period that the King had found an opportunity of preferring him, and then made him Bishop of Peterborough. He was a man of a fair character, esteemed rather a Tory in his principles. It may not be unentertaining to mention another instance of the King's good fortune in being able to promote an old friend. General Legonier one day went and offered his Majesty the nomination to a living in his gift. The King expressed the greatest joy and gratitude, and said, "There is one I have long tried to make a Prebendary, but my Ministers never would give me an opportunity; I am much obliged to you, I will give the living to him."

Chapter 10

> 1753, and Part of 1754.
> Vernon. Then for the truth and plainness of the case,
> I pluck this pale and maiden blossom here,
> Giving my verdict on the white rose' side.
> Lawyer. Unless my study and my books be false,
> The argument you held, was wrong in you;—(To Somerset)
> In sign whereof I pluck a white rose too.
> Shakesp. first Part of *Henry VI.*

This year, soon made remarkable by some extraordinary occurrences, opened quietly; at least with events scarcely worth recording. A few independents of Westminster attempted, on the death of their representative, Sir Peter Warren, to revive an opposition to the Court, by again presenting Sir George Vandeput to the mob; but the idol's holiday was past; and he himself soon declined the contest. The Earl of Marchmont, adopted into the Court, moved the Address in the House of Lords, but coldly and unanimated; the fire and acrimony which made him shine in Opposition were gone, and no grace had succeeded. In the other House, Lord Egmont reflected on the Address, which he said, he expected would have been prudent and discreet, but found some parts of it improper and vain-glorious: that he believed the measures were well intended, but would prove unsuccessful; that the College of Princes had objected to an election of a King of the Romans; that the new memorial of the King of Prussia, outwardly relative to the Silesian loan, was founded, he believed, on that Prince's dissatisfaction with our conduct in the affair of the election; that he desired to avoid petulance, but thought it improper to give approbation to measures as wise, in which no wisdom had appeared, and that therefore, in wording the Address, he would omit the words *wisdom as well as* goodness; that he acknowledged the goodness, not the wisdom. Mr. Pelham replied, that he thought the noble Lord (*who was as accurate as anybody in writing*)[220] had made a false emendation; that the purpose of maintaining peace was all that was aimed at in the speech; who would not own the wisdom as well as the goodness of his Majesty in this? This is all the speech says: is it good in the King or in Ministers to pursue bad measures? there cannot be great goodness and little wisdom.

Feb. 9th.—Lord Egmont, in the course of the Mutiny Bill, moved to have oaths administered to evidences on regimental Courts Martial. He still combatted the giant of military power: Sir Henry Erskine, the old companion of his chivalry, was now the first to oppose him. The consideration, at the motion of Lord George Sackville, was deferred till the report.

13th.—The Duke of Bedford moved to have the accounts of Nova Scotia laid before the House. Lord Halifax added, that all letters to and from the Secretary of State relative thereto should be produced. The Duke of Newcastle opposed this, and desired that only extracts might be brought. The Duke of Bedford artfully inflamed this contest, praised Lord Halifax, and acquiesced.

15th.—Was published the Duke of Newcastle's answer to the Memorial presented by Mons. Michell, Secretary of the embassy from the King of Prussia. This Memorial and other papers had been presented in November and December of the preceding year, and was a pretended justification of the Prussian King's conduct in stopping the last payment of the money due to the subjects of Great Britain on the Silesian loan. This money had been borrowed of private persons in the year 1734 by the Emperor Charles VI., and he had mortgaged to them as a security his Revenues arising from the Duchies of Upper and Lower Silesia, for payment of principal and interest, till the whole debt should be discharged,

---

[220] Lord Egmont had written some pamphlets against the Pelhams.

which was fixed to be in the year 1745. But no sooner was the Imperial debtor dead, than the King of Prussia seized the province of Silesia, on the cession of which to him in form by the treaty of Breslau in 1742, he agreed to take the debt upon himself, and to stand exactly in the place of the Emperor; and actually did continue to discharge part of it; but being intent on erecting himself into a naval Power, and as intent on traversing the views of his uncle, he had involved himself in squabbles with England by transporting and furnishing naval and hostile stores to France on board his Embden ships, some of which had been taken by our men of war, some condemned, some restored. These discussions not turning out to his satisfaction, or he being determined not to be satisfied, at length resolved to detain the last payment on the Silesian loan; that is, after a certain balance had been liquidated by his own Ministers, he stopped about 30,000*l.* of 45,000*l.* which were due, and offered to our subjects to pay the remainder, provided they would give a full and authentic discharge for the whole debt: a transaction the more arbitrary and unjustifiable, as his complaints were not dated till 1746, and the whole debt ought to have been discharged the year before. The measure was violent and insulting, and a glaring comment on the inconveniences resulting from our connections with the Continent. The great superiority of the navies of Great Britain over the baby fleet of Prussia, the only arms by which nations so separated could come to any discussion of interests, was too evident for that Prince to have dared to hazard his infant hopes in so unequal a contest, had he not been sensible that we had a pawn on the continent with which he might indemnify himself for any exertion of British resentment;—and indeed, while we have this pledge staked for our good behaviour, every petty Prince who is a match for Hanover is too powerful for England; nor is it a question any longer what nations can cope with Great Britain, but, what little Landgrave is too formidable to the Electorate?

With the Duke of Newcastle's letter was delivered a confutation of the Memorial, drawn up by Sir George Lee, Dr. Paul, the King's Advocate for Civil Law, Sir Dudley Rider, Attorney, and Mr. Murray, Solicitor General. The examination was made in concert by all, the composition solely by the last; and perhaps few pieces in any language can stand in comparison with it, for elegance, perspicuity, art, and argument. The genius of the author did honour to his country in a performance of such notoriety; but perhaps the dignity of England had been less hurt, if we had been made appear to be less in the right. What advantage was there in having the better of the argument against a Prince, who lay out of danger from the resentments of Great Britain, while Hanover lay at his mercy? It is unseemly for great nations to combat with the pen; and except in the scholastic reign of James the First, England never dictated to other kingdoms by a superiority in controversy. What is still more striking, and a remark that I might, but will not often make, scarce a murmur followed this supineness of conduct. Even those who suffered in that tender point, their interest, seemed contented with our pedantic victory. In the year 1743, a yellow sash worn by the King in the field, and one or two Hanoverian prejudices as trifling, were on the brink of raising a Civil War in this country. In the year 1753, both national honour and national avarice could not, did not attempt to raise so much as a Debate in the House of Commons in their own defence! A little spark, in comparison, kindled the flame that followed.

At the end of the last year, while the dissensions in the tutorhood had been carried so high, an anonymous Memorial,[221] pretended to have been signed by several Noblemen and Gentlemen of the first rank and fortune, had been sent to five or six particular persons: it ran in these words:

> A Memorial, &c.
>
> The Memorialists represent,
>
> That the education of a Prince of Wales is an object of the utmost importance to the whole nation.
>
> That it ought always to be entrusted to Noblemen of the most unblemished honour, and to Prelates of the most disinterested virtue, of the most accomplished learning, and of the most unsuspected principles, with regard to government both in Church and State.
>
> That the misfortunes, which this nation formerly suffered or escaped under King Charles the First, King Charles the Second, and King James the Second, were owing to the bad education of those Princes, who were early initiated in maxims of arbitrary power.

---

[221] It was written by the Author of these Memoirs.

That, for a Faction to engross the education of a Prince of Wales to themselves, excluding men of probity, property, and wholesome learning, is unwarrantable, dangerous, and illegal.

That, to place men about a Prince of Wales, whose principles are suspected, and whose belief in the mysteries of our Holy Faith is doubtful, has the most mischievous tendency, and ought justly to alarm the friends of their country, and of the Protestant Succession.

That, for Ministers to support low men, who were originally improper for the high trust to which they were advanced, after complaints made of dark, suspicious, and unwarrantable means made use of by such men in their plan of education; and to protect and countenance such men in their insolent and unheard of behaviour to their superiors, is a foundation for suspecting the worst designs in such Ministers, and ought to make all good men apprehensive of the ambition of those Ministers.

That, it being notorious that books inculcating the worst maxims of government, and defending the most avowed tyrannies, have been put into the hands of the Prince of Wales, it cannot but affect the Memorialists with the most melancholy apprehensions, when they find that the men who had the honesty and resolution to complain of such astonishing methods of instruction are driven away from Court, and that the men who have dared to teach such doctrines are continued in trust and favour.

That the security of this Government being built on Whig principles, and alone supported by Whig zeal; that the establishment of the present Royal Family being settled on the timely overthrow of Queen Anne's last Ministry, it cannot but alarm all true Whigs, to hear of schoolmasters of very contrary principles being thought of for Preceptors; and to see none but the friends and pupils of the late Lord Bolingbroke entrusted with the education of a Prince, whose family that Lord endeavoured by his measures to defeat, and by his writings to exclude from the Throne of these kingdoms.

That, there being great reason to believe that a noble Lord has accused one of the Preceptors of Jacobitism, it is astonishing that no notice has been taken of a complaint of so high a nature; on the contrary, the accused person continues in the same trust, without any inquiry into the grounds of the charge, or any steps taken by the accused to purge himself from a crime of so black a dye.

That no satisfaction being given to the Governor and Preceptor, who, though a nobleman of the most unblemished honour, and a Prelate of the most unbiassed virtue, have been treated in the grossest terms of abuse, by a menial servant in the family, is derogatory to his Majesty's authority, under which they acted, is an affront to the Peerage, and an outrage to the dignity of the Church.

That whoever advised the refusal of an audience to the Lord Bishop of Norwich, who was so justly alarmed at the wrong methods which he saw taken in the education of the Prince, is an enemy to his country, and can only mean at best to govern by a faction, or is himself influenced by a more dangerous faction, who intend to overthrow the Government, and restore the exiled and arbitrary House of Stuart.

That to have a Scotchman of a most disaffected family, and allied in the nearest manner to the Pretender's First Minister, consulted on the education of the Prince of Wales, and entrusted with the most important secrets of Government, must tend to alarm and disgust the friends of the present Royal Family, and to encourage the hopes and attempts of the Jacobites.

Lastly, the Memorialists cannot help remarking, that three or four low, dark, suspected persons are the only men whose situation is fixed and permanent, but that all the great offices and officers are so constantly varied and shuffled about, to the disgrace of this country, that the best affected apprehend that there is a settled design in those low and suspected persons to infuse such jealousies, caprices, and fickleness into the two Ministers whose confidence they engross, as may render this Government ridiculous and contemptible, and facilitate the Revolution, which the Memorialists think they have but too much reason to fear is meditating.

God preserve the King!

Of these papers, one had been sent to General Hawley, and another to Lord Ravensworth. The former immediately carried one copy of his to the Duke, who gave it to the King, and another to the Duke of Newcastle, whose fright was only equalled by the noise raised by other copies of the Memorial, which was soon dispersed. Whoever was ill at or discontented with the Court, whoever was popular, whoever was remarkably Whig, were said to be in the number of the Memorialists. But why Hawley was selected for one of the first copies, was not so easily guessed. It was well said, by somebody, that it was judiciously intended by the author, if he meant to have it propagated; for as Hawley could not read, he must of necessity communicate it to others. Why Lord Ravensworth received one was obvious. He was reckoned one of the warmest and honestest Whigs in England. His being reckoned so, was a reason for the authors of the Memorial to address one to him; perhaps not their only reason; perhaps their thinking him rather a factious and interested, than an honest Whig, was the chief inducement to them to sow their seeds of discontent in a rank soil, which did indeed produce an ample crop.

In the beginning of February, Lord Ravensworth came to town, and acquainted Mr. Pelham that he had strong evidence of Jacobitism to produce against Stone, Murray, the Solicitor-General, and Dr. Johnson, Bishop of Gloucester. The notification was not welcome; yet could not be overlooked nor stifled. Lord Ravensworth had already communicated his intention of having the affair sifted to the Duke of Devonshire, the Chancellor, Lord Anson, and Mr. Fox, the latter of whom he had consulted, whether he should carry the notice to the King or to the Duke. Mr. Fox told him that the Duke never meddled out of his own province, the Army. The Ministry determined, against the opinion of Lord Granville, that the Cabinet Council should hear Lord Ravensworth's information.

On the 15th, 16th, and 17th, the Cabinet Council sat long and late, but with much secrecy, inquiring into this affair. The first night Lord Ravensworth was heard for four hours. The purport of his accusation was, that some few weeks before at Durham, one Fawcett, an Attorney, reading the newspaper which mentioned the promotion of Dr. Johnson to the Bishopric of Gloucester, said "He has good luck!" Being asked what he meant by that expression, he had replied, "Why, Johnson has drunk the Pretender's health twenty times with me and Mr. Stone and Mr. Murray." Dr. Cowper, Dean of Durham, who had been present at this dialogue, was called, and in a short and sensible manner confirmed Lord Ravensworth's account. The conversation made no noise at the time; only Dr. Chapman, master of Magdalen College in Cambridge, gave private intelligence of it to Harry Vane, a creature of the accused triumvirate, and he, by Mr.

Pelham's order, wrote to Fawcett to know the meaning of this imputation. Fawcett denied what he had said, and acquitted the Bishop of the charge. The clamours against Stone, on his quarrel with the Bishop of Norwich and Lord Harcourt, and the Memorial reaching Lord Ravensworth soon after this conversation happened, he determined to signalize his zeal, and hastened to London, Fawcett having confirmed to him what he had denied to Vane, but begging not to be produced as an accuser.

16th, Fawcett was examined: never was such an instance of terror and confusion! yet with reluctance and uncertainty he owned that what he had uttered at Durham was true. The substance of his evidence was, "that, about twenty years ago, Murray, then a young Lawyer, Stone, then in indigence, and himself, had used to sup frequently at one Vernon's, a rich Mercer, a noted Jacobite, and a lover of ingenious young men. The conversation was wont to be partly literature, partly treason; the customary healths, *The Chevalier* and *Lord Dunbar*."

Had the greater part of the Council not wished well to the accused, it must have shocked them to hear a charge of such consequence brought after an interval of twenty years, brought on memory, the transactions of a private company, most of them very young men, at worst flattering an old rich bachelor of no importance, and, in their most unguarded moments, never rising beyond a foolish libation to the healths of their imaginary Monarch and his Minister. Considering the lengths to which party had been carried for the last twenty years; considering how many men had been educated at Oxford about that period, or had been in league with every considerable Jacobite in the kingdom, if such a charge might be brought after so long a term, who almost would not be guilty? Who almost would be so innocent as not to have gone beyond a treasonable toast? It was necessary to be very Whig to see Lord Ravensworth's accusation in an honourable light.

17th, Lord Ravensworth and Fawcett were called to sign their Affidavits: the latter asked if he might alter his? The Chancellor told him he might add for explanation, but not make two Affidavits. He said, "My lords, I am fitter to die than to make an Affidavit." He contradicted many things that he had told Lord Ravensworth, and behaved so tragically, yet so naturally, that the Council were too much moved to proceed, and adjourned.

The accused were warm and earnest in denying the charge: Stone in particular affirming, that he would allow the truth of all that had been alleged against him for the last six months, if he had so much as once drunk the Pretender's health in the most envenomed companies, even when a student at Oxford; adding many menaces of prosecuting Fawcett for calumny. Such minute assurances from one so suspected, or such strains of prudence in his very youth, did not much contribute to invalidate Fawcett's testimony in the eyes of the world.

19th, the House of Commons went on the supply for Nova Scotia, as opened by Lord Duplin. Colonel Cornwallis, just returned from that Government, gave a short and sensible account of the colony, where, he said, the trade and improvements had been carried to as great a height as could be expected in the time. Beckford spoke strongly in behalf of the colony, and for attending to the West Indies, where all our wars must begin and end; that till we attended to our Navy, we had done nothing in the last war; how preferable this, to flinging our money into the gulf of Germany! He commended Cornwallis, and the Board of Trade. Sir Cordel Firebrace inquired into the state of the civil government; Cornwallis gave it. Gray spoke for improving it. Mr. Pelham desired to have it remembered, that the support of the colony was the sense of the House; and he told Beckford, that if he would praise oftener where it was deserved, his reproofs would be more regarded.

The Council sat late again that night: Fawcett collected more resolution; said, that Lord Ravensworth had been in the right to call upon him; that it was fact that he had been with the three accused when the treasonable healths were drunk; that at such a distance of time, he could not swear positively that they drank them; but he would endeavour with time to recollect particular circumstances.

21st and 22nd, the Council continued sitting, and heard Mr. Stone purge himself, who, with other articles of defence, called Bishop Hay Drummond to the character of his principles.

On the 23rd, Mr. Murray appeared before them, but rejected impetuously the reading of the Depositions: he said, he was positive to their falsehood, be they what they might: as he was aware that suspicions might arise from the connections of his family, he had lived a life of caution beyond even what his principles would have dictated.

Lord Ravensworth grew unquiet. Fawcett's various and uncertain behaviour distressed him: though the world was willing to believe the accused Jacobites, the evidence did not tend to corroborate the opinion: was drinking a treasonable health all the treason committed by men from whom so much danger was apprehended? Were no proofs of disloyalty more recent than of twenty years to be found against men who were supposed involved in the most pernicious measures? If no acts of a treacherous dye could be produced against them since they came into the King's service, might it not well be supposed, that their views and establishment under the present Government had washed out any stains contracted by education or former adulation? and it did appear that Vernon the Mercer had actually made Murray the heir of his fortunes. Lord Ravensworth consulted the Speaker, who advised him to establish his own truth, in having received the advertisement from Fawcett—but neither was that denied, nor the drinking the healths disbelieved, though both Stone and Murray at the last session of the Council on the 26th, when the latter made an incomparable oration, took each a solemn oath, that the charge was absolutely false.

The Council made their report to the King, signed unanimously, that Fawcett's account was false and scandalous—yet the Duke of Grafton, one of the unanimous, owned to Princess Emily, that Fawcett being asked if he had seen Mr. Murray since he had been in town, confessed he had, that he had been sent to him by Harry Vane. "What did Mr. Murray say to you?" "He advised me to contradict what I had said." And the Chancellor, who communicated the whole transaction to the Duke of Bedford, seemed to own Mr. Murray guilty. How his jealousy of Murray, and his mean court to Stone, made him choose to distinguish between them, will appear still more strongly hereafter.

Chapter 10

The King's acceptance of Lord Ravensworth's zeal was by no means gracious. Whether those frowns provoked, whether the Cabinet censure might inflame, whether disappointment from the ill success of such notable policy had soured, or whether he was still persuaded that the House of Hanover was in danger by employing men who had had such dangerous connections in their youth with a Jacobite Mercer, Lord Ravensworth was eager and busy in blowing up farther and more public inquisition. His temper was naturally hot; he was reckoned honest; two strong motives to prevent his acquiescing calmly to the disgrace he had received. His manner of prosecuting his measure, whatever was the end, was neither warm nor over-righteous. He tampered with the Duke of Bedford, communicated his papers to him, and even told him that it would not be disagreeable to him to be called upon in the House of Lords to explain his conduct. Yet to others he protested that he had no dealings with the Duke. His Grace was warned of this intricate behaviour; yet being still warmer than Lord Ravensworth, and incapable of indirect policy himself, he slighted the notice; and on March 16th, acquainted the Lords, that on the Thursday following he should move for the papers relating to the examination of Stone and Murray. This was a strain of candour a little beyond what was exacted by honour or policy. If the notification exceedingly embarrassed the Ministry, it must be owned that the measures they concerted, from the time given them by the Duke, were as discreet and artful as could be devised.

The 22nd was the day of expectation. The House was crowded. The Duke of Bedford began with observing that the public attention had been so engrossed by the late Cabinet Councils, that he was not surprised at the multitude he found assembled to hear the discussion, or at least to get some light into an affair, which, though touching the public so nearly, had been wrapt in such mysterious secrecy: such solemn councils held on treason, yet so little known of either accusation or process!—the effects indeed, the acquittal and the continuation of confidence, were divulged and notorious. His difficulties in a disquisition of this tender nature were great; difficult it was for him, after repeated obligations, to name the name of his Majesty— yet, if ever he should suggest a doubt, he could only mean his Majesty's

Ministers. It is the very spirit of the Law, the King can do no wrong—and not only the language of Law and of Parliament, it was the language of his heart—his experience of the King had taught it him: his Majesty cannot err, but when facts are not fairly stated to him. Those who state them unfairly, may misrepresent me. "The notoriety," said the Duke, "that an inquest of treason had been in agitation, made me conclude that it must be brought hither for our advice—could I doubt but it would? What other Judicature is there for crimes and criminals of this high nature? The incompetence of the Lords who had been assembled for this trial was evident: can the Cabinet Council condemn? Can they acquit? if they cannot condemn nor acquit, can they try? or who that is accused, is innocent, till he has had a more solemn purgation than their report can give him? But if no character can be purified by their verdict, what becomes of their own? My Lords, what a trust is reposed in the Cabinet Council! Can they be at peace till their opinions are sanctified by our sentence? But why do I talk of their satisfaction? the nation has a right to be satisfied. Here is an accusation of treason brought against men in such high and special trust, that the Councils of his present Majesty, and the hopes of the nation in the successor, are reposed in them: and this charge brought by a Lord of Parliament, who—but it is not for me to enter upon facts; the Lord himself is present, and has given me leave to call upon him: he showed me papers, though he said, he was fully satisfied that he had cleared his own character—I call upon that noble Lord to give your Lordships the necessary information."

Lord Ravensworth, not from want of any facility of expressing himself, for his manner was natural and manly, but from perplexity of mind, whether to own or not to own that he had instigated the Duke of Bedford to this examination, was ambiguous and unsatisfactory; and he endeavoured to cover his ungenerous behaviour to that Duke with frankness and candour. He said, that by the King's consent, he had received what papers he thought necessary, that is, he had received his own examination and the report—indeed, he had not been permitted to have a copy even of Harry Vane's letter. For his part, he had determined to proceed no farther. When the Duke of Bedford asked him, he had shown him the examination, not the report. That he had told his Grace that it would not be disagreeable to him to have the whole world know the story, and let them judge on it. That he should never have sought this discussion, yet could not but be glad of it. That so many aspersions had been thrown on him, that he believed his story had never been twice told in the same manner. That he had represented to the Ministers, as was his duty, what he had heard, and had left it to them to proceed upon as they should think proper—that, now he was called upon, he was willing to lay open the whole to their Lordships, provided they would allow him to name a Lord of Parliament, who was concerned in the affair, and was now present—but must first desire that they would let himself be sworn to the strict veracity of what he should say.

The Duke of Bedford told him, that as the Lord was present, he might name him, unless it was opposed; that the Lord, if he thinks proper, may retire: that it would be very irregular for Lord Ravensworth to be sworn. The Duke of Newcastle said, that he supposed it proceeded from the Bishop's ignorance of the forms of the House, that he had not risen and given leave to be named; but that he would answer for his Lordship's permission. The Bishop of Gloucester (the person hinted at) pleaded ignorance of forms, and consented to the free mention of his name. Lord Ravensworth told him, that as he was perfectly acquitted, the Lords would be ready to do him justice. Lord Ravensworth then told the story shortly, clearly, well: that company having dined with the Dean at Durham on the King's birth-day, as two of them, Fawcett and a Major Davison, were drinking coffee with the Dean in the evening, and reading a newspaper which mentioned a report that Dr. Johnson was to be Preceptor[222] to the Prince of Wales, Fawcett said, "He has good luck! twenty years ago he was a Jacobite." That this conversation had seemingly been forgot: but that on the 12th of January following, as he (Lord Ravensworth) was at a Club at Newcastle with Fawcett, the latter had showed him a letter from Harry Vane, inquiring into the meaning of those words. That he recollected no

---

[222] Lord Ravensworth at first, as is mentioned, p. 266, thought that Fawcett's observation on Dr. Johnson's promotion, had been in relation to the Bishopric; but on recollection and discussion, it appeared to have related to the intention of making him Preceptor to the Prince of Wales.

particulars of the letter—and he said with emphasis, *This letter, my Lords, I have not*. It only, as far as he remembered, expressed that Mr. Vane was desired and authorized by Mr. Pelham to inquire into that conversation, as it had occasioned some talk. He dwelt on his great regard to Mr. Pelham, and said, that urged by that motive, he had desired Fawcett to come to him the next day; that he had exhorted him to stick to the truth, and in four several conversations had always found him uniform. In those conversations he added the names of Mr. Stone and Mr. Murray—then, my Lords, I took it up; it then grew important. I feel none higher, none of more moment than Mr. Stone. That he had advised Fawcett to write no answer, but to go to Mr. Pelham; he went. That what tended to confirm his own suspicions, and led him to believe the imputed connection, was his finding, upon inquiry, that Vernon had been a notorious Jacobite; that Mr. Murray had been Vernon's sole heir. That some other incidents had not weakened his doubts; that Mr. Murray had advised Fawcett to let the affair drop; that Bishop Johnson said Fawcett had acquitted him in a letter written to him; the letter had been written to the Bishop, but his Lordship stood by while Fawcett wrote it. That soon afterwards the Bishop would have persuaded Mr. Fawcett to add these words, *and this is all I can say consistent with truth*. Fawcett refused. He concluded with saying, "My Lords, I was not the accuser; I told the Ministers, that, having come to the knowledge of the accusation, I was determined to bring the affair to light in some shape or other. I did it from duty and from zeal, not, as has been said, to revenge the quarrel of a noble Lord,[223] my friend, who has quitted a shining post on some disgusts with some of the persons involved in this charge."

The Duke of Bedford observed, that Lord Ravensworth had made some omissions in his narration, of which, as he had given him leave, he would put him in mind—to which the other replied hastily, that he had communicated nothing to the Duke from the last papers he had received, only from his own examination. The Duke owned that he had not seen the report; but took notice that Lord Ravensworth had forgot to mention that Fawcett had kept no copy of Vane's letter, and that Fawcett had owned to

---

[223] Lord Harcourt.

the Council that he had given Lord Ravensworth all the information which the latter affirmed to have received from him. The Chancellor, who was to conduct the solemn drama of the day, took care to keep off all episodes that might interfere with the projected plan of action, and interrupted the two Lords, by laying it down for order, that Lord Ravensworth must not repeat what he had only *heard* passed in Council. But this authoritative decision was treated as it ought to be by the Duke of Bedford, who with proper spirit launched out upon the indecent assumption of power in the Council, a step that added double weight to the reasons for bringing this matter before Parliament. That indeed even the Chancellor's supposing it had been brought before the *Council* was an unfounded assertion; that he denied its being the *Council*; it was only a private meeting of certain Lords—were they a Committee of Council? as such was it, that they arrogated the power of tendering oaths, and listening to voluntary evidences? if they were, the President of the Council should have presided—but here was no President, no forms, no essence, no authority of Council. In their own persons only these Lords were respectable. The Secretary of State is no Justice of Peace. An unheard-of jurisdiction had been attempted to be erected, unknown to this country, derogatory from the authority of this House! Before this revived Star-chamber, this Inquisition,—different indeed from the Inquisition in one point, for the heretics of this court were the favourites of it!—before this court the accused were admitted to purge themselves upon oath—a leading step to the introduction of perjury! But what was the whole style of their proceedings? mysterious! secret! arbitrary! cruel! The minutes are secreted; the witnesses were held in a state of confinement:[224] Lord Ravensworth was required to deliver up letters: orders for filing informations against Fawcett were given—or said to be given—"for I doubt the intention of carrying them into execution," said the Duke: "though, if they are pursued, the hardship on Fawcett will be the greater, as he is already pre-judged." The report, concise as it was, was three-fold: it

---

[224] The Dean of Durham (Dr. Cowper) and the others were literally detained privately in separate rooms for several hours; yet Murray, one of the accused, as it appeared, had evidently tampered with Fawcett the accuser, and seen him at his own house; so had Dr. Johnson.

pronounces Fawcett's accusation false and malicious; it pronounces the accused innocent; it justifies Lord Ravensworth, the accuser! how many powers assumed! Fawcett, though a lawyer, was terrified at such a court!

"It was their proceedings," the Duke said, he blamed; he had great regard for more than half of the Lords concerned, yet he must say they had erred greatly, if their proceedings were anything more than preparatory. However, these transactions did not strike him more than the high rank of the accused. Mr. Stone stands in as public a light as any man in Britain—there are other points in which the public should be satisfied too—for his part he had never conferred with the reverend and noble Lords,[225] who had lately retired from that important turbulent scene, yet he owned their resignations had already filled him with suspicions. They had been dismissed for no misbehaviour: he hoped they would vouchsafe to lay their motives before the House, that, *in this acquitting age*, they too may be disculpated—nay, the Council too should be disculpated; it should be manifest that they were not biased, and that their report is fit to see the light. Seen to be sure it will be; it cannot be meant to be secreted. Till it is produced, the world is left to perplexity, to argue in the dark—till more is known, one is apt to dwell on the uniformity of Fawcett's behaviour for four different times—no deviation, no inconsistency in his narrative, till after his interviews with Bishop Johnson and Mr. Murray—then it grew retrograde—then he faltered in his evidence—this gives suspicion; this calls for the whole system of the Council's procedure—how to produce that properly he did not know.

"You all wish the accused may be cleared; assist me, my Lords, in dragging into light every testimonial of their innocence: it is our natural business; and at the same time no business more arduous on which to give the King advice. Here he may want it; sinister advices may make our unbiased, honest opinions more necessary, more welcome." The noble Lord who presided lately over the education of the Prince, has been as well replaced as possible; the choice was the more acceptable, as it was his Majesty's own—*he* can do no wrong; he always acts right, when he acts

---

[225] Bishop of Norwich and Lord Harcourt.

himself. The time is proper for inquiring into this affair; it is no longer under examination; nor could he be told, as he generally was, "*we have a clue: don't stop us: these are the King's secrets.*" This inquiry can be attended with no inconvenience; it may be attended with good: the King desires to have the accused persons cleared. For the papers that are denied, they must be produced in Westminster-hall, if Fawcett is prosecuted— there *the King's secrets* must come out. That now was not merely the proper, it was the only time for searching into the character of the person entrusted with the education of the Prince—should a minority happen (and sorry he was he had not been able to be present and to give his dissent to a Bill of so pernicious a precedent and nature as the Regency Bill!) if that dreaded contingency should happen, might not they who are possessed of the person and authority of the King,—might not they, however suspected, however accused, shelter themselves under the clause of præmunire; a clause calculated not to guard the person of the Prince, but the persons of his Governors from danger? He moved for all the papers, examinations, and letters, that had been before the Cabinet Council.

The Chancellor, with acrimonious tenderness, began with protesting, that he should have taken this for a factious motion, had it not come from a Lord of so unsuspected a character—but he would enter at once into the matter. Lord Ravensworth had applied to have the affair examined, and his Majesty had ordered his Council to inquire into it. Mr. Stone had made the deepest asseverations of his innocence; nay, he went so far as to beg that the distance of time might be thrown out of the question, and that if the least title of the accusation could be proved against him, his guilt might be considered as but of yesterday. That the term *Cabinet* Council, said to be borrowed from France, was no novelty; that it was to be found in the Journals of Parliament. That the Duke of Devonshire being added by his Majesty's particular order on this occasion, was not unprecedented. That it had been called by our ancestors, sometimes the Cabinet for Foreign Affairs; sometimes the Cabinet for Private. How they corresponded as a Council in Queen Elizabeth's time might be seen in Forbes's State Papers. That they had not proceeded by compulsory summons: that it had been determined in Westminster-hall, that a Secretary of State may administer oaths. That Magistrates indeed might not accept the oath of an accused person: here in truth their oaths had been accepted now by an act of grace, which was the more excusable, as they were subject to no punishment from the Council that examined them. That this had been an inquiry for satisfaction, not for prosecution: that their oaths was the only satisfaction to be obtained: Vernon was dead; nobody else was present at these pretended treasonable meetings, (this was false, for he presently afterwards urged in their favour, that Mr. Cayley, who is living, and used to be present, had been examined, and could remember no such passages;) that the oaths had not been administered by authority, but admitted at their own desire. He commended the great solemnity of the proceedings, and added, we have all of us the King's leave to answer any questions.

He dwelt on the prevarications and inconsistence of Fawcett's behaviour, who had often said that he could not charge anybody but himself. He then turned to encomiums on the zeal and conduct of Mr. Stone during the Rebellion; and mentioned Mr. Cayley's evidence. Slightly he mentioned Mr. Murray, who, he said, had always behaved in his court in an irreproachable and meritorious manner from the year 1742. (Servile was this court to Stone; envious this transient approbation of Murray!) He added, that no orders had been given for the prosecution of Fawcett—but in a higher tone he talked of the impropriety of the Motion: that no prerogative was so appropriate to the King as the government of his own family: that ten Judges had declared for it[226]—therefore, you will not wantonly invade it—have you any distrust of the Lords who have sifted this matter? to what good end would further inquiry tend? That much he was surprised how the Regency Bill came to be drawn into the question! Is there one word in that Bill of the Governors of the Prince of Wales? He never knew that the noble Duke had disapproved that Bill. He reflected with pleasure on the many converts that had been made from Jacobitism, and hoped that by raking into old stories their Lordships would not prevent and discourage change of principles: that it would make those who were willing to come over to the pale of loyalty dread parliamentary inquiries

---

[226] In the late King's reign, on the difference between his Majesty and the Prince.

hanging over their heads: they would never think themselves safe: and it would be ungenerous to exclude men of any principles from enjoying the sunshine and blessings of such a Reign and Government—for his part he hated names and distinctions, and to stifle any attempts for reviving them would give his negative to the Motion.

Lord Harcourt rose next, and though a little abashed as never accustomed to speak in public, said, with great grace and propriety, that he thought the King had the best right to judge in his own family; that he had communicated to his Majesty alone the reasons of his dissatisfaction in the government of the Prince: his Majesty had not thought his reasons good; he had therefore resigned a post which he thought he could not hold with credit and reputation.

If the decency and consistency of this speech had wanted a foil, it would have found it in Lord Talbot's subsequent harangue; who said, that if the Motion had come from a person of less known integrity, he should have thought it dictated by a spirit of confusion. That some indeed love the Crown, some a jumble of Administrations. That a very sensible man drunk, may make a very good Jacobite: that he knew Fawcett, and had had a good opinion of him; but that often where he thought there was most perfection, he had found least. That he would not have acted like Lord Ravensworth— yet—(what a *yet* after such a prelude!) shall a private Council exclude the activity of the greater? The management of the Royal Children is of public import: shall the Council engross the direction of them? Hereafter, if this precedent is suffered, a cabal of Ministers will be worse than the Star-chamber. The precedent will be used to stifle all inquiries against sycophants, by applying to the Crown to appoint a trial by the Cabinet Council.

Hayter, Bishop of Norwich, the late Preceptor, with no less decency than Lord Harcourt, but with a little more artful desire of inflaming the prejudice against Stone and Murray, said that he would not declare the reasons of his resignation till he should be forced. That all he would say was, that he had met with obstructions from inferiors, *most cruel obstructions*. That he did not think himself at liberty to appeal from the King, *yet would willingly tell if he was obliged to it*. This insinuating offer the Duke of Bedford had not the presence of mind to take up; and the Bishop's gauntlet not being challenged, he could not with propriety go any farther. Perhaps the Ministry had not more reason to triumph on the event of the day, than on the Duke of Bedford's overlooking so fair an opening into their most vulnerable part!

At last rose the Bishop of Gloucester. If provocation often sharpens the genius, it did not in his case. Yet he was not confused, he was insolent: he spoke like a man that had governed children,[227] not like one fit to govern them. His language and circumstances were vulgar and trivial; he dwelt more on his housemaid letting in Mr. Fawcett when he came to him, than on any part of his defence. He said, he did not doubt but their Lordships would treat this accusation with the abhorrence it deserved. That for himself, he yielded to many on the Bench for capacity, he would not to any in loyalty. That he had had promises of favour formerly from his Grace of Bedford, and hoped he had not forfeited them: that it was not true that there had long been a scheme of making him Preceptor; that [he] himself had never heard of it till he was at the Hague, and then he was told of such a design by a noble Duke, who had heard it from a noble Lord, who had heard such a report—but not one of his own friends had thought of it for him: that if his Majesty had designed it, he did not know it. That in the Roman state, when informers were most rife, yet nothing had happened of this kind. He insisted on the badness of Fawcett, and affirmed that he did not dictate to him the letter for himself, though he owned he stood by while Fawcett wrote it; and that two days afterwards, when he desired Fawcett to add some words to it, they were not, *This is all I can say consistent with truth*, but, *This is the truth*.

Lord Ravensworth entirely acquitted the Bishop, and added this extraordinary problem, that Fawcett's character was so bad only from its being so good. He desired to know of all the Lords, whether they did not acquit him; and whether they did not believe that Fawcett had told him all he had announced.

---

[227] He had been one of the Masters of Westminster School.

Of the Duke of Newcastle's speech, an hour in length, I shall touch but a few of the most remarkable passages, such as, after acquitting Lord Ravensworth, were his panegyric on Harry Vane, *who never said a false thing, or did a bad one*! and another, scarce less exaggerated, on the Duke of Devonshire's *sagacity*, for which his Majesty had ordered him to be added to the Council. Of his own immediately going to the King, and saying, "Sir, I am come to keep my promise; that you should be the first to hear any complaints against Stone; if he is a Jacobite, he is a greater traitor to me than to you." How Stone, who had had the fate of kingdoms in his breast, had desired to have the accusation examined, and to be sequestered from his attendance on the Prince of Wales, till he should be acquitted; and lastly, how these stories had been propagated by cabal and intrigue, and by the anonymous Memorial sent assiduously all over the kingdom, full of falsities and irreverence to the King; and which General Hawley, as was his duty, had brought to him within an hour after receiving it.

At last opened the solemnity of the scene! the Chancellor's hackneyed sophistries, the Bishop of Gloucester's pedantic scorn, and the Duke of Newcastle's incongruous volubility, were rightly judged or foreseen to want a proper weight on so serious an occasion. To raise the comely pompous dignitaries of the Cabinet Council, and make them break their long mystic silence in favour of the accused, was a resource that did honour to the policy, as it effectually did the business, of the secret junto. The Duke of Marlborough first, and then the Archbishop, rose and gave short accounts of their having fully agreed in the sentence and report of the Council. Lord Waldegrave, with decency and spirit, commended Stone, spoke highly of the young Prince, and added, that he would not act a moment longer as Governor, than he should find Mr. Stone a man of honour, principles, and integrity. Dr. Hay Drummond, Bishop of St. Asaph, and brother of Lord Duplin, made a very elegant and eloquent speech in behalf of the accused. The Marquis of Hartington and the Duke of Dorset gave their testimonials, like the two former,[228] to the acts of the Cabinet Council. Lord Granville added to his, "That innocence was no

---

[228] The Duke of Marlborough and the Archbishop.

defence against temporary clamour; it will blow over: but I don't like Mr. Stone's desiring to have it heard any farther; it would be making ourselves an inquisition. Some often accuse others, to come at a third person. I love my Lord Harcourt for what he said." The Duke of Grafton, too, bore his testimony.

The Duke of Bedford rose again, and said, that if he had been angry, he had had time to cool: and must say, on the utmost deliberation, and with the greatest attention to what he had heard, that he had not found sufficient reason to acquit the accused persons, and for this strong reason, amongst others, that it remains evident that the Bishop of Gloucester had tampered with Fawcett—do the innocent tamper with evidence? as little could he agree with the Duke of Newcastle, who said he would be guilty to be so acquitted by the Chancellor—Newcastle interrupting him, that he had only said, he would be suspected; the Duke of Bedford rejoined, that when his Grace had gone so far, it was no wonder if he had gone a little farther; but so far from agreeing even to that modification, he would not be suspected by one man, to be acquitted by that whole House. That, when he had been of the Cabinet Council, he had never known such a thing as their sitting on a trial. That the Duke of Newcastle had told them almost the whole examination; what can induce their Lordships still to refuse to ask for it? That he had been particularly called upon to make this Motion; that the nation demands it; that the very Parliament of Paris would go into such an examination. That if any, in so high a trust as the care of the Prince of Wales, are suspected, can it be called a point of domestic concern only? can it be deemed so domestic as to forbid public inquiry? That he must still urge that Fawcett had never prevaricated, till the Bishop had been with him—but if his Lordship is really desirous of purging himself of this charge, let him promote this Motion: here he will be sure of the most impartial trial, of the most open, and consequently of the most satisfactory acquittal. "To prompt witnesses to prevaricate—to stifle inquiry—these arts will not quiet the suspicions of mankind. A more manly way it had been to have said, we did drink these healths, we were as Jacobite as it is pretended we were, but we are converted—but, my Lords," concluded the

Duke, "it is not to prove that these healths were drunk that I contend—if any part of the charge is true, more is true."

Lord Bath objected to any farther examination of a man who had so prevaricated with the Cabinet Council, whose proceedings, he said, were not only sufficient, but not unprecedented. That he had once been examined so himself, with Sir Paul Methuen and Mr. Cholmondeley, and that they had been examined separately; it was in relation to one Lewis, a clerk to Lord Oxford, who, by mistake for one Levi, a Jew, had been suspected of negotiations with the Court of St. Germains: it was in the Queen's time, and she had referred it to the Cabinet Council.

Lord Northumberland perceiving it was a day for great men to stand forth, thought it a good opportunity to announce his own dignity; but he said little to the purpose. Still less was said by the young Marquis of Rockingham, though he had prepared a long quotation from Tacitus about informers; and opened with it.

The Duke of Argyle sneered at Ministers out of place—not at future Ministers, for he was profuse in flattery to Stone, who, till lately, he had never heard had an enemy! that, during the Rebellion, happening to be at the Secretary's office, two men came to solicit Mr. Stone for a place; the refused went away the better pleased of the two, from Mr. Stone's gracious manner of refusing!

Lord Anson bore his testimony to the unanimity and report of the Cabinet Council. Dr. Madox, of Worcester, ungraciously and rudely said, that though it might be right to countenance converts, yet would it be wrong to entrust the whole to one, who had been a Jacobite. That there were great dissatisfactions already: what would ensue, if a Star-chamber were erected to protect the most unpopular? why not remove Mr. Stone to any other employment? let him come and take his place among your Lordships. He added, that great would be the hardship on Fawcett, if tried in Westminster-hall; for what Jury but would be influenced by the authority and decision of the Council? Lord Holderness notified his assent to the proceedings of the Cabinet Council. The Bishop of Worcester and Lord Sandys had some jarring; and then Lord Ravensworth put a period to this solemn mummery, in which he had acted such various parts, by saying that he was satisfied with his acquittal; that he thought nothing farther necessary to his honour; would take no farther part; did not desire anybody else would; would leave it here—and went away! A silence of confusion ensued for some minutes; nobody rising to speak, the Duke of Bedford, Lord Townshend, Lord Harcourt, and the Bishop of Worcester, went below the bar to divide, and the Bishop of Norwich was going; but no more following, they gave it up without telling the House; all the Tory Lords keeping their seats to vote for Stone and Murray.

Chapter 11

About this time was taken in Scotland, Dr. Archibald Cameron, a man excepted by the Act of Indemnity. Intelligence had been received some time before of his intended journey to Britain, with a commission from Prussia to offer arms to the disaffected Highlanders, at the same time that ships were hiring in the north to transport men. The fairness of Dr. Cameron's character, compared with the severity he met from a Government, most laudably mild to its enemies, confirmed this report. That Prussia, who opened its inhospitable arms to every British Rebel, should have tampered in such a business was by no means improbable. That King hated his uncle—but could a Protestant Potentate dip in designs for restoring a Popish Government?—of what religion is policy? to what sect is royal revenge bigoted? The Queen-dowager, though sister of our King, was avowedly a Jacobite, by principle so—and it was natural: what Prince but the single one who profits by the principle can ever think it allowable to overturn sacred hereditary right? It is the cause of sovereigns that their crimes should be unpunishable. Two sloops were stationed to watch; yet Cameron landed; and was taken with difficulty: an officer and ten men pursued him: they divided—yet wherever they turned, they found children posted, who ran swiftly and screamed to give notice. At last they overtook a boy who had hurt his foot; and by him were directed to a house in a wood; yet the Doctor was gone; but, on the wood being surrounded, was taken.

By the very loyal, consequences equally threatening were feared from a new amour of the King of France, who had taken a mistress of Irish extraction, the daughter of a shoemaker, formerly a life-guardsman: her name, Murphy, and of signal beauty. Madame Pompadour was a friend to peace and England. This deviation in the Monarch's constancy was, however, of transitory duration. With scarce complaisance, with no affection, he had for many years confined himself to his homely, elderly, unattractive queen. All the intrigues of a gallant Court, or of interested factions, had not been able to undermine his conjugal regularity, for it was no more. Accident threw him into the arms of Madame de Mailly, a sensible woman, a fine figure, but very plain; he demanded not beauty, and became as regular as with the Queen. To engage him more, that is, to govern him, Madame de Mailly associated to their suppers her sister, Madame de Vintimille, a woman of great wit, but exceedingly ill-proportioned with beauty—a great oversight in an ugly woman, who had dispossessed an ugly one. The coadjutrix soon displaced her introductress; but died in labour; of poison, as the state of intrigues would of course suppose. The Monarch hankered about the same family, and took a third sister, who was gloriously beautiful, and whom he created Duchesse de Chateauroux. In the triumph of her concubinage, the King fell ill at Metz. Fitz-James, Bishop of Soissons, attacked a frightened piety, which was natural, and only subdued by constitution. The mistress was not only discarded, but publicly affronted, the Monarch permitting it; and the Queen, who was sent for, made a foolish triumphal entry to thank the Lord for the recovery of the King's soul and body—but as soon as the latter was re-established, the Queen was sent to her prayers, the Bishop to his diocese, and the Duchess was recalled—but died suddenly. Though a jealous sister may be supposed to dispatch a rival, can one believe that Bishops and Confessors poison?

Madame Pompadour, the wife of a Fermier General, succeeded: grace, beauty, address, art, ambition, all met in that charming woman. She governed him more than he had ever been governed but by Cardinal Fleury: she engaged in all politics, she gave life and agreeableness to all; she amassed vast treasures herself, she was the cause of squandering vast treasures, in varying scenes of pleasure to divert the gloom of a temper which was verging nearer to the age of devotion. The Clergy hated her, for she countenanced the Parliament; the people imputed oppressions to her; the Dauphin, who was a bigot, and who loved his mother, affected to shock her: yet the King, who was the best father in the world, bore with great mildness so unpleasant an attack on royal and parental authority.

The session of Parliament was languishing towards a conclusion, when a Bill sent down from the Lords to the Commons, and which had passed almost without notice through the former House, having been carried by an hundred Lords against the Duke of Bedford and eleven others, raised, or gave occasion to raise, extraordinary heats. This was the famous *Marriage Bill*; an Act of such notoriety, and on which so very much was said at the time, and on which so much has been written since, that it would be almost impossible, at least very wearisome, to particularize the Debates, and very unnecessary to enter much into the state of the question. Some of the most particular passages, such as tend to illustrate or explain the characters, the politics, and the factions of the time, I shall, according to my custom, succinctly touch.

The Bill had been originally moved by my Lord Bath, who, attending a Scotch cause, was struck with the hardship of a matrimonial case, in which a man, after a marriage of thirty years, was claimed by another woman on a pre-contract. The Judges were ordered to frame a Bill that should remedy so cruel a retrospect. They did; but drew it so ill, and it was three times printed so inaccurately, that the Chancellor was obliged to give it ample correction. Whether from mere partiality to an ordinance thus become his own, or whether in shaping a law, new views of power opened to a mind fond of power, fond of dictating; so it was, that the Chancellor gave all his attention to a statute into which he had breathed the very spirit of aristocracy and insolent nobility. It was amazing, in a country where liberty gives choice, where trade and money confer equality, and where facility of marriage had always been supposed to produce populousness,— it was amazing to see a law promulged, that cramped inclination, that discountenanced matrimony, and that seemed to annex as sacred privileges to birth, as could be devised in the proudest, poorest little Italian principality; and as if the artificer had been a Teutonic Margrave, not a little lawyer, who had raised himself by his industry from the very lees of the people; and who had matched his own blood with the great house of *Kent*!

The abuse of pre-contracts had occasioned the demand of a remedy—the physician immediately prescribed medicines for every ailment to which the ceremony of marriage was or could be supposed liable! Publication of banns was already an established ordinance, but totally in disuse except amongst the inferior people, who did not blush to obey the law. Persons of Quality, who proclaimed every other step of their conjugation by the most public parade, were ashamed to have the intention of it notified, and were constantly married by special licence. Unsuitable matches in a country where the passions are not impetuous, and where it is neither easy nor customary to tyrannize the inclinations of children, were by no means frequent: the most disproportioned alliances, those contracted by age, by dowagers, were without the scope of this Bill. Yet the new Act set out with a falsehood, declaiming against clandestine marriages, as if they had been a frequent evil.

The greatest abuse were the temporary weddings clapped up in the Fleet, and by one Keith,[229] who had constructed a very Bishopric for revenue in Mayfair, by performing that charitable function for a trifling sum, which the *poor* successors of the Apostles are seldom humble enough to perform out of duty. The new Bill enjoined indispensable publication of banns, yet took away their validity, if parents, nay, if even guardians, signified their dissent, where the parties should be under age—a very novel power!—but guardians are a limb of Chancery! The Archbishop's licence was indeed reserved to him. A more arbitrary spirit was still behind: persons solemnizing marriages, without these previous steps, were sentenced to transportation, and the marriage was to be effectually null—so close did congenial law clip the wings of the prostrate priesthood! And as if such rigour did not sufficiently describe its fountain and its destination, it was expressly specified, that where a mother or a guardian should be *non compos*, resort might be had to the Chancellor himself for licence. Contracts and pre-contracts, other flowers of ecclesiastic

---

[229] Being deprived of this income, Keith swore he would be revenged of the Bishops—that he would buy a piece of ground and outbury them.

Chapter 11

prerogative, were to be totally invalid, and their obligations abolished: and the gentle institution was wound up with the penalty of death for all forgeries in breach of this statute of modern Draco. Quakers, Jews, and the Royal Family had the only toleration.

May 14th.—The Bill came down to the Commons. Nugent took it to pieces severely and sensibly, pointed out the impropriety of it in a commercial nation, and the ill-nature and partiality of the restrictions. He showed himself a great master of political disquisitions, and it seemed that a desire of displaying that learning was the sole cause of any opposition to the Bill. This was all that passed material the first day, and the Bill was read on a majority of 116 to 55.

21st.—A second adversary appeared against the Bill. This was Charles Townshend, second son of my Lord Townshend, a young man of unbounded ambition, of exceeding application, and, as it now appeared, of abilities capable of satisfying that ambition, and of not wanting that application: yet to such parts and such industry he was fond of associating all the little arts and falsehoods that always depreciate, though so often thought necessary by, a genius. He had been an early favourite of Lord Halifax, and had already distinguished himself on affairs of trade, and in drawing plans and papers for that province; but not rising in proportion to his ambition, he comforted himself with employing as many stratagems as had ever been imputed to the most successful statesmen.

His figure was tall and advantageous, his action vehement, his voice loud, his laugh louder. He had art enough to disguise anything but his vanity. He spoke long and with much wit, and drew a picture, with much humour at least, if not with much humility, of himself and of his own situation, as the younger son of a capricious father, who had already debarred him from an advantageous match: "were new shackles to be forged to keep young men of abilities from mounting to a level with their elder brothers?" Nugent had not shone with more parts the preceding day; Nugent on no day discovered less modesty. What will be their fates I know not; but this Mr. Townshend and Mr. Conway seemed marked by nature for leaders, perhaps for rivals in the Government of their country. The quickness of genius is eminently with the first, and a superiority of application; the propriety and amiableness of character with the latter. One grasps at fortune, the other only seems pleased to accept fortune when it advances to him. The one foresees himself equal to everything, the other finds himself so whenever he essays. Charles Townshend seems to have no passion but ambition; Harry Conway not even to have that. The one is impetuous and unsteady; the other, cool and determined. Conway is indolent, but can be assiduous; Charles Townshend can only be indefatigable. The latter would govern mankind for his own sake; the former, for theirs.

The speeches hitherto had only been flourishes in the air: at last the real enemy came forth, Mr. Fox; who neither spared the Bill nor the author of it, as wherever he laid his finger, it was not wont to be light. He was supported by Fazakerley and Sir William Yonge. Mr. Pelham, the Attorney and Solicitor, Lord Hilsborough, Hampden, and Lord Egmont, supported the Bill, and it was carried that day by 165 to 84.

On the 23rd and 25th, the House sat late each day on the Bill, Mr. Fox attacking and Mr. Pelham defending with eager peevishness. The former repeated his censures on the Chancellor, which old Horace Walpole reproved; Nugent was absurd; and the measure growing ministerial, the numbers against the Bill diminished.

28th.—The Committee sat till half an hour past three in the morning, on the clause for annulling marriages that should be contracted contrary to the inhibitions in the Bill. The Churchmen acquiesced in the Legislature's assuming this power in spirituals, as they had done in the single case of the young King's marriage in the Regency Bill: but however commendable the moderation of the Clergy might be, the Pontific power arrogated by the head of the Law, and his obstinate persisting to enforce a statute, by no means calculated or called for by general utility, was most indecent. The Speaker argued with great weight against the clause; Wilbraham, well for it. Mr. Fox, at one in the morning, spoke against it for above an hour, and laid open the chicanery and jargon of the Lawyers, the pride of their Mufti, and the arbitrary manner of enforcing the Bill. A motion for adjournment was moved, but was rejected by above 80 to 40 odd.

Chapter 11

30th.—The Committee went upon the clause that gave unheard-of power, in the first resort to parents and guardians, and then to the Chancery, on the marriages of minors. Fox spoke with increasing spirit against this clause too; and on Wilbraham's having said, if you have a sore leg, will you not try gentle remedies first? he drew a most severe picture of the Chancellor, under the application of the story of a Gentlewoman at Salisbury, who, having a sore leg, sent for a Country Surgeon, who pronounced it must be cut off. The Gentlewoman, unwilling to submit to the operation, sent for another, more merciful, who said he could save her leg, without the least operation. The Surgeons conferred: the ignorant one said, "I know it might be saved, but I have given my opinion; my character depends upon it, and we must carry it through"—the leg was cut off. Charles Yorke, the Chancellor's son, took this up with great anger, and yet with preciseness, beginning with these words, "It is new in Parliament, it is new in politics, it is new in ambition;" and drew a lofty character of his father, and of the height to which he had raised himself by his merit; concluding with telling Fox, how imprudent it was to attack such authority, and assuring him that he would feel it. Mr. Fox replied with repeating the sententious words: "Is it new in Parliament to be conscientious? I hope not! Is it new in politics? I am afraid it is! Is it new in ambition? It certainly is, to attack such authority!" Mr. Pelham answered him well. Mr. Fox once more replied, urging how cruel and absurd it was to force the Bill down: that he knew he should not be heard by above one-third of the House, but would speak so loud that he would be heard out of the House. That from the beginning to the end of the Bill, one only view had predominated, that of pride and aristocracy. There was much of truth in this. At the very beginning, on the Duke of Newcastle's declining to vote in the Bill, the Chancellor told Mr. Pelham, "I will be supported in this, or I never will speak for you again." As the Opposition had at that time been inconsiderable, this breathed a little more than a mere spirit of obstinacy, and foretold a Bill to be framed not without an interested meaning: at least a legislator is uncommonly zealous for the public good, who forgets the philosophy of his character to drive on his honest ordinances by political menaces!

The next day the Committee finished without a division. Sir Richard Lloyd, a Lawyer, who had spoken against the Bill, voted for it afterwards, without assigning any reason for his change of opinion. Captain Saunders, who had said that he would go and vote against the Bill, for the sake of the sailors, having once given forty of his crew leave to go on shore for an hour, and all returned married, was compelled by Lord Anson, the Chancellor's son-in-law and his patron, to vote for it. Henley and the Solicitor-General declaring of the same words, the one, that they could not be made clearer; the other, that they were as clear as the sun at noonday, though each gave a totally different interpretation of them, were well ridiculed by Fox; as a serious speech of Lord Egmont was with much humour and not a little indecency by Nugent.

June 1.—The report was made of the Bill, and the House sat till ten. On one clause only there was a division of 102 to 20.

2d.—A new anti-ministerial Paper appeared, called the Protester, supported at the expense of the Duke of Bedford and Beckford, and written by Ralph, a dull author, originally a poet, and satirized in the Dunciad: retained, after his pen had been rejected by Sir Robert Walpole, by Doddington and Waller; but much fitter to range the obscure ideas of the latter, than to dress up the wit of the former: from them, he devolved to the Prince of Wales in his second opposition, and laboured long in a paper called the Remembrancer, which was more than once emboldened above the undertaker's pitch, by Lord Egmont and others. Ralph's own turn seemed to be endeavouring to raise mobs by speculative ideas of government; from whence his judgment at least may be calculated. But he had the good fortune to be bought off from his last Journal, the Protester, for the only Paper that he did not write in it.

4th.—The Marriage Bill was read for the last time. Charles Townshend again opposed it with as much argument as before with wit. Mr. Fox, with still more wit, ridiculed it for an hour and a half. Notwithstanding the Chancellor's obstinacy in maintaining it, and the care he had bestowed upon it, it was still so incorrect and so rigorous, that its very body-guards had been forced to make or to submit to many amendments: these were inserted in Mr. Fox's copy in red ink: the Solicitor-General, who sat near him as he was speaking, said, "How bloody it looks!" Fox took this up with spirit, and said, "Yes, *but you cannot say I did it; look what a rent the learned Casca made*, (this alluded to the Attorney,) *through this the well-beloved Brutus stabbed*!" (Mr. Pelham)—however, he finished with earnest declarations of not having designed to abuse the Chancellor, and with affirming that it was scandalous to pass the Bill—but it was passed by 125 votes to 56.

6th.—The Bill being returned to the Lords, the amendments were read. The Duke of Bedford, who began to attack the whole Bill, was obstructed by the Chancellor, who would have confined him to the mere amendments; but the Duke, appealing to the House whether he might not argue against the face of the whole Bill as it now stood, the Chancellor seemed to acquiesce; but the Duke, not finding any disposition to support him, soon dropped the cause; objecting chiefly to the last clause on not extending the act to Foreign Countries. The Chancellor replied, that he was sorry the clause was there; but the Bill was too good to be lost, and might have much good engrafted on it hereafter.[230] Lord Sandys declared that he would agree to all the amendments made by the House of Commons, against any that should be offered by anybody else. An absurd declaration, founded on the design of proroguing the Parliament on the morrow, which would leave no time for returning the Bill to the Commons; and a plain indication of the indigested manner in which a law of such importance was hurried on. On its being urged that several women could not write, the Bishop of Oxford, with a sophistry that would have distinguished him in *any* church, replied that the Clergyman might write to himself, and give it to the woman, and she to him again, for that the Bill did not say, that when she gave her consent in writing, it must be of her own writing! Lord Bath said, the opposition had proceeded from faction and party. The Duke of Bedford replied, that his opposition had arisen from conscience, that he had not troubled himself about what the House of Commons did; yet he had perceived that the Bill had been crammed down both Houses.

---

[230] Yet no amendment was ever made in it, and all its clauses and faults supported by the utmost rigour of the power of Chancery.

At last the Chancellor—not, as he has been represented,[231] in the figure of *Public Wisdom speaking*, but with all the acrimony of wounded pride, of detected ambition, and insolent authority. He read his speech; not that he had written it to guard himself from indecency; or that he had feared to forget his thread of argument in the heat of personality: he did not deign an argument, he did not attempt to defend a Bill so criticized. He seemed only to have methodized his malice, and noted down the passages where he was to resent, where to threaten. He introduced himself with just allowing conscience and candour to the Duke of Bedford; but what he had to complain of had passed without those walls, and in another place. That, as to the young man, (Charles Townshend,) youth and parts require beauty and riches, flesh and blood inspire such thoughts, and therefore he excused him—but men of riper years and graver had opposed; that the first, (the Speaker,) was a good, well-meaning man, but had been abused by words— that another, (Fox,) dark, gloomy, and insidious genius, who was an engine of personality and faction, had been making connections, and trying to form a party, but his designs had been seen through and defeated. That in this country you must govern by force or by law; it was easy to know that person's principles, which were to govern by arbitrary force. That the King speaks through the Seals, and is represented by the Chancellor and the Judges in the Courts where the Majesty of the King resides; that such attacks on the Chancellor and the Law was flying in the face of the King: that this behaviour was not liked: that it had been taken up with dignity,[232] and that the incendiary had been properly reproved; that this was not the way to popularity or favour; and that he could take upon him to say, that person knows so by this time; a beam of light had broken in upon him; but, concluded he, I despise his scurrility, as much as his adulation and retraction. This *Philippic* over, the Bill passed. Lord Granville, who had threatened to oppose it, did not attend.

The prorogation of the Parliament prevented any farther open war. Mr. Fox seemed wantonly and unnecessarily to have insulted the Chancellor, and had even manifested some fear at having done so. Indeed, he who had

---

[231] An expression of Lord Lyttleton on Lord Hardwicke.
[232] Meaning by his son, Charles Yorke.

always been rash and resolute, now first discovered some symptoms of irresolution; and the time advanced but too fast, when the provocation offered to Yorke, and the suspicion of his want of a determined spirit, were of essential detriment to him. He could not but feel the Chancellor's haughty scorn of the atonement he had offered; yet, though he let slip both sentences of resentment and indications of an ambition that began to aspire higher, he soon yielded to a silent pacification. Mr. Pelham affected to be rather ignorant of the heights to which the rupture had openly been carried; and on the King's being told, that Mr. Fox's behaviour had been concerted with the Duke of Bedford, Mr. Pelham protested to Fox, that he had assured the King that the latter, on some proposal of union about elections from that Duke, had refused any such connection while he should remain in the King's service. For the storm between Fox and the Chancellor, Mr. Pelham said it would blow over, "Yet neither of you," said he to the former, "will forgive." Mr. Fox, in return, who gave no credit to this affected candour, reproached him in strong terms with the Chancellor's (and by necessary implication, with the Duke of Newcastle's) treachery to Sir Robert Walpole.

The Duke's conversation on this occasion with Mr. Fox was remarkable. "The Chancellor meaned me," said he, "by arbitrary force." Mr. Fox thought not. "Why," said the Duke, "do you think that he imagines you would govern by an Army without me?" "Sir," said Fox, "how will the King act on what has happened?" "The King," replied the Duke, "would part with you, or even with me, to satisfy them: but if you can maintain yourself for six months, he will like you the better for what has passed, for he thinks you a man, and he knows none of the rest have the spirit of a mouse." Mr. Fox said, "If they turn me out, I shall not acquit Mr. Pelham, nor shall I spare him. Let him raise up Murray; Mr. Pelham knows he has betrayed him, but is willing to forget it. I know he fears me still more; he has often told me I was like Mr. Pulteney. It may be vanity, but if I am stronger than Murray, I am ten times stronger than Mr. Pelham." "Mr. Pelham," replied the Duke, "has neither candour, honour, nor sincerity. Fox, how do you think I have been entertaining myself this morning? It was poor pleasure, but I had no better. The Duke of Newcastle asked me how I would have the warrant for Cranborn[233] drawn. I thanked him, but heard Mr. Pelham was uneasy that I had not thanked him; so to-day I met them together, and thanked the Duke of Newcastle again, and only asked t'other when he went to Esher." The Duke concluded with advising Fox to speak to the King, and not let him brood on it: "He will talk on the Bill," said the Duke: "let him; and you, who could not be convinced in the House, be convinced by him."

The King was civil to Fox at his next levee: afterwards in his closet Mr. Fox beginning to say, "Sir, last Wednesday the Chancellor"—the King interrupted, "Oh! sir, I believe you had given him cause; it is now pretty even." Mr. Fox said, "Sir, I shall only beg to be heard as to there being any faction or intrigue in my behaviour: I give you my honour it is not true." "The moment you give me your honour," replied the King, "I believe you; but I must tell you, as I am no liar, that you have been much suspected." He then repeated to him accusations of such low caballing, of balls given at Holland House to the Duchess of Bedford, to which Mr. Pelham's daughters had not been invited, of persons who were disagreeable to the Pelhams being invited; in short, accusations of such feminine and peevish trifles, that if Mr. Pelham was not the whisperer of them, and the Chancellor was, the latter had certainly very tender sensations, when they could extend themselves to the dancing disgusts of his friend's wife and daughters! Mr. Fox answered these cursorily, disclaimed any political connections with the Bedfords, and repeated with emphasis, "Such intrigues, Sir, would be worse in me, while in your service, than in any man living, as nobody blamed such intrigues in those who undermined Sir Robert Walpole so much as I." This dialogue ended so well, that Mr. Fox asked for a little place for one of his dependents, and obtained it.

7th.—Dr. Archibald Cameron suffered death at Tyburn. He had been forced into the Rebellion by his brother Lochiel, whom he had tried to confine, to prevent his engaging in it: not that Lochiel had taken arms voluntarily: he was a man of great parts, but could not resist the desperate honour which he thought the Pretender did him, in throwing himself into

---

[233] The King had just given Cranborn Lodge in Windsor Forest to the Duke.

his arms, and demanding his sword and interest.[234] The Doctor, who was a man of learning and very valuable humanity, which he had displayed in endeavours to civilize that part of a barbarous country, and in offices of benevolence to the soldiers employed on the Highland roads, and to the mine-adventurers established at Strontean, was torn from these sweet duties, from his profession, from a beloved and large family, and attended his rash brother at Prestonpans and Falkirk, escaped with him, and was appointed physician to Lochiel's regiment in the French service. He ventured back, was taken as mentioned above, and underwent a forced death with as much composure as a philosopher could affect at dying a natural one.

During the course of the summer the troubles in Ireland increased. Lord Kildare returned thither towards the end of June, after having presented a Memorial to the King against the administration of the Duke of Dorset, and the ascendant of the Primate. Nothing could be worse drawn: he was too weak to compose better, and too obstinate to submit to any correction. No facts were alleged against the Lord Lieutenant, nor any crime pretended in the Primate but that he was a Churchman. Yet these no accusations, he told the King he would return to prove whenever he should be required, and would answer that the Irish House of Commons would stand by him. He had no experience; nor knew that many men will say with party heat what they will not support with party steadiness. Lord Holderness, by the King's command, wrote to the Chancellor of Ireland, telling him, that the King had sent the Duke of Dorset to govern them, because he had pleased them so much formerly, and because he had the good of Ireland so much at heart: that his Majesty wondered at any man taking upon himself to answer for a nation; and that he expected that all who loved him would support the Lord Lieutenant: that his Majesty permitted this letter to be communicated to Lord Kildare, to anybody. Thus the absurdity of the Memorial was balanced by the haughtiness of the mandate. Lord Kildare had transfused into a State Manifesto the most

---

[234] "Il marche en philosophe, où l'honneur le conduit,
  Condamne les combats, plaint son maître, et le suit."
  Henriade.

licentious topics of party libels: the English Ministers adopted, in the King's answer, the most exalted diction of French prerogative.

Whatever might be the temper in Ireland, the increasing servility in England encouraged such a spirit in the Court. Mr. Pelham, who went to Scarborough this summer for his health, received the extravagant and unprecedented compliment of being desired to recommend a member to that borough, which happened to be vacant. The people of Bristol proceeded so far as to offer the same nomination to the King himself on this occasion: riots had happened there on the erection of new turnpikes; a citizen knocked down one of the rioters, and another stabbed him. The jury brought it in willful murder in the first. The Attorney-General moved in the King's Bench to reverse the judgment. This so pleased both parties in that city (the condemned person being a chief Tory), that they acknowledged it by this offer, so repugnant to all ideas of freedom of elections. What followed was only ridiculous. The King recommended Nugent: the Bristol men begged to be excused, as Nugent had been the principal promoter[235] of the Bill for a General Naturalization.

Some little time before the Irish Parliament met, the Speaker's friends gave out, that the Primate had made acknowledgments to him of his concern for the confusion that was likely to follow, that he would meddle no more with the House of Commons, but would give all his interest and influence there to the Speaker: that the latter had replied, the Primate had such underhand ways, and had deceived him so often, that he could not trust him; and for his influence he despised it. All this passed by the intervention of Luke Gardiner, who, on the Primate's party denying it, being called on, avowed the message. However, as it was decent for the Speaker to act candour and contrition too, he went to the Duke of Dorset, and told him, that he had got a majority in the House of Commons, and that they were determined to omit in the Address to the King the usual thanks for sending his Grace; and that if his Grace would acquiesce in that omission, they would make the rest of the session easy to him. The Duke, as hardhearted as the Speaker had been to the Primate, would by no means

---

[235] Vide Appendix.

give his own consent to being stigmatized. An hour before he went to open the Parliament, the Speaker returned and acquainted him that he had prevailed on his friends to suffer the usual Address—and it was made.

The English Parliament, which opened on the 15th of November, was employed till the end of the year in an affair which showed how much the age, enlightened as it is called, was still enslaved to the grossest and most vulgar prejudices. The year before an Act had passed for naturalizing Jews. It had passed almost without observation, Sir John Barnard and Lord Egmont having merely given a languid opposition to it, in order to reingratiate themselves with the mobs of London and Westminster. The Bishops had honestly concurred in removing such absurd distinctions, as stigmatized and shackled a body of the most loyal, commercial, and wealthy subjects of the kingdom. A new general election was approaching; some obscure men, who perhaps wanted the necessary sums for purchasing seats, or the topics of party to raise clamour, had fastened on this Jew Bill; and in a few months the whole nation found itself inflamed with a Christian zeal, which was thought happily extinguished with the ashes of Queen Anne and Sacheverel. Indeed, this holy spirit seized none but the populace and the very lowest of the Clergy: yet all these grew suddenly so zealous for the honour of the prophecies that foretell calamity and eternal dispersion to the Jews, that they seemed to fear lest the completion of them should be defeated by Act of Parliament: and there wanted nothing to their ardour but to petition both Houses to enact the accomplishment. The little Curates preached against the Bishops for deserting the interests of the Gospel; and Aldermen grew drunk at county clubs in the cause of Jesus Christ, as they had used to do for the sake of King James. Yet to this senseless clamour did the Ministry give way; and to secure tranquillity to their elections, submitted to repeal the Bill.

It is worthwhile to recapitulate some instances of the capriciousness of the times. An inglorious peace had been made, and the first hostages imposed that ever this country gave: not a murmur followed. The Regency Bill, with the tremendous clause of *præmunire*, had been passed without occasioning a pamphlet. The Marriage Bill, that bane of society, that golden grate that separates the nobility from the plebeians, had not excited a complaint from the latter. A trifling Bill, that opened some inconsiderable advantages to a corps of men, with whom we live, traffic, converse, could alarm the whole nation—it did more: a cabal of Ministers, who had insulted their master with impunity, who had betrayed every ally and party with success, and who had crammed down every Bill that was calculated for their own power, yielded to transitory noise, and submitted to fight under the banners of prophecy, in order to carry a few more members in another Parliament.

I shall be very brief on the Debates that attended this repeal; the topic was foolish, the chief speakers not considerable, the events not memorable.

On the very day the Houses met, the Duke of Newcastle moved to repeal the Bill, which, he said, had only been a point of *political policy*. The Bishop of Oxford undertook the apology of his Bench, and (though in a manner too ironic) defended them well, for having given way to a Bill, which they had considered only in a political light, had never much liked, and were glad to have repealed, to quiet the minds of good people. Drummond of St. Asaph, sensibly and in a more manly style, urged that the Bishops could not have opposed the Bill without indulging a spirit of persecution, abhorrent from the spirit of the Gospel. Lord Temple, with his accustomed warmth, opposed the repeal, grew zealous for the honour of a Ministry which he wanted to censure, and protested against the Legislature listening to clamour, which was less intended to serve the Protestant Religion, than to wound the Protestant Succession. Loved he did the Liberty of the Press, yet thought the abuse in the Daily Papers ought to be noticed. He had never listened to popular clamour, nor always thought that the voice of the people was the voice of God. That the approaching general election had given foundation to this uproar, and therefore should not have wondered at a repeal being consented to by the other House, but for the Lords to consent, would be subscribing to the accusation. Lord Temple was still more violent on the second reading; pronounced the clamour disaffection clothed in superstition, and a detestable high-church spirit: trembled lest the Plantation Act should be repealed; trembled lest fires should be rekindled in Smithfield to burn Jews; shuddered at our exceeding the heinous days of Charles the Second, who, though he oppressed

Presbyterians, encouraged Jews. That to give way to this spirit, would invite persecution against the Presbyterians. For him, he acted on the principles on which he had been bred, had lived, and would die. The Chancellor replied to him with temper, and defended the measure of a free government giving way. That the longer Bills of Naturalization existed, the more difficult they grow to repeal, as they have been hanging out invitation to Foreigners to accept the advantages of them: was earnest against any thought of repealing the Plantation Act, which had subsisted thirteen years, and allows seven years for settling: that as Jews are chiefly concerned in remittances, it would undo our colonies to repeal Bills made in favour of that people.

On the 21st, the Duke of Bedford said he had been against the Bill, and was now against the repeal, which was an effect of the imbecility of the Administration. Lord Temple again spoke against it, and well. Lord Granville with humour turned the whole into ridicule; said he remembered many religious Bills in which religion had nothing to do; they were made or repealed from clamour. When the Schism Bill passed, Lord Harcourt, then *not* Chancellor was for it; afterwards against it, and then pleaded, that it was only a Bill to make school-mistresses take the Sacrament three times a year, and what was that to Government? The Uniformity Bill was rejected after being carried so high by party, that it was not regarded whether a man was for peace or for war, but whether he was for or against that Bill. That it had been afterwards brought in by the Whigs to gain a single Lord, Lord Nottingham; that when it was objected that a persecuting Bill was surely paying dear for one man, a grave Whig Lord replied, "It is true; but let our friends be persecuted sometimes, or they will not think they want us." That undictated by religion as those Bills were, or the clamour against them, they breathed the very essence of it, compared to this Jew Bill, which, with its clamour, was the nothingness of a nothing. Lord Temple commended the Bench, but feared there might be Toryism lurking in some corner of it; and then painted the Bishop of London, who, he said, he had heard, was disposed to a repeal even of the Plantation Act.

He would not suffer Jews even in that diocese[236] of his—he did not know whether he ought strictly to call it his diocese: the Plantations were subjected to his Lordship's pastoral jurisdiction; but perhaps he had not taken out his patent; it might cost fourscore or an hundred pounds! He talked again of disaffection, and said he had been raking into the London Evening Post, that Augæan stable of filth and calumny—thus was Lord Temple at once a zealous Whig, and scandalized at libels! Whigs have not generally disliked libels, nor had he, but it was when he was less Whig. The Bishop of Oxford answered for his brother of London, and denied that he was averse to the Plantation Act. The Chancellor said, that the only imbecility of the Administration was in tolerating such libels; that the liberty of the Press could not give liberty to print what a man may not write; that what a man could not justify to do, he could not justify to print; that he thought the libels on this Bill ought to be prosecuted; that the Lords and Commons might trust themselves with looking into the licence of the Press.

22d.—On the third reading of the Bill, Lord Temple made a very bad obscure speech; tried to answer Lord Granville; tried to encourage the Tories to continue the clamour; tried to excuse his invective on the Bishop of London; but succeeded in none of those points, and the repeal passed.

In Ireland, the new parties from personalities turned to matters of government. A Bill had been prepared to enable them to dispose of an overplus of the Revenue for the benefit of the kingdom; and it was specified in the preamble that it was with the King's consent. The Opposition refused to admit this preamble: the Castle were afraid to proceed to a division, and suppressed the preamble, but sent over the Bill, depending on the English Ministry not suffering such a diminution of the prerogative. The next day, on a trifling question about some words relating to Neville Jones, the Castle stood a division, and had a majority, though but of three votes. As the parties were so equally balanced, the animosities did not flag, but proceeded to great extremities, both in the English manner of abuse, and in the Irish of duels.

---

[236] The plantations are reckoned in the diocese of London.

27th.—Lord Temple, after having mysteriously summoned the Lords to an affair, as he told them, of great importance, moved to have the Judges asked, if Jews could purchase land, and whether it would legally descend to their children. The Chancellor, Lord Cholmondeley, Lord Granville, and the Duke of Argyle opposing the Motion, and nobody supporting it, Lord Temple gave it up.

The same day the repeal was agitated in the other House; Northey proposed to have the words in the preamble, *have taken occasion to raise clamour*, altered to *have raised clamour*. He was seconded by Prowse, Lord Egmont, and Admiral Vernon. On the other side Nugent, Sir W. Yonge, Sir Richard Lloyd, Mr. Pelham, old Horace Walpole, and Mr. Pitt, who was just come abroad again after a year of sullen illness, defended the words and the repeal, and it passed by a majority of 150 to 60.

28th.—Letters came from Ireland with an account of the first Parliamentary victory obtained there by the Opposition over the Court. Neville Jones had been voted guilty of abuse in his office[237] by 124 to 116. The strangers in the gallery of the House huzzaed; the city was crowded by the triumphant mob. Lord Kildare, the popular hero, was an hour passing to his own house at eleven at night.

Dec. 4th.—A call of the House being appointed, Lord Harley and Sir James Dashwood moved for a repeal of the Plantation Act. Martin, the West Indian, opposed the Motion in a speech of wit. He said, this Act had been made thirteen years ago; had occasioned no clamour then, nor since. Foreigners would begin to think that there was no combustible matter left in England but these poor miserable Jews. One hundred and eighty-five have taken the benefit of the Act. He had been so idle, he said, as to read all the pamphlets and papers on the late Act, and must pronounce that no subject ever occasioned the spilling so much nonsense. That America can only be peopled by Foreigners, unless you would drain your own country, over and above those valuable colonists, the transported.

---

[237] [He was consequently dismissed, and, with an allusion to his profession of architect, said, with much good humour and pleasantry, "So, after all, I shall not be Inigo, but *Out I go*, Jones."]—E.

Sir Roger Newdigate spoke for the last moved repeal. Nugent ridiculed it, and said, that if once the principle was admitted, there would be no stopping. Why have 130 Jews been naturalized in Jamaica, and none in Barbadoes? because three parts of the former are desert, and no part of the latter. Would you drive them out of the desert? Spanish Jews are the most proper, because they can best support the climate. That noble pirate, the Knight of Malta, says, Make perpetual war with perpetual enemies: so says the Inquisition—imitate them—and you will only lose your Mediterranean trade. Then break with those who league with the enemies of your religion, as Spain does with Denmark[238]—but no; you have done what you meaned to do; stop here: a Christian knows no perpetual enmity. The most prosperous, happy man here has the best chance for the next world. They who made this clamour, now smile with us; if we gave way, would laugh at us.

Sir John Barnard made a short, bad speech, and went away. Mr. Pelham said, to repeal the Plantation Act would be to tell the people, We will repeal this law, not because it has, but because it ought to have made you uneasy. But it would be too serious to pay such attention even to clamour: who part with their wealth, part with their strength. Such a repeal would revive the principle of the Church, which has had such pernicious effects—but no encouragement must be given to that spirit, though it has been laboured by some who can only figure in a hot contest, and who can thunder out their ecclesiastic anathemas, but have nothing to say when they come to preach on morality. Pitt carried this still further; and though he did not act like, yet he affected to speak with the same spirit of Whiggism as his friend, Lord Temple. He had not expected, he said, that this would be the first return to Parliament for their condescension in repealing the late act. Here the stand must be made, or *venit summa dies*! we should have a Church spirit revived. He believed the late clamour was only a little election art, which was given way to genteelly; that the other Bill was not a toleration of, but a preference given to, Jews over other sects. That his maxim was, never to do more for the Church than it now enjoys: that now

---

[238] For making a league with the Algerines.

you would except the Jews in the opposite extreme. It is the Jew to-day, it would be the Presbyterian to-morrow: we should be sure to have a septennial Church clamour. That we are not now to be influenced by old laws enacted before the Reformation: our ancestors would have said, "A Lollard has no right to inherit lands." But we do not fear indulging Jews; they will never be great purchasers of land; they love money, and trade with it to better advantage. This silly effort of old prejudices was baffled by 208 to 88. Not that even eighty-eight men were actuated by such monkish principles; some were obliged to espouse them to secure their approaching elections.

The heats in Ireland increased with the success of the Opposition. The Speaker was adored by the mob; they worshipped him under the name of *Roger*. They made bonfires of reproach before the door of the Primate: they stopped coaches, and made them declare for England or Ireland. The Hackney Chairmen distinguished their patriotism by refusing to carry any fare to the Castle. A Dr. Andrews of the Castle-faction, reproaching a Mr. Lambert at the door of the House of Commons, with forfeiting a promise of bringing him into Parliament, and proceeding to a challenge, Lambert said, "I will first go into the House, and vote against that rascal Neville Jones." Dr. Andrews repeating the insult, Lambert went in and complained, and Andrews was ordered into custody; Carter, Master of the Rolls, saying, "What, would that man force himself into a seat here! and for what? only to prostitute his vote to a man,[239] the known enemy of this country! I need not name him, you all know whom I mean." Malone's brother, a rising young man, on Lord George's imputing the prosecution of Neville Jones to the rage of party, said, "He did not believe there subsisted any such thing; but if there did, it was more laudable than threats, bribes, and promises, which that Noble Lord had used to procure a majority." The accusation was not groundless; Sir James Hamilton, a very indigent member, refused an offer from the Castle of 2000*l*. and 200*l*. per annum for life. Satires and claret were successful arms even against corruption! The Money Bill was

---

[239] Lord George Sackville.

sent back from England, with the preamble re-instated, but was rejected in Ireland by a majority of five.

1754. The new year began with orders sent to Ireland to prorogue the Parliament, and to disgrace the most obnoxious, at the discretion of the Lord-Lieutenant; but the Duke was moderate. He contented himself with obtaining an adjournment for three weeks, and with displacing Carter, the Master of the Rolls; Malone, Prime Serjeant, (a convert from Popery), Dilks, Quarter-Master and Barrack-Master General; and with stopping the pension of Bellingham Boyle, Register of the Prerogative Court, and a near relation of the Speaker. Andrew Stone was inclined to temporize, but Murray counselled, and drove on measures of authority.

February 7th.—Sir John Barnard, on the view of the approaching elections, and their concomitant perjury, moved to repeal the Bribery Oath; and was seconded by Sir William Yonge. But the consideration that the repeal would avow permission of bribery prevailed over the certainty of bribery heightened by perjury, and the Motion was rejected without a division. In the other House, the next day, the Bishop of Worcester had as little success in another moral attempt: he moved for reformation and a fast—in vain.

19th.—There was a Debate on the Bill for subjecting to military law the troops going to the East Indies; but it passed on a division of 245 to 50.

March 4th.—The Duke of Bedford offered a Bill to postpone the activity of the Marriage Bill, till it should be maturely considered and amended. The Chancellor opposed it dictatorially; and it was rejected by 56 Lords to 10.

These were the last occurrences in the life of that fortunate Minister, Henry Pelham, who had surmounted every difficulty, but the unhappiness of his own temper. The fullness of his power had only contributed to heighten his peevishness. He supplied the deficiencies of genius by affected virtue; he had removed superiors by treachery, and those of whom he was jealous, by pretexting, or administering to the jealousies of his brother: but the little arts by which he had circumvented greater objects, were not applicable even to his own little passions. He enjoyed the plenitude of his Ministry but a short time, and that short period was a scene of fretfulness. He had made a journey to Scarborough in the summer for scorbutic complaints, but receiving little benefit from a short stay, and being banqueted much on the road, he returned with his blood more disordered. It produced a dangerous boil, which was once thought cured; but he relapsed on the third of March, and died on the sixth, aged near sixty-one.

It would be superfluous to add much to the character already given of him in the former part of these memoirs. Thus much may be said with propriety: his abilities, I mean, parliamentary, and his eloquence cleared up, and shone with much greater force, after his power was established. He laid aside his doubling plausibility, which had at once raised and depreciated him, and assumed a spirit and authority that became him well. Considering how much he had made it a point to be Minister, and how much his partizans had proclaimed him the only man worthy of being Minister, he ought to have conferred greater benefits on his country. He had reduced interest, and a part of the National Debt; these were his services. He had raised the name of the King, but he had wounded his authority. He concluded an ignominious peace; but the circumstances of the times made it be thought, and perhaps it was, desirable. The desertion of the King in the height of a Rebellion, from jealousy of a man with whom he soon after associated against some of the very men who had deserted with him, will be a lasting blot on his name—let it be remembered as long, that, though he first taught or experienced universal servility in Englishmen, yet he lived without abusing his power, and died poor.

Chapter 12

1754.
Plus on étudie le monde, plus on y découvre le ridicule.
La Bruyere.
Les exemples du passé touchent sans comparaison plus les hommes que ceux de leur siècle. Nous nous accoutumons à ce que nous voyons; et je ne sçai si le consulat du Cheval de Caligula nous auroit autant surpris que nous nous l'imaginons.—*Card. de Retz.*

Having never proposed to write a regular history, but to throw together some anecdotes and characters which might cast a light on the times in which I have lived, and might lead some future and more assiduous historian to an intimate knowledge of the men whose counsels or actions he shall record, I had determined to lay down my pen at the death of that Minister, whose fortune, situation, and genius had superinduced a very new complexion over his country, and who had composed a system of lethargic acquiescence, in which the spirit of Britain, agitated for so many centuries, seemed willingly to repose. But as the numbness of that enchantment has been dispelled by the evanition of the talisman, though so many of its mischievous principles survive, I shall once again endeavour to trace the stream of events to their secret source, though with a pen more unequal than ever to the task. A Monkish writer may be qualified to record an age of barbarity and ignorance; Sallust alone was worthy to snatch the rapid episode of Catiline from oblivion; Tacitus, to paint monsters whose lives surpassed caricatura; Livy, to embrace whole ages of patriots and heroes. Though no Catiline, I trust, will rise in my pages, to deform his country by his horrid glory; though our present minister,[240] notwithstanding he has the monkey disposition of Heliogabalus, is happily without his youth or lusts, and by the character of the age that disposition is systematized into little mischiefs and unbloody treacheries; though we have no succession of incorrupt senators; yet the times beginning to wear in some lights a more respectable face, it will require a steadier hand, and more dignified conceptions, than served to seize and to sketch out the littlenesses and trifles that had characterized the foregoing period.

The style, therefore, of the following sheets will perhaps wear a more serious aspect than I have used before: yet shall I not check a smile now and then at transient follies; nor, as much appropriated as gravity is to an historian, can I conceive how history can always be faithful, if always solemn. Is a palace a perpetual shrine of virtue, or incessantly a tribunal of severity? do not follies predominate in mankind over either virtues or vices? and whoever has been conversant in a Court, does he not know how strongly the cast of it verges towards ridiculous? Besides, I am no historian: I write casual Memoirs; I draw characters; I preserve anecdotes, which my superiors, the historians of Britain, may enchase into their weighty annals, or pass over at their pleasure. In one point I shall not vary from the style I have assumed, but shall honestly continue to relate the blemishes of material personages as they enter upon the scene: and whoever knows the interior of affairs, must be sensible to how many more events the faults of statesmen give birth, than are produced by their good intentions.

If I do not forbid myself censure, at least I shall shun that frequent poison of histories, flattery. How has it preponderated in most writers! My Lord Bacon was almost as profuse of his incense on the memory of dead Kings, as he was infamous for clouding the living with it. In the reign of Henry the Seventh, the whole strain of his panegyric (and it is more justly to be called so than Pliny's, whose patron was really a good Prince), is to erect that sordid Monarch's tyranny into prudence, nay, his very knavery into policy! Comines, a honester writer, though I fear by the masters whom

---

[240] The Duke of Newcastle. This was written in 1756.

he pleased, not a much less servile Courtier, says, that the virtues of Louis the Eleventh preponderated over his vices! Even Voltaire, who feels for Liberty more than almost ever any Frenchman did, has in a manner purified the dross of adulation, which cotemporary authors had squandered on Louis the Fourteenth, by adopting and refining it after the tyrant was dead. In his war of 1741, he paints that phantom of Royalty, the present King, extinguishing at Metz, with as much energy of concern, as if he was describing the death-bed of a Titus or an Antonine.

But how unpardonable is a flattering history!—if anything can shock one of those mortal divinities (and they must be shocked before they will be corrected), it would be to find that the truth will be related of them at last. Nay, is it not cruel to them to hallow their bad memories? one is sure they will never *hear* truth; shall they not even have a chance of *reading* it?

It may be wondered that I, who know and have drawn the emptiness of present Royalty, should, in the exordium to a new period, in which surely the effulgence of Majesty has not been displayed with any new lustre, detain the reader with reflections on a pageant which has so little operation on the reality of the drama. But I must be pardoned: though I now behold only a withering King, good, as far as acquiescing to whatever is the emergent humour of his people, and by no means the object of jealousy to his subjects, yet I am sensible that, from the prostitution of patriotism, from the art of Ministers who have had the address to exalt the semblance while they depressed the reality of Royalty, and from the bent of the education of the young Nobility, which verges to French maxims and to a military spirit, nay, from the ascendant which the Nobility itself acquires each day in this country, from all these reflections, I am sensible, that prerogative and power have been exceedingly fortified of late within the circle of the Palace; and though fluctuating Ministries by turns exercise the deposit, yet there it is; and whenever a Prince of design and spirit shall sit in the Regal Chair, he will find a bank, a hoard of power, which he may play off most fatally against this constitution. That evil I dread—the steps to that authority, that torrent which I should in vain extend a feeble arm to stem, those steps I mean to follow and record.

My reflections led me early towards, I cannot quite say Republicanism, but to most limited Monarchy; a principle as much ridiculed ever since I came into the world, as the profligacy of false patriots has made patriotism—and from much the same cause. Republicans professed to be saints, and from successful sainthood became usurpers: yet Republicanism, as it tends to promote Liberty, and Patriotism as far as it tends to preserve or restore it, are still godlike principles. A Republican who should be mad, should be execrable enough to endeavour to imbrue his country in blood merely to remove the name of a Monarch, deserves to excite horror; a quiet Republican, who does not dislike to see the shadow of Monarchy, like Banquo's ghost, fill the empty chair of state, that the ambitious, the murderer, the tyrant, may not aspire to it; in short, who approves the name of a King, when it excludes the essence; a man of such principles, I hope, may be a good man and an honest; and if he is that, what matters if he is ridiculous? A Republican, who sees monarchy realizing, who observes all orders of men tending to exalt higher, what all orders had concurred to depress; who has found that the attempts of the greatest men to divert the torrent, have been turned afterwards to swell it; who knows the inefficacy of all endeavours to thwart the bent of a nation, and who is but too sensible how unequal his own capacity and virtue would be to so heroic a character; such a man may be pardoned, I hope, if he contents himself with the silent suffrage and wishes of his heart, though he has not the parade of martyrs, nor the courage of a Roman, in as *un-Roman*—(why should it be beneath the dignity of history to say?) in as *un-British* an age as ever was.

Mr. Pelham's death was unexpected; he was healthy, and not old: all men had concurred to serve under him; none had prepared any intrigues to succeed him. The King had found it comfortable to be governed absolutely, as long as the *viceroy*[241] *over him* could govern the kingdom as absolutely: being told of his Minister's death, he said with a sigh, that could not excite much compassion, "I shall now have no more peace!"

---

[241] Expression of Shakspeare in the Tempest, in one of the scenes of sailors.

Figure 2. M^R. Pelham. London. Henry Colburn, 1846.

The Houses, who certainly were not to be consulted on the successor, adjourned themselves for a week—who *should* be consulted, was the question—for nobody pretended to suppose that the Sovereign was to choose his delegate himself. What was as ridiculous as this state of doubt, was the measure taken for solving it—the Duke of Devonshire was sent for—a proper dictator, had the only business of the State been to drive a nail into a wall! The event put the finishing stroke to the ridicule. In the meantime, the Lord Chief Justice Lee was appointed Chancellor of the Exchequer, the forms depending on that office not admitting an interregnum. Lord Chief Justice Pratt had been supplied in like manner on the demission of Aislabie.[242]

As the temper of the age did not admit the ancient folly of that presumptuous officer called a King's favourite; and as Ministers in late times had towered to power from ascendants gained by abilities or address in the House of Commons, it was natural for the nation to turn its eyes thither: three subjects there presented themselves before the rest, as candidates for the first Ministership; but each attended with almost insuperable difficulties: these were Fox, Pitt, and Murray. The Chancellor hated the first: the Scotch and the Law, two formidable bodies, whom Fox had wantonly and repeatedly provoked, readily listed under that banner: the Princess could not love him from his connection with the Duke; and though he had been the ostensible second to Mr. Pelham, he had never lived upon any terms with the Duke of Newcastle: but he was the ablest man in Parliament, at least the craftiest Parliament-man, had acted steadily with the Whigs, and had in their eyes the seeming right of succession. Pitt had, or had unluckily acted, very ill health; and was now at Bath. Mr. Pelham, who had adopted him, had, however, died without removing, probably without trying to remove, his Majesty's excommunication; and that was now allowed all its force, as Pitt had no party that wished his elevation. Murray was a Scot, and too lately been the object of clamour on the worst species of Scotch principles. The Chancellor was already jealous of him; and both Fox and Pitt would have concurred for his exclusion. He was timid himself, and always waving what he was always courting. This Gordian Knot was soon cut; and the world that had pretended to look out for a genius worthy to govern them, in six days descended from their ambition, and submitted to be ruled by no abilities at all.

Fox acted reserve and retirement, and expected to be wooed. His enemies indulged this humour, and deceived him. Stone went to him, and in Murray's name disclaimed all emulation of that kind, that he never meant to quit his profession, that he aspired *only* to be Chancellor. The Chancellor on his part contributed: he sent Lord Anson to Fox, to offer

---

[242] In the reign of George the First.

reconciliation, though justifying himself on the former quarrel. Between the King and Fox several messages passed by the intervention of Lady Yarmouth. The Princess, however, expressed her dislike; and the Duke of Argyle was warm against his promotion. The late beloved Minister was in the meantime totally forgot, or only remembered by daily discoveries of the duplicity of his conduct. Even his brother, who whimpered for him like a child during the first hours, like a child forgot him, as soon as he had formed the plan of inheriting his power: and nothing tended so much to unravel the mystery of devotion which the nation had conceived for Mr. Pelham, as its appearing, that it had not been the genius of the man, but the servility of the times, which had established his authority—in a fortnight the whole country was prostrate before his brother.

The Duke of Newcastle, who for thirty years together had sapped every Administration, could not resist having courage enough to seize it for himself now it lay so exposed. A faint offer was made to the Duke of Devonshire to sit at the head of the Treasury, which he declining, on the 12th of March at night, only six days after the death of Mr. Pelham, to the astonishment of all men, yet only to their astonishment, it was settled that the Duke of Newcastle should take the Treasury, with Legge for Chancellor of Exchequer, and that Mr. Fox should be Secretary of State, with the management of the House of Commons. Those solemn personages, the Cabinet Council, were directed to offer this disposition to his Majesty, as the result of their wisdoms and opinion—an opinion, that in two days more they were reduced to disavow. The King confirmed this establishment, with this salvo to his Royalty, that Legge should never enter his closet; to so scanty a space was his kingdom shrunk! That very night Lord Hartington was sent to notify the new regulation to Mr. Fox, with this supplement, not imparted to the Council, that his Grace would reserve to himself the disposal of the Secret-Service Money, though he would always exactly communicate to Mr. Fox how it had been employed.

The next morning, the Marquis carried Mr. Fox to the Chancellor, where a reconciliation was completed; though, as this sincere man told Lyttelton and Granville, he had made peace with Fox, yet would never act in concert with him. From thence they went to the new Vizier. On opening upon terms and measures, Mr. Fox mentioned the Secret-Service Money—the Duke cut him short with saying, that his brother had never disclosed the disposal of that money, nor would he. Mr. Fox represented, that if he was kept in ignorance of that, he should not know how to talk to members of Parliament, when some might have received *gratifications*, others not. The Duke answered ministerially, that though he would not inform Mr. Fox, he would inform no one else. Lord Hartington ventured to urge that this was not the message on which he had been sent; and Mr. Fox pushing for further explanation, asked who was to have the nomination to places? Newcastle replied, "I myself." Fox, "Who the recommendation?" N. "Any member of the House of Commons." Fox then inquired into the projected measures for securing the approaching Parliament, and what list Mr. Pelham had left for composing it. The Duke said, "My brother had settled it all with Lord Duplin." Fox replied, "Not all;" and named some unsettled boroughs. The Duke said hastily, "No, no, all was settled." Fox said, "I will come and look over the list with your Grace." He answered, "No, I will look it over with Duplin, and then show it to you." They came away.

Before I prosecute this barter for power, let me make one reflection. How avowed was become the traffic for Parliaments! how extensive the breach of the constitution, since Pym and Hampden presented their bosoms to cover and close the gap! Yet what has befallen this country, but what is common to sublunary establishments? How few years had rolled away between the age of Cato's Brutus's, Cicero's, and the domination of that Imperial fiddler, Nero? Within how small a period did the stock-jobber, Julianus, purchase the very Empire which Trajan had extended to its utmost limits? The auction of votes is become an established commerce, and his Grace did nothing but squabble for the prerogative of being sole appraiser.

Fox felt he was bubbled—yet was irresolute. He seemed unaccountably to have lost the spirit which the Duke seemed as unaccountably to have acquired. But in this transaction, and in many subsequent instances, it appeared, that his timidity was consistent with extreme rashness: his brother's timorousness more unallayed, had predominated, and given the colour of fear to their joint Administration.

The Duke left to himself, always plunged into difficulties, before he shuddered for the consequences: the other had possessed more foresight.

Lord Hartington acquainted the Chancellor with what had passed. He seemed struck; but, as if conscious to the violation of the terms, or determined at once to profit of it, said, he could not see the Duke that evening, but would next morning. At night, the Duke sent for Lord Hartington; not repentant; he was not apt to repent of advantageous treachery. He would not deny the breach of his engagements, but honestly declared he would not stand to them. Lord Hartington, as if avowal of treachery repaired it, expressed no resentment. His impartiality was ludicrous; he thought he displayed sufficient friendship to Fox, by publishing the Duke of Newcastle's breach of faith; and he knew he should not offend the latter, by adhering to a simple relation of his perfidy.

Fox in the meantime consulted his friends. The Duke of Cumberland dissuaded his complying with terms infringed ere ratified. Horace Walpole, the younger, laid before him the succession of the Duke of Newcastle's wiles and falsehoods; and being persuaded that this coalition was intended only to prejudice Mr. Fox, and that he would be betrayed, mortified, disgraced, as soon as the new Minister should have detached him from his connections, and prevented his strengthening them, urged him to refuse the Seals. Sir Charles Williams, who happened to be in England, and whose interest as a Minister in Foreign Courts, indubitably pointed to make him wish Mr. Fox Secretary of State, yet with great honesty laboured in the most earnest manner to tear him back from the precipice on which he stood. He yielded, yet never[243] forgave Sir Charles Williams, whose dissuasion having been most vehement, had made most impression on him. He sent the following letter by Lord Hartington to the Duke of Newcastle:

March 14th, 1754.
My Lord Duke,
As your Grace intends to wait upon his Majesty to-day, I must lose no time to desire your Grace would not acquaint his Majesty that I have

---

[243] [There are no traces of this in Mr. Fox's papers. On the contrary, he and Sir Charles continued intimate friends till the illness and death of the latter.]—E.

accepted the office of Secretary of State. But, if his Majesty has already been acquainted with my acceptance of it, your Grace will, I hope, tell his Majesty that I purpose, with the utmost submission, to beg his Majesty's leave to decline it. It is impossible his Majesty could think of raising me to so exalted a station, but with a design that I should, with and under your Grace, have the management of his affairs in the House of Commons. This was the whole tenour of your Grace's messages by Lord Hartington, which, in your Grace's conference with Lord Hartington and me yesterday morning, and with Lord Hartington last night, have been totally contradicted. Unable, therefore, to answer what, I dare say, is his Majesty's expectation (though your Grace has frankly declared it not to be yours), that I should be answerable for his Majesty's affairs in the House of Commons, I beg leave to remain where I am, heartily wishing success to his Majesty's affairs, and contributing all that shall be in the power of a single man towards it. I am, &c.

On 16th, Fox saw the King. The former said, with humility, that in seven years he had never presumed to enter first on other affairs than of his province. The King interrupted him, "It was a great place I designed for you; I thought I did much for you; many Dukes have had it." Fox answered, "Sir, your Majesty has been told that I asked for too much." The King said, "You did; the Secret Service money has never been in other hands than the person's at the head of the Treasury." "Perhaps, Sir," replied Fox, "I did ask too much; but they were more in fault who promised and broke their word: Lord Hartington is witness. I shall speak with truth, not with modesty. I might be a great man in the House of Commons, if I would be Secretary of State at the head of an Opposition— but I prefer serving your Majesty as a private man, without seeing the Duke of Newcastle. He promised me his confidence: I never can believe him more. I am honest, he is not." The King concluded, "I know it cannot be made up; you are not apt to depart from your resolution—it is a great office! but I have learned *nemini obtrudere beneficium*."

The triumphant Duke having disabled Fox, and being possessed of Murray, or rather the agent of power for him, had little trouble with the remaining competitor. Sir George Lyttelton, whose warmest prayer was to go to heaven in a Coronet, undertook to be factor for his friends. Unauthorized, he answered for Pitt's acquiescence under the new plan. He obtained a great employment for himself, overlooked Lord Temple, and if he stipulated without commission for George Grenville, at least it was for a preferment, large beyond the latter's most possible presumption.

All impediments thus removed, Newcastle obtained his full list of preferments; and the rest of the month was employed in forming and establishing his new court. Legge, as has been said, was made Chancellor of the Exchequer—unwillingly: he preferred his own more profitable place, less obnoxious to danger and envy. The meanness of his appearance, and the quaintness of his dialect, made him as improper for it as unwilling. Sandys's solemn dullness had made men regret Sir Robert Walpole's cheerful dignity: Legge's arch gravity struck no impression after Mr. Pelham's peevish authority: men had no notion of an epigrammatic Chancellor of the Exchequer. Lord Barnard, Lord Duplin, and Nugent composed the rest of the Treasury. George Grenville succeeded Legge as Treasurer of the Navy. Sir George Lyttelton was made Cofferer; Lord Hilsborough Comptroller of the Household, and Lord Barrington Master of the Great Wardrobe, in the room of Sir Thomas Robinson, who, to give some relief to Lord Holderness, and no possibility of umbrage to the fretful Duke, was nominated to the Seals, which Mr. Fox had declined.

Sir Thomas had been bred in German Courts, and was rather restored than naturalized to the genius of that country: he had German honour, loved German politics, and could explain himself as little as if he spoke only German. He might have remained in obscurity, if the Duke of Newcastle's necessity of employing men of talents inferior even to his own, and his alacrity in discovering persons so qualified, had not dragged poor Sir Thomas into light and ridicule; yet, if the Duke had *intended* to please his master, he could not have succeeded more happily than by presenting him with so congenial a servant: the King, with such a Secretary in his closet, felt himself in the very Elysium of Herenhausen!

The Chancellor's sincerity and services were crowned with an Earldom; but, as Roman Consuls in the very car of Victory were coupled with a slave, to remind them of their mortality, Harry Vane (lately become

Lord Barnard by the death of his father,) was created Earl of Darlington at the same hour.

While England was re-settling into a calm, the troubles continued in Ireland. A dangerous tumult was raised at the theatre; the audience called for a repetition of these lines in a translation of Voltaire's Mahomet:

> —— if, ye powers divine,
> Ye mark the movements of this nether world,
> And bring them to account; crush, crush these vipers,
> Who, singled out by a community
> To guard their rights, shall, for a grasp of ore,
> Or paltry office, sell them to the foe.

Diggs, the actor, refused, by order of Sheridan, the manager, to repeat them: Sheridan would not even appear on the stage to justify the prohibition. In an instant, the audience demolished the inside of the house, and reduced it to a shell. The Lord Mayor was sent for; he said he was sick: the High-Constable; he was said to be out of town. At the same time, the King issued the contested money by his own authority; for, as the whole currency of Ireland does not amount to above 500,000*l.*, the specie in question was necessary to carry on the circulation. The Castle wore so little a spirit of pacification, that the Duke of Dorset wrote to press the disgrace of the Speaker: but the English Ministry would have conjured down the storm by pressing the Earl of Hertford to go Lord Deputy, when the Duke of Dorset should return, which would have avoided the ungracious renewal of the Primate's share in the Regency. But this was a most unwelcome measure, not to that Prelate only; Lord George Sackville foresaw that Mr. Conway, a kind of contemporary rival, and brother of Lord Hertford, would necessarily share the popular merit of restoring tranquillity; and accordingly, as was supposed, instigated the Irish Chancellor to write to England, that, if he was to carry the Seals before Lord Hertford, he should desire to come to England during that period. Not content with this, the Duke himself wrote to prevent having Lord Hertford for Deputy. The Duke of Newcastle and the Chancellor were much inclined to the pacific method, but the faction of Stone and Murray prevailed, of whom the latter always counselled authoritative measures. It was the Duke of Newcastle's turn to be bullied. As the latter had usurped England, and the Duke of Argyle had wormed himself into the sole power in Scotland, Dorset asserted and maintained his ascendant in Ireland. The Speaker was removed, and Mr. Hill, uncle of Lord Hilsborough, was made Chancellor of the Exchequer in his room. The Primate, the Chancellor, and Lord Besborough, were constituted Lords Justices on the Duke's return to England.

On the 8th of April, the Chief-Justice Lee died: Sir Dudley Rider succeeded him; Murray rose to Attorney-General, and Sir Richard Loyd was made Solicitor. The same day the English Parliament was dissolved; and on the 31st of the following month, the new Parliament, chosen in the very spirit of the Pelhams, met and sat for five or six days in order to pass one Bill, and constitute their essence; for, by the Regency Bill, the last Parliament that should sit in the life of the King, was to revive on his death; and the new one was too acceptable to the Ministry, not to be insured. Mr. Legge presided at the Cockpit meeting, for reading the King's Speech to the Court members. The little man lost his temperance of spirit, and began to deceive himself into an opinion of being a Minister: the Duke of Newcastle, as severe a monitor to Ministers of their nothingness as the most moral preacher, and more efficacious, soon shuffled him out of his dream of grandeur, and having raised him as high as was necessary to his own views, took an immediate turn of depressing and using him ill. At the Treasury Board, the Duke gave papers cross him to Lord Duplin to read, and even sent the latter into the city to negotiate the money affairs for the Government. The obsequiousness of his creatures could not exempt them from his Grace's jealousy, as oft as he approached them too near to his own person. Legge gave an artful turn to his disgust, and vaunted to the Whigs that his want of favour was owing to his refusal of acting in concert with Stone and Murray: "But that would have been a stain," said he, "which I thought no time could wash away."

Pitt came to town much in discontent: Newcastle asked him his opinion of the new settlement: he declined answering; on being pressed, he replied, "Your Grace will be surprised, but I think Mr. Fox should have been at the head of the House of Commons." Their mutual discontents soon led Pitt and Fox to an explanation on their situation, and on all who had endeavoured to inspire them with jealousy. Pitt complained most of Mr. Pelham, who, he said, had always deprecated, but always fomented their variance. The Chancellor, ever since Pitt's return, had falsely boasted to him of having proposed him for Secretary of State.

The halcyon days of the new Administration soon began to be overcast by foreign clouds. The pacific genius of the house of Pelham was not unknown to France, and fell in very conveniently with their plan of extensive empire. They had yielded to a peace with us, only to recover breath, and to recoil with greater force after a few years of recruited strength; yet even in the short term lapsed since the treaty of Aix-la-Chapelle, they had not been unactive. Complaisance in Europe was to cover encroachments in both Indies. Mr. Pelham was willing to be the dupe. If the nation demanded no redress, he would neither propose nor seek it. Redress could be procured but by arms; armaments must be furnished by money; money to be raised might create murmurs; opposition might ensue—were national honour or interest worth hazarding that? And having had the merit of lessening the National Debt, he had the more justifiable and reasonable excuse of dreading to augment it again, when it was still so burthensome. In the East Indies we had lost Madras in the late war; and since the peace, under pretence of the two nations engaging on different sides in support of two contending Nabobs, hostilities had continued with various success.

During Mr. Pelham's rapid decline of health, a small fleet had been fitted out to protect a trade, which the numerous reinforcements dispatched by the French East India Company, with equal countenance from their Crown, had already rendered very precarious, indeed desperate. In Africa, they debauched our Allies, erected forts, and aimed at embracing the whole Gold Coast and Guinea trade. But their attempts in America grew daily more open, more avowed, more alarming, indeed extended to nothing less than by erecting a chain of garrisons from Canada to the mouths of the Mississippi, to back all our settlements, cut off our communication with the Indians west of that river, and inclose and starve our universal plantations and trade: it would not be necessary to invade them, they would fall of course. The discussions left unsettled by the precipitate peace of Aix-la-Chapelle, and proposed to be adjusted by those most ineffective of all negotiators, Commissaries, gave, not a pretence, rather an invitation to the French, to dispatch by force of arms the liquidation of an affair which might be explained to their disadvantage. The fatal treaty of Utrecht had left but too many of our interests in the West Indies problematic: the impetuosity of Lord Bolingbroke to betray Europe left him no moments, could inspire him with no zeal to assert our pretensions in America. The rights of either nation, as adjudged by treaties and mutual concessions, and more easily still to be defined by their actual establishments, were capable of being made tolerably clear: if explored to their source, they were mere pretensions in both. The topic, striking as it is to a mind that can philosophise, abstractedly from connections with any particular country, is too common to be enlarged upon.

A sea captain first spying a rock in the fifteenth century; perhaps a cross, or a coat of arms set up to the view of a few miles of coast by an adventurer, or even by a shipwrecked crew, gave the first claims to Kings and archpirates over an unknown tract of country. This transitory seizure sometimes obtained the venerable confirmation of an old priest at Rome (who, a century or two before, had in his infallibility pronounced that the existence of such a country was impossible), or of a still more politic, though not less interested Privy Council at home. Sometimes, indeed, if the discoverers were conscientious, they made a legal purchase to all eternity, of empires and posterity from a parcel of naked natives, for a handful of glass beads and baubles. Maryland, I think, was solemnly acquired at the extravagant rate of a quantity of vermilion and Jew's-harps: I don't know whether the authentic instrument may not be recorded in that Christian depository the Court of Chancery. By means so holy, a few Princes, who would be puzzled to produce a legitimate title to their own dominions in Europe, were wafted into rights and prerogatives over the boundless regions of America. Detachments were sent to take possession of the new discoveries; they peopled the seaports, they sprinkled themselves over the coasts, they enslaved or assisted the wretched natives to butcher one another, instructed them in the use of firearms, of brandy, and the New Testament, and at last, by scattered extension of forts and colonies, they have met to quarrel for the boundaries of Empires, of which they can neither use nor occupy a twentieth part of the included territory.

What facilitated the enterprises of the French was the extreme ignorance in which the English Court had kept themselves of the affairs of America. That department is subjected to the Secretary of State for the Southern Province, assisted by the Board of Trade. That Board, during Sir Robert Walpole's administration, had very faultily been suffered to lapse almost into a sinecure; and during all that period the Duke of Newcastle had been Secretary of State. It would not be credited what reams of papers, representations, memorials, petitions, from that quarter of the world lay mouldering and unopened in his office. West Indian Governors could not come within the sphere of his jealousy: nothing else merited or could fix his mercurial inattention. He knew as little of the geography of his province as of the state of it: when General Legonier hinted some defence to him for Annapolis, he replied with his evasive lisping hurry, "Annapolis, Annapolis! oh! yes, Annapolis must be defended; to be sure, Annapolis should be defended—where is Annapolis?" When the French invasions forced him to arouse a little from this lethargy, he struggled to preserve his inactivity, by ordering letters of the most abject and submissive import to be written to our Governors, who pressed for instructions, nay, for permission to defend themselves. Somewhat more of this will appear hereafter. But if he sacrificed the dignity of the Crown with one hand, he thought to exalt it with the other: the prerogative was strained unwarrantably over the Assemblies: the instructions to Sir Danvers Osborn, a new Governor of New York, seemed better calculated for the latitude of Mexico and for a Spanish tribunal, than for a free rich British Settlement, and in such opulence and of such haughtiness, that suspicions had long[244] been conceived of their meditating to throw off their dependence on their mother country.

---

[244] [If as the Author asserts, this was written at the time, it is a very remarkable passage.]—E.

Chapter 12

Lord Halifax, who now presided at the Board of Trade, and who, among the concessions of the Pelhams, had wrenched much American authority from the Secretary of State, was fond of power and business, was jealous of his own and country's honour, encouraged and countenanced plans and lights for preserving and extending our trade and dominion in that hemisphere, and as much as he could counteracted the supineness of the Administration. Had the Rulers of the State been as alert, the season was favourable; and uncommon incidents threw occasions into their hands of dispelling the dangers that hung over them from the French. Spain was revolved to its true interest; the rudder of Bourbon no longer steered their Court. The ambitious Queen Dowager, who by money, intrigues, and by the prospect of her son Carlos's succession, as the King was likely to have no children, had preserved a potent faction in the Ministry, was sinking into impotence of power, and saw all her schemes blasted. Don Caravalho and Lancaster, the Prime Minister, died in April this year: the Duke d'Huescar succeeded, and had raised his friend General Wall to be Minister for Foreign Affairs. It is not to be told with what regret the latter quitted England, which had become his country as much by affection as by extraction. He and the Duke were fortunately old Spaniards in principle, and being obnoxious to, were consequently averse to, the Queen Dowager and her French party. One of the first effects of this new Ministry was the fall of Ensenada, the creature of the Queen Dowager. Sir Benjamin Keene discovered, and imparted by the means of General Wall to the King, that Ensenada had sent orders to their West Indian Governors to fall on our ships, and had lent great sums of the Royal treasure to the French East India Company. He was disgraced, but with great lenity, and exiled to Granada.

While the Duke of Newcastle neglected such real opportunities of popularity, he was entering into little details in the Treasury, and threatened great reformations in trifles. The first abuses to be moderated or rooted out were pensions and quarterings on places; the former to gratify his Majesty, the latter to please public opinion. This lasted a fortnight: to support his vain power, both abuses were in his very second year, as will be seen, pushed to enormity.

In August came news of the defeat of Major Washington in the Great Meadows on the western borders of Virginia: a trifling action, but remarkable[245] for giving date to the war. The encroachments of the French have been already mentioned; but in May they had proceeded to open hostilities. Major Washington with about fifty men attacked one of their parties, and slew the commanding Officer. In this skirmish he was supported by an Indian half king and *twelve* of his subjects, who in the Virginian accounts, is called a very considerable Monarch. On the third of July, the French being reinforced to the number of nine hundred, fell on Washington in a small fort, which they took, but dismissed the Commander with military honours, being willing, as they expressed it in the capitulation, to show that they treated them like friends! In the express which Major Washington dispatched on his preceding little victory, he concluded with these words; "I heard the bullets whistle, and believe me, there is something charming in the sound." On hearing of this letter, the King said sensibly, "He would not say so, if he had been used to hear many." However, this brave braggart[246] learned to blush for his rodomontade, and desiring to serve General Braddock as Aide-de-camp, acquitted himself nobly.

The violence of this proceeding gave a reverberation to the stagnated politics of the Ministry: in a moment, the Duke of Newcastle assumed the hero, and breathed nothing but military operations: he and the Chancellor held Councils of War; none of the Ministers, except Lord Holderness, were admitted within their tent. They knew too well how proper the Duke was to be consulted: of course they were jealous, and did not consult him. Instead of him, they summoned one Gates,[247] a very young officer just returned from Nova Scotia, and asked his advice. He was too sensible of their absurdity, and replied, that he had never served but in Nova Scotia, and it would be impertinent to give his opinion; he was ready to answer any

---

[245] And as remarkable for being the first action in which Washington was mentioned, who near thirty years afterwards became the principal figure in America.

[246] [It is wonderful that Lord Orford should have allowed this expression to remain after he had lived to witness and admire the subsequent career of that great man, General Washington.]—E.

[247] This young man also was afterwards a considerable person in America.

questions. They knew not what to ask. When this lad would not be a Marshal, they next consulted one Hanbury, a Quaker, and at his recommendation determined upon Sharpe, the Governor of Virginia, for their General. They told the King he had served all the last war, though he had never served, and that the Duke had a good opinion of him: the Duke said, "So good, that if Sharpe had been consulted, I am sure he would have refused." We must defer the history of the campaign till its proper season.

No other event happened before the meeting of the Parliament except the decision of a famous cause. The inhabitants of Richmond and the neighbouring gentlemen, even instigated underhand by the Duke of Newcastle, had commenced a suit against Princess Amelie[248] for the right and liberty of entering into New Park at their pleasure: the case was this: Charles the First made the park, partly by pecuniary, partly by compulsory methods, and gave great disgusts by it. Queen Anne gave two or more lives in it to her relations, the Hydes, who suffered it to run to great decay. When Sir Robert Walpole became Minister, who was fond of hunting, and wanted occasional retirement and exercise, he persuaded King George the First to buy out the family of Hyde, and obtained the Rangership for his eldest son, which was confirmed to him by the present King for life. It was a bog, and a harbour for deer-stealers and vagabonds. Sir Robert Walpole drained it, and expended great sums upon it himself; but to obtain more privacy and security, he took away the ladders on the walls, and shut up the gates, but settled keepers at them, who were to open to all foot-passengers in the daytime, and to such carriages as had tickets, which were easily obtained. Princess Amelie succeeded his son Lord Orford, but preserved no measures of popularity. Her brother William had incredibly disgusted the neighbourhood of Windsor by excluding them from most of the benefits of the park there. The Princess entirely shut up New Park, except by giving very few tickets. Petitions were presented to her; she would not receive them. They were printed in the public Newspapers, but had as little effect. Subscriptions were formed, conferences were held to no purpose. At last the cause was brought to a trial. Sir John Philipps and the younger

---

[248] His Grace had formerly pretended to be in love with Princess Emily, but hated her now, on her connexion with her brother, the Duke, and the Bedfords.

Beckford presented themselves as tribunes of the people to plead the cause, but instead of influencing the Court, they confounded the rest of their Council. The Princess carried her cause.[249]

The children of the Crown in England have no landed appanages: they naturally covet them: Rangerships for lives are the only territories the King has to bestow. Both the Duke and his sister entered more easily into the spirit of prerogative than was decent in a family brought hither for the security of liberty. To shut up Windsor or Richmond parks, if the law permits, is no violation of the constitution; but when Princes of the Blood (and the race is likely to be numerous) come to stand suits for exclusive privileges, it is easy to foresee into what excesses their ambition or their necessities may make them slide.

Nov. 14th.—The Parliament met. The King's speech endeavoured to inculcate notions of tranquillity, yet with preserving a salvo for demanding supplies hereafter, by just hinting at the preservation of our rights in America. Sir George Lee, who moved the Address in the Commons, spoke plainly on Spain's having given orders for restoring our ships. Mr. Conway, who seconded him, went a little farther, and descanted on the increase of France. Potter ridiculed Ministerial Addresses well; called them the late lullabies that always acquainted us with the disposition of all the European powers to preserve the peace—but France indeed had spoiled that part of the speech for this year: yet he would agree to the Address, and consider measures hereafter. The Ministers did not know which should act Minister for the day: at last Murray pushed up Legge, who said a few words without dignity; the tenour and point of which was that our conduct was to be *fortiter in re, suaviter in modo*. Beckford said, that we had had such an order for restitution from Spain two years ago; and therefore he should not trust to this. That the marine and colonies of France had not increased in proportion to ours. That we should exert naval strength instead of alliances. With those great alliances in the last war we had run thirty millions in debt. Queen Elizabeth, in her distress, did not go about begging and buying alliances.

---

[249] She carried her cause against a road for coaches and carts, but some few years afterwards lost a suit commenced against her for a footway, on which she abandoned the park.

Mr. Conway replied in a few words elegantly, that Beckford had mistaken him; that he had not said that the colonies of France had increased in proportion to ours, but along with their landed power in Europe; however, that he was far from not thinking them very formidable in America; for, if we considered their extent of country along the rivers and lakes, it was like a net, which, if drawn a little tighter, might shuffle us into the sea. Lord Egmont, who always larded, or composed his speeches with speculative topics of government, went back to the Revolution, which, he said, was Rebellion, if anything more than restitution of the old constitution. That he would not oppose the Address, because we wanted unanimity, but that too languid a spirit prevailed. That it was thought so necessary to keep peace in the Administration, that we dared not take great steps: yet now was the time, when the House was no longer under any ministerial influence: however, we must take care not to provoke France, when part of the King's dominions (Ireland) was so discontented. Murray observed, that the new members must wonder at a Debate without a question or opposition: but, said he, how will all this be represented abroad? to Spain, that we don't believe their offers: to Germany, that we would shake off all our Allies: to France, that we reckon the peace broken; and that we make no distinction between our rights and our possessions. For the Colonies, he believed they would sacrifice everything rather than submit to France: yet was it judicious in Lord Egmont to throw out notions of discontents? The Address passed without a negative.

About this time came unwelcome news to the King: his son-in-law, Frederic, Hereditary Prince of Hesse Cassel, was discovered to be turned Papist. He was a brutal German, obstinate, of no genius, and after long treating Princess Mary, who was the mildest and gentlest of her race, with great inhumanity, had for some time lived upon no terms with her: his father, the Landgrave William, protected her: an arbitrary, artful man, of no reputation for integrity. The hereditary Prince was devoted to France and Prussia. It was not an age when conversions were common; nor were his morals strict enough to countenance any pretence to scruples; it was necessary to recur to private or political reasons for his change, and, from what has been said, it appears in what numbers they presented themselves.

Yet even the King of Prussia acted zeal for the Protestant cause. The Landgrave was as outrageous as if he felt for it too. No obstructions being offered by the Catholic powers, the Landgrave and States, with the concurrence of the King, enacted heavy restrictions on the Prince, whenever he should succeed his father.

The scene began to darken at home. As the Duke of Newcastle had secured by employments almost every material speaker in Parliament, it was hoped that the session would be amused, and pass off with regulating controverted elections: there was one of much expectation. The majority in all late Parliaments, and still more in this devoted one, had been composed solely from boroughs: counties were too extensive to be ventured upon in the way of expense, and had been left to their own ill humours, and to the country gentlemen: Oxfordshire in particular had long been a little kingdom of Jacobitism. The Duke of Marlborough, prodigal, and never judicious in his extravagance, would not content himself with the offer made to him by the county, of electing his son as soon as he should be of age: he determined to choose both representatives from his own party. Mr. Pelham had received the proposal with joy: that Duke was led by Fox: if the contest succeeded, Mr. Pelham would command two more members; if it miscarried, Fox and the Duke of Marlborough would labour under all the unpopularity. After unbounded expense, the four candidates were all returned, and the House was to decide on the merits, which must take up several weeks.

There was another election depending, of still nicer discussion; that of Mitchell, in Cornwall. Lord Sandwich had long dictated there, upon the interest of his nephew, Courtney, a minor. The Duke of Newcastle had now encouraged the Boscawens and Edgcumbes to oppose him. Lord Sandwich secured the returning officer, but a petition was lodged against his members. Fox, who sought all opportunities, where the King's name could not be pretended, of crossing the Duke of Newcastle, warmly and openly espoused Lord Sandwich. Pitt, as ill disposed, was neuter in this; but in the Reading election pretended connections with Lord Fane, Lord Sandwich's brother-in-law, and declared on the same side. In this temper the Parliament had opened; and Pitt, who, though ready to give words in change, was not a man to take them, had already come to some explanation with the Duke of Newcastle, and had even said to him, "Fewer words, my Lord, if you please, for your words have long lost all weight with me."

21st.—A day was to be appointed for hearing the Mitchell election: Lord Sandwich, who tried to defer its being heard, was beat with 127 by 154.

25th.—Another petition being in agitation, the House thin and idle, a younger Delaval had spoken pompously and abusively against the petitioner, and had thrown the House into a laughter on the topics of bribery and corruption. Pitt, who was in the gallery, started, and came down with impetuosity, and with all his former fire said, "He had asked what occasioned such an uproar; lamented to hear a laugh on such a subject as bribery! Did we try *within* the House to diminish our own dignity, when such attacks were made upon it from without? that it was almost lost! that it wanted support! that it had long been vanishing! scarce possible to recover it! that he hoped the Speaker would extend a saving hand to raise it: he could only restore it—yet scarce he! He called on all to assist, or else *we should only sit to register the arbitrary edicts of One too powerful a subject*!" This thunderbolt, thrown in a sky so long serene, confounded the audience. Murray crouched, silent and terrified. Legge scarce rose to say with great humility, "That he had been raised solely by the Whigs, and if he fell sooner or later, he should pride himself in nothing but in being a Whig."

The evening of this novel day was still more tempestuous. The Committee of Elections opened. Mr. Gray, a steady but plausible Tory, favoured by the Chancellor and Sir George Lyttelton, desired to have the petition against him from Colchester deferred, till it was sure of being heard. Sir Thomas Robinson said, "That might be soon, for the Reading election, which was to precede it, could not last long; there was but a majority of one vote for Lord Fane, and it was a poor cause." Pitt sprung up, and attacked Sir Thomas fiercely; told him how ignorant he was to talk in that style of a cause unheard; that he was not to be thus taught his duty by any man; but if the first officer in the State could make so gross a supposition, there would be short work with elections: he never thought to see so melancholy a day! Sir Thomas replied with pomp, confusion, and warmth, that spirit should be shown: could gentlemen, could merchants, could the House bear, if eloquence alone was to carry it? he hoped words only would not prevail! that for himself, he executed an office, of which he had never been ambitious. Pitt replied with cool art, and showed that he had only aimed the stroke at the Duke of Newcastle, through Sir Thomas, to whom he now spoke with respect, and with esteem of his integrity; adding, *that he thought him as able as any man that had of late years filled that office, or was likely to fill it*. The weapons that Pitt laid down Fox took up, and exercised them with still more inveteracy and warmth on poor Sir Thomas and his ignorance: "If one of the greatest men in the House pronounced it a poor cause, it would indeed be a poor cause; but he imputed it to his inexperience: he was the first great man, and he hoped would be the last, that ever pronounced so on a cause unheard!" It was plain that Pitt and Fox were impatient of any superior; and as plain by the complexion and murmurs of the House in support of Sir Thomas Robinson, that the inclinations of the members favoured neither of them.

27th.—The Committee sat on the Army, late but without a division; and in general the Debate was dull: the subject had long been exhausted, and during the former Opposition had been a constant day for teaching young and callow orators to soar. The younger Beckford, who had been announced for a genius, and had laid a foundation for being so, by studying magazines and historical registers, made a tedious harangue against standing armies; and moved for 15,000 men, instead of the old number of 18,800. Lord Barrington answered him well, and told him how little difference it would make to the constitution; if eighteen thousand intended to overturn it, fifteen might. That none of the usual number could be spared; from whence could they? The licentiousness of the capital, the mutinous miners and colliers, the smugglers, the destroyers of turnpikes, all the outlaws that increase of riches and licence produces and encourages, all were to be kept in awe. And so far from soldiers being a burthen, the country rejoices in being under their protection. That instead of squabbling for trifles, everybody should unite at this conjuncture to make the late great man as little missed as possible. That the great men he has left will show spirit; and spirit never brought on a war. His Majesty has the hearts of the people, of all who can feel gratitude or the benefits of their own situation. The Ministry have popularity, and it must be owing to Beckford's absence in Jamaica, that he did not know that the period which he had wished to see of a popular King and Administration, was actually arrived—but perhaps Jamaica Newspapers were as faulty as our own. Fox told the elder Beckford, that if he was Sheriff next year, he hoped he would not keep the resolution he had declared, of not calling in the military, if they are wanted: and added, that the soldiers behave so discreetly, that in eight years that he had been Secretary at War, he had not received three complaints in a year, even from innkeepers.

Nugent added in reply to Beckford (who had said that the Opposition were Whigs and the Ministry Tories,) that he hoped he had not taken his idea of Whigs from those who refused King William his Dutch troops: if he had, he did not wonder that he mistook the Ministers for Tories. He applied the old apologue of the hen and ducklings; and then flew out into this gross and barefaced strain, *that there did not exist an honester man than the Duke of Newcastle!* professing that he should be the most crouching slave if he meant this for flattery. Pitt, only smiling at this Drawcansir in adulation, and bent to pursue the humiliation of Murray, said that the moderation of the Estimate was a proof of the Crown's attention to economy; but he could by no means agree in our opulence, and would recommend it to gentlemen not to deceive themselves or others. We are in reality a distressed people: he hated declamation, and was as little given to anger, but nothing should hinder him from asserting what he felt, and from averring what he knew. Young members may allow too much to what is spoken in that place: when anybody says he don't believe that Jacobitism exists, he would tell him to his face he did not believe what he said. Nugent called him to order.

Pitt was a little disconcerted, but resuming himself said, "For the nursing mother, the hen, he had been bred under such a one,[250] and he would tell the House what she had been doing for these twenty years; she

---

[250] Oxford.

had been raising a succession of treason—there never was such a seminary! but he would throw himself into the gap, and would as cheerfully make his protest alone, as in the most applauding assembly. He knew what he was; he knew what he would be; and was too cool not to know what he said. That the body he meant (Oxford) was learned and respectable: so much the more dangerous! he would mention what had happened to himself the last summer on a party of pleasure thither. They were at the window of the Angel Inn; a lady was desired to sing *God save great George our King!* The chorus was re-echoed by a set of young lads drinking at a college over the way, but with additions of rank treason. He hoped, as they were lads, he should be excused from not having taken more notice of it. After this, walking down the High Street, in a Bookseller's shop he observed a print of a young Highlander with a blue ribbon: the Bookseller, thinking he wanted to buy it, held it out to him—but what was the motto!—*hunc saltem everso Juvenem!*—This was the prayer of that learned body—for it was in Latin!" Colours, much less words, could not paint the confusion and agitation that worked in Murray's face during this almost apostrophe! His countenance spoke everything that Fawcett had been terrified to prevaricate away.

Two days after this, an incident happened of a private nature, scarce worth mentioning, but as it served to dissolve the remains of so historic a friendship as that of Mr. Pitt and Sir George Lyttelton, and brought out all the colours of some remarkable characters. Mr. Conway was repeating with concern to the younger Walpole the lamentations of Sir George on Mr. Pitt's coldness[251] and his own apprehensions that the complexion of the times denoted new troubles. Walpole, who had not so pacific a disposition, but whose passion to see a new Opposition had been considerably damped by Mr. Fox's acquiescence under the Duke of Newcastle's sole power, and who loved Mr. Conway enough to sacrifice to his love of peace, when he had little prospect of gratifying his own love of party, owned to him carelessly, that he knew the Duke of Bedford had a

---

[251] Pitt and Lord Temple resented Lyttelton's negotiating for them, though it is certain he had used all his endeavours to serve them—but as they had meant to have the sole power of serving, not to be served, they treated him as ill as if he had sold them.

propensity to reconcile himself to the Court, that the Duchess and her friends were eager for it, and gave Mr. Conway leave to talk it over with Sir George Lyttelton, if by any means they could make use of this disposition to reconcile the growing humours. It was singular, that Horace Walpole, who had so eagerly attacked the promotion both of Pitt and Lyttelton, should, in the most distant manner, negotiate their re-union. However, on reflection (for it is certain that he had dropped this discourse without any), he recollected, that it was not acting handsomely by Mr. Fox, who at least was out of humour, to throw new strength into the Duke of Newcastle; and accordingly went to Mr. Conway to retract the permission he had given, and to desire no mention might be made of what had passed in their conversation—but how was he surprised to meet Mr. Conway coming to him in the greatest anxiety, and begging his pardon, for what indeed Mr. Conway was not to blame.

In short, Sir George Lyttelton, who had before professed to Mr. Conway a resolution of quitting his employment, unless he could hold it with Mr. Pitt's good opinion, had been so struck with the first idea of what he heard of the Duke of Bedford, and saw such an opening to favour by transacting the treaty, that instead of consulting with, or leaving it to Mr. Conway's coolness or fitness to chalk out the path of negotiation, he hurried to Newcastle House, and whispered his intelligence. Newcastle said, with his usual hurry, "My dear Sir George, there is nothing I would not give to accomplish such a reconciliation." Sir George, accepting this declaration as full powers, and forgetting at once that he was aggravating his breach of friendship with Mr. Pitt, and that of all men living he was the most improper to transact with the Duke of Bedford on so nice a point, having quitted him for Newcastle, and being involved in a private family quarrel with him too, posted away to Bedford House, demanded an audience, took no measures to soften the abruptness of his commission, but at once told that Duke, that he understood his Grace was a little mollified, and in the Duke of Newcastle's name, offered him *charte blanche*.—How was the volunteer Ambassador astonished at a flat refusal! The hot little Duke was transported with the importance this gave him; and notwithstanding the solicitation of the Duchess and his Court, whose measures were all overset by Lyttelton's awkward policy, the Duke immediately sent for Mr. Pitt, and communicated the message. Pitt flattered his steady virtue and disinterestedness, and broke openly with Sir George, who was first disavowed by the Duke of Newcastle, and then disavowed his own having gone so far as he had done. Horace Walpole, who would have had art indeed, had he planned and foreseen how the event would blow up the six months' labour of the pacific part of Bedford House, but who had acted merely from inadvertence, laughed and confirmed the Duke of Bedford in his highest opinion of his own importance and steady virtue.

The late impetuous and joint attack on Sir Thomas Robinson had alarmed his principal: the Duke of Newcastle saw his mighty power totter; yet he could not determine to share it. The first thought was to dismiss Pitt. This was too bold a measure to have the preference long: the next, more natural, was to try to sweeten Fox: accordingly, on the morning of the 29th, the King sent for Fox, and reproached him for concurring to worry Sir Thomas Robinson, and asked him if he had united with Pitt to oppose his measures? Fox assured him he had not, and that he had given him his honour he would resign first. "Then," said the King, "will you stand up and carry on my measures in the House of Commons, as you can do, with spirit?" Fox replied, "I must know, Sir, what means I shall have, or I cannot answer for what I cannot answer." "It will be better for you," said the King; "you shall have favour, advantage, and confidence"—but would not explain particulars, only asking, if he would go to the Duke of Newcastle. "I must, if you command me," answered Fox, "go and say I have forgot everything." "No," replied the King: "I have a good opinion of you; you have abilities and honesty, but you are too warm. I will send a common friend, Lord Waldegrave." He told him too, "I have obligations to you that I never mentioned; my son (the Prince) tried you, and you would not join him; and yet you made no merit of it to me."

The negotiation was entrusted to Lord Waldegrave: Stone, probably from perceiving that Murray dared not undertake the rudder of the House of Commons, promoted the treaty—and did himself no service with the Princess, who prevailed on Lord Egmont to accept, and on the King to

Chapter 12

offer him an employment. The Junto, who had laboured to keep Pitt and Fox disunited, more than to secure either of them, were reduced to take the one or the other. The Chancellor had discovered so much of the secret of his breast, as to ask Pitt, "Could you bear to act *under* Fox?" Pitt replied, "My Lord, leave out *under*; it will never be a word between us; Mr. Fox and I shall never quarrel." Originally, Pitt had assured the Chancellor and the Duke of Newcastle that he would not unite with Fox. When he saw that to promote division was their only drift, he sought heartily and sincerely to league with Fox, and told him that they had *formalized* at his professions.

Fox, irresolute, affecting content, borne down by the Duke from opposition, and aspiring at sole power, conferred with Pitt, but would not enter into real measures. The King proposed that Fox should write his demands: he asked for time, waiting to see what should be their decision on Pitt, who set them at defiance. The Duke of Marlborough proposed to Fox, to limit his demands to a Cabinet-Counsellor's place, "For," said he, "you don't mind money." The Duke of Cumberland disapproved the advice: "The King," said his Royal Highness, "could do better and more sensibly than he will, but he will do just as the Duke of Newcastle bids him. He has a good memory; he will remember this; and when he sees a proper occasion, perhaps some years hence, he will tell you you did right—but he will never tell you so till he sees that occasion. I don't know him, but by what you tell me, Pitt is, what is scarce—he is a man. If they should give you this Cabinet-Counsellor's place, and Pitt should hereafter attack the Duke of Newcastle, and you should not defend him, they will say you have broke your word."

The Duke of Marlborough persisted, but advised Fox to add, that he would not oppose Pitt. The Duke approved it with this modification. Fox drew the letter, and showed it to Pitt, who liked it, provided some words were omitted; "For," said he, "if they give a hint to invention that I would do the least thing to keep my place, it would hurt me beyond measure." The letter thanked the King for his goodness, and said, that understanding what his Majesty, who was determined to have no Minister at the head of the House of Commons, required, was, that he (Fox) should act there with spirit, not only in his private but public capacity, he, coveting no lucrative employment, wished only for a feather, to show that his Majesty had done him the honour to ask his assistance. Cabinet-Counsellor was not specified, but was construed to be meant, by Lord Waldegrave, who delivered the letter, and who explained to the King, that Fox would never accept Pitt's place, that it might not be objected to him at his re-election, and that Pitt might not say he answered him for money. He was ready to act *under* Sir Thomas Robinson, "For," said Fox, laughing, "what is acting under *him*? if there is a meeting of the Council, it will be his paper and pens and his green table: if we both rise to speak, I will yield to him." Lord Waldegrave added, that if Fox answered Pitt, it should always be in defence of the measures, but with particular civility. These qualifications were accepted, and the dignity of Cabinet-Counsellor granted a few days afterwards. Yet Fox, on receiving it, privately forswore all connection with Pitt. As the latter came to the knowledge of that secret abjuration, and as it was so much the interest of men so little scrupulous of treachery as the Chancellor and the Duke of Newcastle, to have Pitt apprized of it, it is neither refining nor uncharitable to suspect who divulged it.

The Mutiny Bill coming on, Mr. Fox had showed Lord Egmont a new clause for subjecting the American regiments to English discipline. He took it as gravely as if he were still to oppose, though it was public that he was to succeed the superannuated Lord Fitzwalter, as Treasurer of the Household, and, as he himself had said, by special command of the Princess. The first day he did not attend. December 11th, Oswald and Henley spoke for the clause: Lord Egmont, struck with the old sounds, and forgetting his new engagements, could not resist the impulse of haranguing against a Mutiny Bill. He rose, and spoke on his ancient topics of military law, of massacre and butchery, and of all he had foretold, and said, that everybody must be sensible that, in the situation he stood, he must have had grievances brought to him from every part of the known world; and talked much on the old constitution, the feudal law, and prerogative. Pitt spoke after him, but gently, and not well; Lord George Sackville well. Charles Townshend (who had ambitioned the Treasury on the late settlement, had stuck out for some time, and had then accepted the Admiralty), hurt at a new promotion over his head, started up, and not considering how indecent it was in him, a little Minister, to discourage renegades, fell with warmth and insolence and eloquence on Lord Egmont; pointed out the ridicule of a popular tribune speaking for prerogative, and against revolution principles; then panegyrized the Board of Trade, defended all their acts, even the instructions to Sir Danvers Osborn; and, turning again to Lord Egmont, bade him take the poor American by the hand, and point out his grievances; his Lordship was able, and used to be willing to bring out grievances; he had threatened he would; yet he defied him—if that would not do, he beseeched him—to point out one grievance; for his part, he did not know of one; he should be glad to learn why his Lordship did not intend to mention one *now*: and then, in the most provoking manner, and in terms most intelligible, he attacked him on the place he was going to accept. Lord Egmont was abashed, replied with confusion, said he might state grievances hereafter, but hoped things were going to be redressed. He was over-powered by the attack, and excused himself from accepting the promised employment.

At the conclusion of the year deceased two men in great offices, whose deaths made remarked what their lives might have done; how little they were worthy of their exaltation. The one, Lord Gower, Lord Privy Seal, had indeed a large fortune, and commanded boroughs. Lord Albemarle, the other, died suddenly at Paris, where his mistress sold him to that Court. Yet the French Ministry had little to vaunt; while they were purchasing the instructions of our Embassador, attentive only to acquire the emptiest of their accomplishments, they employed at our Court a man too empty to learn even the dullest of ours. Lord Albemarle made great proficience in the study of their manners, while Monsieur de Mirepoix could not learn even to pronounce the names of one or two of our games at cards, which, however, engaged most of the hours of his negotiation. Our Colonies were to be protected by the copy of a *Petit Maitre*; we were to be bullied out of them by an apprentice to whist! How serious a science, Politics!

Appendix

A.

Constitutional Queries, Earnestly Recommended to the Serious Consideration of Every True Briton, Dispersed in 1751, and Ascribed to Lord Egmont

Whether this capital may not be beset with troops, under such orders and commands, as may render the power of King, Lords, and Commons precarious; and subject our liberties, property, and laws, once more, to a military regulation?

Whether, if alarm posts should be appointed, places of rendezvous assigned, officers have the word, not to be absent, though on no duty, without express leave, and to hold themselves in readiness on a moment's warning, such regulations in time of peace would not have a martial air, by no means becoming the freedom of a British constitution?

Whether disgracing or dismissing old officers, men of family, men of property, in order to make way for the promotion of boys, slaves, and beggars, would not be such a garbling of the Army, as might furnish very melancholy apprehensions of its destination?

Whether such terrifying dispositions ought not to alarm a free people; and might not with too much reason induce them to apprehend, that the time was approaching when some *important blow was to be struck*?

Whether, if a *younger* son of the Crown should ever be invested with absolute power over such an Army; and, at the same time, by a factious connection, make himself master of the Fleet, our lives and fortunes might not be dependent on his will and pleasure, and the *Right of Succession* have no other security than his want of ambition?

Whether adding to this dangerous degree of power the sole direction of affairs in the Cabinet likewise, might not give him such a dictatorial authority as would enable him to expel from his father's Council and person every moderate Minister, true Englishman, and old servant of the Crown, who, though perhaps unable to prevent, might in some measure delay, the execution of his designs?

Whether, during the time of peace, experiment has not been actually made in one part of this country (now under the cloud of prejudice) how far an army may be depended on in usurping a dominion over law?

Whether, if in any country express and positive orders should be generally and circularly given by authority to the troops to execute the law, to seize and imprison the persons of the subjects, upon such information as they should think sufficient, without the concurrence of the civil power, such country might not be deemed under a direct military government in its rankest form?

Whether a successful attempt in one part of a country would not furnish sanguine hopes of reducing the remaining part to the like unconstitutional dominion?

Whether the omnipotence of a commander, joined with the faction, stupidity, and corruption of the times, might not be able to stifle and baffle all regular proof of such notorious acts of arbitrary and tremendous power?

Whether it might not be prudent to reflect on the fatal instances of John of Lancaster and crook-backed Richard?

Whether an abused K—— and kingdom, liberty, property, and the laws, do not all concur to inspire this timely invocation?

God preserve the Succession.

B.

The Following Queries Are Humbly Offered to the Serious Consideration of Every True Englishman

Whether it has not strongly appeared by the late conduct of the House of Commons, that they are more eager and industrious to create and to foment the spirit of party and sedition, than to promote the liberty and happiness of the people?

Whether the leaders of the House have not by open force, as well as private fraud, endeavoured to weaken and reduce even the appearance of a free constitution?

Whether, in the case of Mr. Murray, the House of Commons did not assume a power they had no just right to?

Whether they did not proceed throughout in a most illegal, unconstitutional, unprecedented manner?

Whether they did not try him upon an accusation they knew to be false, scandalous, and groundless?

Whether they did not condemn him in defiance of all law, and in the most open violation of justice?

Whether their proceedings have not made a dangerous encroachment upon the freedom and independency of the British people, as well as brought a lasting dishonour upon the British Parliament?

Whether their daily conduct does not tend, instead of remedying the distractions of a jarring people, to throw them into a continued confusion, and to make resentment and rebellion become habitual to Britain?

Whether there is not reason to expect that we shall soon be deprived of the most valuable right a British subject can enjoy, the right of election?

Whether we are not bound upon the most conscientious motives by any means in our power to defend it?

Can we patiently look upon these fresh endeavours to abuse and to divide the nation? can we patiently bear fresh loads of oppression multiplied without measure, and extended without limitation?

C.

This song was written immediately after the loss of the battle of Fontenoy, and was addressed to Lady Catherine Hanmer, Lady Falconberg, and Lady Middlesex, who were to act the three goddesses with Frederick Prince of Wales, in the Judgment of Paris, whom he was to represent, and Prince Lobkowitz, Mercury.

SONG,
BY FREDERICK, PRINCE OF WALES.

1.
Venez, mes cheres Deesses,
Venez, calmer mon chagrin;
Aidez, mes belles Princesses,
A le noyer dans le vin.
Poussons cette douce ivresse
Jusqu'au milieu de la nuit,
Et n'écoutons que la tendresse
D'un charmant vis-à-vis.

2.
Quand le chagrin me devore,
Vite à table je me mets,
Loin des objêts que j'abhorre,
Avec joie j'y trouve la paix.
Peu d'amis, restes d'un naufrage,
Je rassemble autour de moi,
Et je me ris de l'étalage
Qu'a chez lui toujours un Roi.

3.
Que m'importe que l'Europe
Ait un ou plusieurs tyrans?
Prions seulement Calliope
Qu'elle inspire nos vers, nos chants.

Laissons Mars et toute la gloire,
Livrons nous tous à l'amour;
Que Bacchus nous donne à boire;
A ces deux faisons la cour.

4.
Passons ainsi notre vie,
Sans rêver à ce qui suit;
Avec ma chere Silvie[252]
Le tems trop vite me fuit.
Mais si par un malheur extreme,
Je perdois cet objêt charmant;
Oui, cette compagnie même
Ne me tiendroit un moment.

5.
Me livrant à ma tristesse,
Toujours plein de mon chagrin,
Je n'aurois plus d'allegresse
Pour mettre Bathurst[253] en train.
Ainsi pour vous tenir en joie,
Invoquez toujours les Dieux,
Qu'elle vive et qu'elle soit
Avec nous toujours heureux.

D.

SONG.
THE CHARMS OF SYLVIA.
BY THE PRINCE OF WALES ON THE PRINCESS.

'Tis not the liquid brightness of those eyes,
That swim with pleasure and delight,

---

[252] The Princess.
[253] Allen, Lord Bathurst.

Nor those heavenly arches which arise
O'er each of them to shade their light:

'Tis not that hair which plays with every wind,
And loves to wanton round thy face;
Now straying round the forehead, now behind
Retiring with insidious grace:

'Tis not that lovely range of teeth so white,
As new-shorn sheep equal and fair;
Nor e'en that gentle smile, the heart's delight,
With which no smile could e'er compare:

'Tis not that chin so round, that neck so fine,
Those breasts that swell to meet my love,
That easy sloping waist, that form divine,
Nor ought below, nor ought above:

'Tis not the living colours over each
By nature's finest pencil wrought,
To shame the full-blown rose, and blooming peach,
And mock the happy painter's thought:

No[254]—'tis that gentleness of mind, that love
So kindly answering my desire;
That grace with which you look, and speak, and move,
That thus has set my soul on fire.

The elegy alluded to was probably the effusion of some Jacobite royalist. That faction could not forgive the Duke of Cumberland his excesses, or successes, in Scotland; and not content with branding the Parliamentary Government of the House of Brunswick as usurpation,

---

[254] Sir George Lyttelton, who was out of favour with the Prince, made a parody on this copy of verses: two of the lines were,
  No—'tis that all-consenting tongue,
  That never puts me in the wrong.

indulged in frequent, unfeeling, and scurrilous personalities on every branch of the reigning family.

> Here lies Fred,
> Who was alive, and is dead;
> Had it been his father,
> I had much rather:
> Had it been his brother,
> Still better than another;
> Had it been his sister,
> No one would have missed her;
> Had it been the whole generation,
> Still better for the nation;
> But since 'tis only Fred,
> Who was alive, and is dead,—
> There's no more to be said.

Note.—[The following, which is styled "Brief account of George Bubb Doddington, Lord Melcombe," is written in Horace Walpole's printed copy of the Diary; and as it contains some traits of character, and other anecdotes of a person who is often mentioned in the Memoirs, and who has himself related many of the same transactions, it is here subjoined to the work, though no injunctions to that purport were left by the author.]

George Bubb Doddington was son of an apothecary at Carlisle, by a sister or near relation of Mr. Doddington of Eastberry, in Dorsetshire, who bequeathed him his estate and name, with obligation to finish the vast seat at Eastberry, designed by Vanbrugh; and which was pulled down by Richard Grenville, first Earl Temple, on whom it was entailed, in case of Bubb's having no issue, as happened. Doddington had a great deal of wit, great knowledge of business, and was an able speaker in Parliament, though an affected one, and though most of his speeches were premeditated. He was, as his diary shows, vain, fickle, ambitious, servile, and corrupt. Early in his life, he had been devoted to Sir Robert Walpole, and in an epistle to him, which Pope quotes, had professed himself,

In power a servant, out of power a friend.

At a much later period of life he published an epistle to Lord Bute, whom he styled Pollio. Mr. Wyndham, editor of his Diary, wrote to Dr. Joseph Warton, in 1784, that he had found, among Doddington's papers, an old copy of that poem, *but inscribed to Sir Robert Walpole*. He fell more than once under the lash of Pope, who coupled him with Sir William Yonge in this line—

The flowers of Bubbington and flow of Yonge.

Soon after the arrival of Frederick Prince of Wales in England, Doddington became a favourite, and submitted to the Prince's childish horse-play, being once rolled up in a blanket, and trundled down stairs; nor was he negligent in paying more solid court, by lending his Royal Highness[255] money. He was, however, supplanted, I think, by George, afterwards Lord Lyttelton, and again became a courtier and placeman at St. James's; but once more reverted to the Prince at the period where his Diary commences. Pope was not the only poet who diverted the town at Doddington's expense. Sir Charles Hanbury ridiculed him in a well-known dialogue with Gyles Earle, and in a ballad entitled "A Grub upon Bubb." Dr. Young, on the contrary, who was patronized by him, has dedicated to him one of his satires on the love of fame, as Lyttelton had inscribed one of his cantos on the progress of love. Glover, and that prostitute fellow Ralph, were also countenanced by him, as the Diary shows.

Doddington's own wit was very ready. I will mention two instances. Lord Sundon was Commissioner of the Treasury with him and Winnington, and was very dull. One Thursday, as they left the board, Lord Sundon laughed heartily at something Doddington said; and when gone, Winnington said, "Doddington, you are very ungrateful; you call Sundon stupid and slow, and yet you see how quick he took what you said." "Oh,

---

[255] "This is a strange country, this England" (said his Royal Highness once); "I am told Doddington is reckoned a clever man; yet I got 5000*l*. out of him this morning, and he has no chance of ever seeing it again."

no," replied Doddington, "he was only laughing now at what I said last Treasury day."—Mr. Trenchard, a neighbour, telling him, that though his pinery was expensive, he contrived, by applying the fire and the dung to other purposes, to make it so advantageous, that he believed he got a shilling by every pine-apple he ate. "Sir," said Doddington, "I would eat them for half the money."—Doddington was married to a Mrs. Behan, whom he was supposed to keep. Though secretly married, he could not own her, as he then did, till the death of Mrs. Strawbridge, to whom he had given a promise of marriage, under the penalty of ten thousand pounds. He had long made love to the latter, and, at last, obtaining an assignation, found her lying on a couch. However, he only fell on his knees, and after kissing her hand for some time, cried out, "Oh, that I had you but in a wood!" "In a wood!" exclaimed the disappointed dame; "what would you do then? Would you *rob* me?" It was on this Mrs. Strawbridge that was made the ballad,

> My Strawberry—my Strawberry
> Shall bear away the bell;

to the burthen and tune of which Lord Bath, many years afterwards, wrote his song on "Strawberry Hill."

Doddington had no children. His estate descended to Lord Temple, whom he hated, as he did Lord Chatham, against whom he wrote a pamphlet to expose the expedition to Rochfort.

Nothing was more glaring in Doddington than his want of taste, and the tawdry ostentation in his dress and furniture of his houses. At Eastberry, in the great bedchamber, hung with the richest red velvet, was pasted, on every panel of the velvet, his crest (a hunting-horn supported by an eagle) cut out of gilt leather. The foot-cloth round the bed was a mosaic of the pocket-flaps and cuffs of all his embroidered clothes. At Hammersmith[256] his crest, in pebbles, was stuck into the centre of the turf before his door. The chimney-piece was hung with spars representing icicles round the fire, and a bed of purple, lined with orange, was crowned

---

[256] His house is since called Brandenburgh House.

by a dome of peacock's feathers. The great gallery, to which was a beautiful door of white marble, supported by two columns of *lapis lazuli*, was not only filled with busts and statues, but had, I think, an inlaid floor of marble; and all this weight was above stairs.

One day showing it to Edward, Duke of York, Doddington said, "Sir, some persons tell me that this room ought to be on the ground." "Be easy, Mr. Doddington," replied the Prince, "it will soon be there."

In the approach to his villa at Hammersmith, Mr. Doddington erected a noble obelisk, surmounted by an urn of bronze, to the memory of his wife, who died before him. Mr. Wyndham, his heir, took down the obelisk, and sold it. The Diary was certainly not published entire. A gentleman, who saw it five years before it was published, missed some particular passages.—H. W., June 7th, 1784.

Another instance of Doddington's wit. Doddington was very lethargic: falling asleep one day, after dinner, with Sir Richard Temple, Lord Cobham, the General, the latter reproached Doddington with his drowsiness; Doddington denied having been asleep, and to prove he had not, offered to repeat all Lord Cobham had been saying. Cobham challenged him to do so. Doddington repeated a story, and Lord Cobham owned he had been telling it. "Well," said Doddington, "and yet I did not hear a word of it; but I went to sleep because I knew that about this time of day you would tell that story."

In the Sackville family a son of talents had frequently succeeded a father below mediocrity. The following epigram, founded on that circumstance, was ascribed to Sir Charles Hanbury Williams, but never acknowledged by him, or included in the manuscript copies of his poems. The last stanza was unjust, as well as severe; but there is so much arch humour in the first, that it is worth preserving:—

> Folly and sense in Dorset's race
> Alternately do run,
> As Carey one day told his Grace,
> Praising his eldest son.

But Carey must allow for once
Exception to this rule;
For Middlesex is but a dunce,
Though Dorset be a fool.

The following inscription, though professedly written on a Swedish nobleman, the English reader will at once apply to a certain great statesman of British manufacture:—

"Hic situs est
Senatus Princeps, et Regni Præfectus;
Vir nobilis, splendidus, affabilis, blandus,
At animo non magno, nec magnâ corporis dignitate.
Cujus nomen et laudes tota jamdiu celebrat Academia;
Quem sacerdotes aulici omnes imprimis observant;
Quem reverendissimi Præsules, ut Deum colunt.

Qui cibi conquisitissimi perquàm intelligens,
Et convivia sumptuosè apparandi unicus instructor,
Doctissimos Trimalchionis coquos,
Mercede amplissimâ conductos,
In patriam, inque patriæ, scilicet, honorem,
Primus curavit arcessendos.

Qui indisertus, loquax, obscurus,
Disertissimos oratores, et sapientissimos
Non modò vicit omnes,
Sed hos ipsos semper habuit
Sententiæ suæ astipulatores.

Quippe populi captandi, et corrumpendi mirus artifex,
Atque ad conservandam, quam consecutus est, potentiam,
Ut alius nemo, callidus,
Summam Imperii diu tenuit.
Rei tamen publicæ administrandæ,
Perinde atque suæ,
Minimè peritus.

Tria millia talentûm ex agris et fortunis suis,
Totidemque fortasse e regio, cui præest, ærario
Exhausit, et dissipavit.
Neque quemquam hominem probissimum,
Deque republicâ, aut re literariâ optimè meritum,
Liberalitate suâ decoravit, aut adjuvit.

Solus ex omnibus
Belli et pacis arbiter fuit constitutus:
At belli legitimè suscipiendi, et persequendi,
Aut pacis honestè retinendæ, aut firmandæ
Solus ex omnibus expers et ignarus.

Semper vehementissimè occupatus,
Ac res permagnas visus agere,
Omninò nihil agit.
Semper festinans, properansque,
Atque ad metam tendere prorsùm simulans,
Nunquam pervenit.

Hæc fortassis, Viator, rides:
Sta verò et tristem lege Epilogum;
Hujus unius hominis inscitia
Tantum impressit dedecus,
Tantum attulit detrimentum reipublicæ,
Ut omnibus appareat,
Nisi Sueciæ Genius, siquis est, sese interponat,
Sueciam futuram non esse."

Henrietta, daughter of Sir Henry Hobart, was first married to Colonel Henry Howard, afterwards Earl of Suffolk, by whom she had an only son, Henry, who succeeded his father, but died a young man. Mr. Howard and she travelled in very mean circumstances to Hanover before the accession of that family to the Crown; and after it, she was made a Woman of the Bedchamber to the Princess; and being *confidante* of the Prince's passion for a lady, who was in love with, and soon after privately married to, a Colonel, Mrs. Howard had the address to divert the channel of his inclination to herself. Her husband bore it very ill, and attempted to force her from St. James's, but was at last quieted with a pension of 1200*l*. per annum. Yet Mrs. Howard had little interest with the King. The Queen persecuted whoever courted her; and Sir R. Walpole directing all his worship to the uncommonly-powerful wife, Mrs. Howard naturally became his enemy, and as naturally attached herself to Lord Bolingbroke; the more intimate connection of which intercourse, carelessly concealed by a mistress that was tired, and eagerly hunted out by a wife still jealous, was unravelled by the Princess Emily at the Bath, and at last laid open by the cautious Queen; the King stormed; the mistress was glad he did, left him in his moods, and married George Berkeley, brother to the late Earl, by whom she was again left a widow in 1746.

King George the Second has often, when Mrs. Howard, his mistress, was dressing the Queen, come into the room, and snatched the handkerchief off, and cried, "Because you have an ugly neck yourself, you love to hide the Queen's!" Her Majesty (all the while calling her "*My good Howard*,") took great joy in employing her in the most servile offices about her person. The King was so communicative to his wife, that one day Mrs. Selwyn, another of the Bedchamber Women, told him he should be the last man with whom she would have an intrigue, because he always told the Queen. Their letters, whenever he was at Hanover, were so long, that he has complained when she has written to him but nineteen pages; and in his, at the beginning of his amour with Lady Yarmouth, he frequently said, "I know you will love the Walmoden, *because she loves me*." Old Blackbourn, the Archbishop of York, told her one day, "That he had been talking to her Minister Walpole about the new mistress, and was glad to find that her Majesty was so sensible a woman as to like her husband should divert himself." Yet with the affectation of content, it made her most miserable: she dreaded Lady Yarmouth's arrival, and repented not having been able to resist the temptation of driving away Lady Suffolk the first instant she had an opportunity, though a rival so powerless, and so little formidable. The King was the most regular man in his hours: his time of going down to Lady Suffolk's apartment was seven in the evening: he would frequently walk up and down the gallery, looking at his watch, for a quarter of an hour before seven, but would not go till the clock struck.

The King had another *passager amour* (between the disgrace of Lady Suffolk and the arrival of Lady Yarmouth) with the Governess to the two youngest Princesses; a pretty idiot, with most of the vices of her own sex, and the additional one of ours, drinking. Yet this thing of convenience, on the arrival of Lady Yarmouth, put on all that dignity of passion, which even revolts real inclination.

E.

Extracts from Letters of Sir Charles Hanbury Williams, during His Ministry at Berlin

TO THE DUKE OF NEWCASTLE.
Berlin, July 11-22nd, 1750.

.... Count Podewils's behaviour to me has been hitherto very cold, and when I meet him at third places, he contents himself with making me a bow, without speaking to me.

I have made one visit to Monsieur Finkenstein, who is the second Minister of State for Foreign Affairs. He has very much the air of a French *petit-maître manqué*, and is extremely affected in everything he says and does: but from what I have been able hitherto to learn, his credit with the King of Prussia increases daily; and that of Count Podewils is not thought to be so good as it formerly was. The former has lately gained a point over the latter: Count Podewils's kinsman, who is at Vienna, was named to be a Minister of State before Count Finkenstein; but Count Finkenstein has got into his employment, and when Count Podewils returns from Vienna, Count Finkenstein will take place of him. Not that his Prussian Majesty gives entire confidence either to Podewils or Finkenstein; he reserves that for two persons that constantly reside with him at Potsdam, and whose names are Heichel and Fredersdorff; the first of whom is his Prussian

Majesty's Private Secretary, and who is always kept under the same roof with his Prussian Majesty, and is so well watched, that a person may be at this Court seven years without once seeing him. The other, who is the great favourite, was once a common soldier, and the King took a fancy to him, while he was yet Prince Royal of Prussia, as he was standing sentinel at the door of his apartment. This person has two very odd titles joined together, for he is styled *valet de chambre*, and *grand tresorier du Roi*. He keeps out of all people's sight as much as Heichel.

But there is lately arose another young man, who has undoubtedly a large share in the King of Prussia's favours: his name is Sedoo: he was not long ago his page, then came to be a lieutenant, and is very lately made a major, and *premier ecuyer de l'ecurie de Potsdam*, and will undoubtedly soon rise much higher.

Another Extract

…. On Thursday, by appointment, I went to Court at eleven o'clock; the King of Prussia arrived about twelve, and Count Podewils immediately introduced me into his closet, where I delivered his Majesty's letters into the King of Prussia's hands, and made the usual compliments to him in the best manner I was able. To which his Prussian Majesty replied, to the best of my remembrance, as follows: "I have the truest esteem for the King of Great Britain's person, and I set the highest value upon his friendship. I have at different times received essential proofs of it; and I desire you would acquaint the King, your master, that I will never forget them." His Prussian Majesty afterwards said something with respect to myself, and then asked me several questions about indifferent things and persons. He seemed to express a great deal of esteem for my Lord Chesterfield, and a great deal of kindness for Mr. Villiers, but did not once mention Lord Hyndford, or Mr. Legge. I was in the closet with his Majesty exactly five minutes and a half.

After my audience was over, the King of Prussia came out into that room where the Foreign Ministers wait for his Prussian Majesty. He just said one word to Count de la Puebla (the Austrian Minister) as he came in, and afterwards addressed his discourse to the French, Swedish, and Danish Ministers; but did not say one word either to the Russian Minister or myself.

Extract from Another Letter, in Cipher

Berlin July, 28, 1750.

.... About four days ago, Mr. Voltaire, the French poet, arrived at Potsdam from Paris. The King of Prussia had wrote to him about three months ago to desire him to come to Berlin. Mr. Voltaire answered his Prussian Majesty, that he should always be glad of an opportunity of throwing himself at his Majesty's feet, but at that time he was not in circumstances to take so long a journey; upon which the King of Prussia sent him back word, that he would bear his expenses; but Mr. Voltaire, not caring to trust the King of Prussia, would not leave Paris till his Prussian Majesty had sent him a bill of exchange upon a banker in that town for 4000 rix-dollars, and he did not begin the journey till he had actually received the money. All that I now write your grace was told me by the Princess Amalie.—(*Author.*)

[The following extracts from the private correspondence of Sir Charles Hanbury Williams will further illustrate the remark in the text, and show the unfavourable view taken by him of the Prussian Court and Frederick the Great.]

Extract of a Letter from Charles Hanbury Williams, from Berlin, 1750

.... 'Tis incredible what care this *Pater Patriæ* takes of his people. He is so good as to meddle in their family affairs, in their marriages, in the education of their children, and in the disposition of their estates. He hates that anybody should marry, especially an officer, let him be of what degree soever, and from the moment they take a wife, they are sure of never being preferred. All children are registered as soon as born, and the parents are obliged to produce either certificates of their deaths, or the male children themselves, at the age of fourteen, in order to be enrolled, and to take the oath of a soldier to the King; and if this is not done, or the children have escaped, the parents are answerable for the escape, and are sent to prison.

No man can sell land throughout all the Prussian dominions without a special licence from the King: and as he does no more give licences, nobody can now dispose of or alienate his possessions. If they could, and were to find fools to purchase them, I believe he would not have ten of his present subjects left in a year's time. They have really no liberty left but that of thinking. There is a general constraint that runs through all sorts of people, and diffidence is painted in every face. All their ambition and desire is to be permitted to go to their Country Seats, where they need not be obliged to converse with any but their own family. But this leave is not easily obtained, because the father of his country insists upon their living at Berlin, and making his Capital flourish. He is never here but from the beginning of December to the end of January, and during that time, Prussians, Silesians, and all his most distant subjects, are obliged to come and make a figure here, and spend all they have been saving for the other ten months. He hates that any subject of his should be rich or easy; and if he lives a few years longer, he will have accomplished his generous design. There are actually but four persons in this great town that live upon their own means, and they are people that can't last long in their present condition.

He (always meaning *Pater Patriæ*) gives very small salaries to all employments, and this is the cause that he can get no gentleman to serve him in a Foreign Legation. His Ministers at every Court are the scum of the earth, and have nothing but the insolence of their master to support them; and, indeed, the Prussian method of treating with every Court is such, as I wonder how Sovereign Princes can bear. Of this, if I had time, I could give you many provoking instances. His Prussian Majesty's Ministers at Berlin—I mean those for Foreign Affairs—make the oddest figure of any in Europe. They seldom or never see any dispatches that are sent to the Prussian Ministers at Foreign Courts; and all letters that come to Berlin from Foreign Courts go directly to the King; so that Mr. Podewils and Count Finkenstein know no more of what passes in Europe than what they are informed of by the Gazettes. When any of us go to them on any business, the surprise they are in easily betrays their ignorance, and the only answer you ever get is, that they will lay what you say before their master, and give you an answer as soon as he shall have signified his pleasure to them. When you return to their houses for this answer, they tell you the exact words which the king has directed, and never one word more; nor are you permitted to argue any point. In short, they act the part of Ministers without being really so, as much as ever Cibber did that of Wolsey upon the stage, only not half so well.

The first of them is reputed to be an honest man, but he is nothing less. He loses that appearance of credit he once had, daily; for verily I believe he never had real weight enough with his master to have made an Ensign in his Army, or a Postillion in one of his Posthouses. His face is the picture of Dullness when she smiles, and his figure is a mixture of a clown and a *petit-maître*. He is a little genteeler than Mons. Adrié, who you may remember to have seen make so great a figure in England.

The other, Count Finkenstein, whom everybody calls Count Fink, is very like the late Lord Hervey, and yet his face is the ugliest I ever saw. But when he speaks, his affectation, the motion of his eyes and shoulders, all his different gestures and grimaces, bring Lord Hervey very strongly into my mind; and, like that Lord, he is the Queen's favourite (I mean the Queen Mother's); and her Majesty, whether seriously or otherwise I can't tell, calls him "*Mon beau Comte Fink.*" He has parts, and is what, at Berlin, is called *sçavant*, which is to say, that he has read all the modern French story books, from *Les Egaremens* down to the history of *Prince Cocquetron*.

The person who has certainly the greatest share of the King of Prussia's confidence is one Heichel. He is his Private Secretary, and writes all that the King himself dictates. But this man I never saw, and people that have lived here seven years have never seen him. He is kept like a State

Prisoner, is in constant waiting, and never has half an hour to himself in the whole year.

[Then follows the account of Fredersdorff, to the same purpose, and nearly in the same words as in the extracts printed above.]

He (Fredersdorff) is his Secretary for all small affairs for his Prussian Majesty.—

> Il fait tout par ses mains, et voit tout par ses yeux.

If a Courier is to be dispatched to Versailles, or a Minister to Vienna, his Prussian Majesty draws, himself, the instructions for the one, and writes the letters for the other. This, you'll say, is great; but if a Dancer at the Opera has disputes with a Singer, or if one of those performers want a new pair of stockings, a plume for his helmet, or a finer petticoat, 'tis the same King of Prussia that sits in judgment on the cause, and that with his own hand answers the Dancer's or the Singer's letter. His Prussian Majesty laid out 20,000*l.* to build a fine theatre, and his music and Singers cost him near the same sum every year; yet this same King, when an opera is performed, wont allow ten pounds per night to light up the theatre with wax candles; and the smoke that rises from the bad oil, and the horrid stink that flows from the tallow, make many of the audience sick, and actually spoil the whole entertainment. What I have thought about this Prince is very true; and I believe, after reading what I say about him, you will think so too. *He is great in great things, and little in little ones.*

In the summer 1749, three Prussian Officers came, without previously asking leave, to see a Review of some Austrian troops in Moravia; upon which the Commanding Officer of those troops, suspecting they were not come so much out of curiosity to see the Review, as to debauch some of the soldiers into the King of Prussia's service, sent them orders to retire. This being reported to his Prussian Majesty, he was much offended, and resolved to take some method to show his resentment, which he did as follows:—Last summer, an Austrian Captain, being in the Duchy of Mecklenburgh, met there with an old acquaintance, one Chapeau, who is in great favour with the King of Prussia. At that time, there was to be a great

Review at Berlin, and as Berlin was in the Austrian's road in his return to Vienna, Chapeau invited him to see the Review; but the Austrian replied, that he would willingly come, but was afraid of receiving some affront, in return for what had been done to the Prussian Officers the year before in Moravia; to which Chapeau replied, that if he would come to Berlin, he would undertake to get the King of Prussia's special leave for him to be present at the Review. Encouraged by this, the Austrian came, and the night before the Review, Chapeau brought him word that the leave was granted, and he might come with all safety. He did accordingly come; but as soon as the King of Prussia had notice of his being there, he sent an Aide-de-camp to him to tell him to retire that moment, which he was forced to do, not without much indignation against Chapeau, who had drawn him into the scrape. The next morning he went to Chapeau, with an intention to demand satisfaction for the affront which, through him, he had received. Chapeau said he would do as he pleased, but first desired him to give him leave to speak for himself; which he did. Chapeau then told him, that immediately upon hearing that he had been sent out of the field in that strange manner, he had rode up to the King, and asked his Majesty whether he had not given him orders to tell the Austrian Officer that he might come to the Review with all security? and that the King had replied, it was very true, he had given such orders; because, if he had not, the Austrian would hardly have ventured to come to the Review; and if he had not come there, he (the King) should not have had an opportunity of revenging the affront that had been offered to some Officers of his own the year before in Moravia.

I must tell you a story of the King of Prussia's regard for the law of nations. There was, some time ago, a Minister here from the Duke of Brunswick, whose name was Hoffman. He was a person of very good sense, and what we call well-intentioned, (which means being attached to the interests of the maritime powers and the House of Austria.) He was, besides, very active and dexterous in getting intelligence, which he constantly communicated to the Ministers of England and Austria. This the King of Prussia being well informed of, wrote a letter with his own hand to the Duke of Brunswick, to insist (and in case of refusal to threaten) that he should absolutely disavow Hoffman for his Minister. The Duke, who is the worthiest Prince upon earth, was so frightened with this letter, that he complied, though much against his will, with this haughty and cruel request. The moment the King of Prussia received this answer, he sent a party of Guards to Hoffman's house, seized him, sent him prisoner to Madgeburgh, where he has now been for above four years chained to a wheel-barrow, and working at the fortifications of that town! He was very near doing the same by a Minister of the Margravine of Anspach's, but that person got timely notice, and escaped out of Berlin in the morning; and when the King of Prussia's Guards came to seize him at night, the bird had luckily flown.

There is at present here a Minister of the Duke of Brunswick, the successor of Hoffman, to whom, in his first audience, the King said, that he advised him to act very differently from his predecessor, and particularly to take care not to frequent those Foreign Ministers that he must know were disagreeable to him; for if he did, he might depend upon it he should deal with him in the same manner as he had done with Hoffman.

I think Hamlet says in the play, "Denmark is a prison;" the whole Prussian territory is so in the literal sense of the word. No man can, or does pretend to go out of it without the knowledge of the King and his Ministers. Very hard is the fate of those who have estates in other dominions besides those of his Prussian Majesty; he will neither permit them to sell their estates in his countries, nor live upon those they have out of them. The distresses which are come on the Silesians (who had estates also in Bohemia) are prodigious. Many people have given them up, or sold them for a trifle, to get out of this land of Egypt—this house of bondage. Six hundred dollars make just one hundred guineas, and I know the King of Prussia thinks that just as much as any of his subjects ought to have, exclusive of what he may give them. In a very few years, I am convinced that no subject of his that has not estates elsewhere will have more left him. But from what he has already done, he begins to find that it is no longer possible to collect the heavy taxes which he imposes on his subjects. I know that the revenues of all his countries, except Silesia, have diminished every year, for these last five years.

A Prussian will tell you, with a very grave face, that their present King is the most merciful Prince that ever reigned, and that he hates shedding blood. This is not true; there are often as cruel and tormenting executions in this country as ever were known under any Sicilian tyrant. 'Tis true, they are not done at Berlin, nor in the face of the world, but at Potsdam, in private. Since my arrival in this cursed country, an old woman was quartered alive at Potsdam, for having assisted two soldiers to desert. But his Prussian Majesty generally punishes offenders with close imprisonment and very hard labour, keeping them naked in the coldest weather, and giving them nothing, for years together, but bread and water. Such mercy is cruelty. Many persons destroy themselves here out of mere despair; but all imaginable care is taken to conceal such suicides. I have heard of one of our Governors in the Indies, who was reproached by his friends, on his return to England, that he put a great number of persons to death; to which that humane Governor replied, "It is not true; I only used them so ill, that they hanged themselves."

F.

Deux Henris immolés par nos braves ayeux,
L'un à la liberté, et Bourbon à nos Dieux,
Te menacent, Louis, d'une pareille entreprise:
Ils revivent en toi ces anciens tyrans:
Crains notre désespoir: la noblesse a des Guises,
Paris des Ravaillacs, le clergé des Cléments.

G.

Though poetry was certainly neither a point of their rivalship, nor of their ambition, it may not be unwelcome to the curious to compare these great men even in their poetic capacities. The following sonnet was written by Sir R. Walpole when a very young man; the elegy, by Lord

Bolingbroke, rather past his middle age. Had they climbed no mountain but Parnassus, it is obvious how far Lord Bolingbroke would have ascended above his competitor, since, when turned of fifty, he excelled in the province of youth.

TO THE HELIOTROPE.[257]
A SONG.

1.
Hail, pretty emblem of my fate!
Sweet flower, you still on Phœbus wait;
On him you look, and with him move,
By nature led, and constant love.

2.
Know, pretty flower, that I am he,
Who am in all so like to thee;
I, too, my fair one court, and where
She moves, my eyes I thither steer.

3.
But yet this difference still I find,
The sun to you is always kind;
Does always life and warmth bestow:
—Ah! would my fair one use me so!

4.
Ne'er would I wait till she arose
From her soft bed and sweet repose;
But leaving thee, dull plant, by night
I'd meet my Phillis with delight.

TO CLARA.[258]

---

[257] I found this song in an old pocket-book belonging to my father, who wrote it, as he told me himself, when he was a very young man, on a sister of Sir William Carew.

[258] This was written on a common woman whom Lord Bolingbroke took into keeping, and who, many years afterwards, sold oranges in the Court of Requests.

BY HENRY, VISCOUNT BOLINGBROKE.

Dear thoughtless Clara, to my verse attend,
Believe for once the lover and the friend;
Heav'n to each sex has various gifts assign'd,
And shown an equal care of human kind.
Strength does to man's imperial race belong;
To yours, that beauty which subdues the strong.
But as our strength, when misapplied, is lost,
And what should save, urges our ruin most;
Just so, when beauty prostituted lies,
Of b***s the prey, of rakes the abandon'd prize,
Women no more their empire can maintain,
Nor hope, vile slaves of lust, by love to reign;
Superior charms but make their case the worse,
When what was meant their blessing, proves their curse.
O nymph! that might, reclin'd on Cupid's breast,
Like Psyche, soothe the God of Love to rest;
Or if ambition move thee, Jove enthral,
Brandish his thunder, and direct its fall;
Survey thyself, contemplate ev'ry grace
Of that sweet form, of that angelic face;
Then, Clara, say, were those delicious charms
Meant for lewd brothels and rude ruffians' arms?
No, Clara, no; that person and that mind
Were form'd by nature, and by Heav'n design'd
For nobler ends; to these return, though late;
Return to these, and so redress thy fate.
Think, Clara, think (nor may that thought be vain!)
Thy slave, thy Harry, doom'd to drag his chain,
Of love ill treated and abus'd, that he
From more inglorious chains might rescue thee.
Thy drooping health restor'd by his fond cares,
Once more thy beauty its full lustre wears.
Mov'd by his love, by his example taught,
Soon shall thy soul, once more with virtue fraught,
With kind and generous truth thy bosom warm,

> And thy fair mind, like thy fair person, charm.
> To virtue thus and to thyself restor'd,
> By all admir'd, by one alone ador'd,
> Be to thy Harry ever kind and true,
> And live for him who more than died for you.

The reader will find a very ludicrous anecdote relating to Mr. Nugent, during his election at Bristol, in a letter from our Author to Richard Bentley, Esq., dated July 9th, 1754. It is printed in the publication of his correspondence with that gentleman, but we do not venture to insert it here.

INDEX

A

Albemarle, Lady, 51
Albemarle, W. A. Van Keppel, Earl of, 51
Aldworth, Mr., 121
Amelie, Princess, 251
Andrews, Dr., 229
Ankram, Lord, 37
Anson, Lord, 23, 42, 72, 117, 120, 121, 160, 191, 207, 216, 238
Anspach, Margrave of, 181
Anstruther, General, 25, 35, 39, 42, 66
Archer, Lord, 5
Argyle, Archibald, Duke of, 25, 26, 103, 112, 130, 158, 161, 163, 172, 173, 174, 207, 227, 239, 245
Augusta, the Lady, 45, 51
Ayscough, Dr., 49, 125

B

Baker, Alderman, 44
Baltimore, Lord, 55
Barnard, Lord, 73, 243, 244
Barnard, Sir John, 27, 33, 83, 131, 136, 160, 223, 228, 230
Barrington, William, 7
Bath, Earl of, 73
Bathurst, Lord, 60, 269
Beaufort, Duke of, 173
Beckford, Mr., 95
Bedford, Duchess of, 2, 220
Bedford, John, Duke of, xviii, xxv, 1, 2, 13, 20, 33, 38, 39, 42, 49, 50, 57, 61, 76, 91, 95, 101, 104, 105, 108, 116, 117, 118, 119, 120, 121, 122, 124, 140, 145, 150, 152, 153, 155, 157, 158, 159, 160, 161, 163, 165, 166, 168, 170, 171, 172, 174, 186, 194, 195, 196, 197, 198, 204, 206, 208, 211, 216, 217, 218, 219, 225, 230, 258, 259
Behan, Mrs., 273
Bentinck, Monsieur, 129
Berkeley, Earl, 61
Bertie, Lord Robert, 59
Bertie, Norris, 83
Berwick, Duke of, 3
Besborough, Earl of, 122
Bettesworth, Dr. John, 57
Blacket, Sir Walter, 153, 159

Blakiston, a grocer, 22
Bland, Dr. Henry, 40
Boyle, Bellingham, 230
Boyle, Lady Charlotte, 122
Boyle, Mr., 175, 176, 177
Braddock, General, 250
Bristol, Earl of, 42
Bruce, Mr., 167
Brunswick, Duchess of, 45
Brunswick, Duke of, 284, 285
Buckingham, Duchess of, 74
Buckinghamshire, John, Earl of, 111
Burdett, Sir Robert, 59
Burlington, Richard, Earl of, 122
Bury, Lord, 51
Bute, Earl of, 28
Butler, Dr., Bishop of Durham, 92
Byng, Admiral, xviii, 3

C

Cameron, Dr. Archibald, 209, 220
Campbell, Alexander Hume, 11
Campbell, General, 162
Canterbury, Archbishop of, 43, 46, 92
Carlisle, Lord, 109
Caroline, her Majesty Queen, 137
Carpenter, Lord, 15, 16, 19, 125
Carteret, Lord, xvii, 103
Cathcart, Lord, 48
Cavendish, Lord John, 122
Chapman, Dr., 191
Chateauroux, Duchesse de, 210
Chesterfield, Philip, Earl of, 3
Cholmondeley, George, Earl of, 109
Cholmondeley, Mr., 207
Churchill, General, 14
Clarges, Sir Thomas, 19
Clarke, Dr., 40
Clement, Jacques, 115

Cobham, Richard Grenville, Lord, 49, 58, 84, 99, 151, 153, 271, 274
Coke, Lord, 10, 12, 16, 17, 130, 131, 132, 163
Cologne, Elector of, 50
Compagni, Don Juan, 36
Conway, Henry Seymour, 24
Conway, Lord, 24
Cooke, Mr., 8, 9, 18, 19, 53
Cope, Sir John, 108
Cornbury, Lord, 145
Cornwallis, Colonel, 39, 193
Cotton, Sir John Hinde, 20
Coventry, Lord, 130
Cowper, Dr., Dean of Durham, 40, 191, 199
Cox, Sir Richard, 177
Crawley, Sir Ambrose, Knt., 20
Crooke, Mrs., 110
Crowle, Mr., 12
Cumberland, HRH William, Duke of, 1, 28, 43, 62, 151, 173, 241, 261, 270
Cummings, Mr., 167
Cust, Sir John, 60

D

D'Esmurs, Eleonora, Duchess of Zelle, 57
Dalrymple, Sir Hugh, 29
Darlington, Earl of, 73, 244
Dashwood, Sir Francis, 6, 16, 76
Dashwood, Sir James, 227
Davidson, Mr., 168
Davison, Major, 197
Delaval, Mr., 38, 77
Denmark, her Majesty the Queen of, 141
Denmark, King of, 65, 141, 159
Devonshire, William, Duke of, xx, 71, 122, 177, 191, 201, 205, 237, 239
Diggs, the actor, 244
Doddington, George Bubb, 55, 271
Doneraile, Arthur St. Leger, Viscount, 46

Dorothea, Sophia, Princess of Zelle, 57
Dorset, Charles Sackville, Duke of, 47, 60
Dorset, Lionel Cranfield, Duke of, 60, 61
Dowdeswell, Mr., 17
Downe, Lord, 59, 130
Drummond, Dr. Hay, 193
Dumfries, Earl of, 163
Dunbar, Titular Earl of, 93, 180
Duncannon, Lord, 122
Dunk, Miss Anne, 124
Duplin, Lord, 9, 16, 36, 39, 130, 193, 205, 240, 243, 245
Durham, Bishop of, 40, 92

E

Edward, Prince, 45, 49, 73, 163, 182
Egmont, John Perceval, Earl of, 21
Elibank, Lord, 10
Elizabeth, Lady, 5, 117, 125, 152
Emily, Princess, 45, 47, 48, 101, 114, 117, 140, 194, 251, 277
Erskine, Sir Henry, 25, 33, 39, 42, 66, 69, 70, 159, 186

F

Fagel, Greffier, 123
Falconberg, Lady, 268
Fane, Lord, 254, 255
Finkenstein, Count, 278, 282
Firebrace, Sir Cordel, 193
Fitzroy, Charles, 113
Fitzwalter, Earl of, 123
Fitzwalter, Lady, 124
Fitzwilliam, Colonel, 24
Fleury, Cardinal, 210
Folkestone, Lord, 76
Fox, Henry, 58
Furnese, Harry, 73
Fynte, Sir Charles, 13

G

Gally, Dr., 30
Gardiner, Luke, 222
Gascoyne, Mr., 15
Gibson, 10, 13, 16, 19
Glenorchy, Lord, 41
Godolphin, Lord, 138
Golding, Mr., 29
Grafton, Charles Fitzroy, Duke of, 29, 113, 194, 206
Graham, Mr., 116
Grantham, Lord, 137
Granville, Earl, 3
Gray, Mr., 255
Grenville, George, 11, 84, 243
Grenville, Richard, 84, 271
Grey, Lady Mary, 41
Grey, Marchioness de, 41
Griffith, Colonel Edward, 3
Guildford, Earl of, 54

H

Haldane, Colonel, 35, 37, 50
Halifax, George Montagu, Earl of, 124
Hamilton, Lady Archibald, 46, 47
Hamilton, Lord Archibald, 47
Hamilton, Sir James, 229
Hanbury, 251, 272, 280
Handasyde, General, 6
Hanmer, Lady Catherine, 268
Harcourt, Simon, Earl of, 178
Harding, Mr., 17, 18, 140
Harley, Lord, 90, 136, 159, 227
Harrington, William Stanhope, Earl of, 2, 3
Hartington, Marquis of, 122, 205
Hawley, General, 64, 190, 205
Hay, Dr., 178, 205
Hayter, Dr., Bishop of Norwich, 54, 178, 181, 182, 190, 192, 200, 203, 208

Hedges, Charles, 47
Henley, Mr., 5
Herbert, Nich., 140
Hereford, Viscount, 72
Herring, Archbishop, 57
Hertford, Earl of, 24, 244
Hervey, Felton, 163
Hesse Cassel, Frederick, Hereditary Prince of, 253
Hesse, Landgrave of, 181
Hill, Mr., 245
Hinchinbroke, Viscount, 125
Hobart, Sir Henry, 111, 276
Holderness, Robert Darcy, Earl of, 123, 150
Home, Lord, 11
Hussey, Mr., 128
Hyndford, Lord, 279

I

Ilchester, Lord, 58, 128
Irby, Sir William, 55
Islay, Lord, 103

J

Jansen, Alderman, 18, 132
Jekyll, Sir Joseph, 41
Johnson, 191, 197, 200
Johnson, Dr., Bishop of Gloucester, 182, 191, 197, 199, 204, 205, 206
Jones, Neville, 176, 226, 227, 229

K

Kaunitz, Count, 62
Keene, Sir Benjamin, 249
Keith, Marshal, 127
Kendal, Duchess of, 32, 137, 138
Kent, Henry, Duke of, 41, 71

Kildare, Earl of, 46
Kneller, Sir Godfrey, 43

L

Lambert, Mr., 229
Lamont, Dr., 30, 53
Laurence, Dr. Thomas, 3
Lee, Chief Justice, 56, 72, 237
Lee, Sir George, DCL., 56, 187, 252
Legge, Mr., 119, 153, 245, 279
Legonier, General Sir John, 64
Leicester, Thomas, Earl of, 130
Leveson, Mr., 121, 140
Levi, a Jew, 207
Lincoln, Henry Clinton, Earl of, 53
Lobkowitz, Prince, 268
Lochiel, 220
London, Dr. Sherlock, Bishop of, 71, 76, 92, 225, 226
Lonsdale, Henry, Viscount, 12
Louis, Monsieur, 111
Lovat, Lord, 161, 167
Loyd, Sir Richard, 67, 94, 245
Lyttelton, Sir George, afterwards Lord Lyttleton, 218

M

Macclesfield, Lord, 31
Madox, Dr., Bishop of Worcester, 74, 207, 230
Mailly, Madame de, 210
Manchester, Duchess of, 128
Marchmont, Earl of, 11, 185
Marlborough, Chas. Spencer, Duke of, 6, 43, 50, 59, 124, 138, 205, 254, 261
Marlborough, Sarah, Duchess of, 58
Martin, Mr., 5
Mary, Princess, 181, 253
Methuen, Sir Paul, 55, 103, 207

Index

Middlesex, Earl of, 47
Middleton, Dr. Conyers, 92
Milton, Lord, 167
Molesworth, Sir John, 59
Moncrief, Mr., 42
Monroe, Sir Harry, 170
Mordaunt, Sir John, 18, 68, 162
Murray, Alexander, 10, 21
Murray, Lord John, 27

N

Newcastle, Thomas Pelham Holles, Duke of, xvii, xx, 1, 2, 4, 5, 13, 28, 29, 38, 39, 42, 43, 53, 54, 56, 62, 71, 72, 74, 80, 97, 100, 101, 102, 103, 104, 107, 112, 114, 115, 119, 120, 124, 132, 146, 150, 154, 155, 157, 160, 172, 175, 178, 186, 187, 190, 197, 205, 206, 215, 219, 224, 234, 238, 239, 241, 242, 243, 244, 245, 248, 249, 250, 251, 254, 256, 257, 258, 259, 260, 261, 262
Newdigate, Sir Roger, 78, 159, 228
North, Lord, 48, 54, 107, 117, 161, 207
Northampton, Earl of, 112
Northumberland, Earl of, 5
Nugent, Mrs., 28
Nugent, Robert, 28

O

Ofarel, Brigadier, 66
Oglethorpe, General, 5, 70, 86
Oldfield, Mrs., 14
Onslow, Lord, 163
Orange, Prince of, 128, 133, 141, 163
Orford, George, Earl of, ix, x, xiii, xiv, 5, 53
Orford, Robert Walpole, Earl of, 14, 32, 53, 65, 73, 74, 100, 101, 103, 105, 106, 107, 112, 114, 137, 143, 144, 145, 146, 173, 251

Orleans, Duke of, 48
Ormond, Duke of, 32
Osborn, Sir Danvers, 248, 263
Oxenden, Sir George, 18
Oxford, Bishop of, 40, 217, 224, 226
Oxford, Earl of, 90

P

Paris, Archbishop of, 135
Paul, Dr., 187
Pavonarius, 44
Pelham, Henry, 230
Penlez, Bosavern, 8
Philipps, Sir John, 251
Pinfold, Colonel, 42
Pitt, Thomas, 58
Pitt, William, afterwards Earl of Chatham, 5, 32, 47, 58
Poland, Augustus, King of, 127, 153
Pompadour, Madame de, 135
Porteous, Captain, 26
Potter, Thomas, 43
Pretender, The, 180
Probyn, Mr., 5
Prussia, Queen of, 110

R

Ravensworth, Lord, 190, 191, 192, 193, 194, 195, 196, 197, 198, 201, 203, 204, 205, 207
Richmond, Duke of, 2
Rider, Sir Dudley, Attorney-General, 161, 187, 245
Rigby, Mr., xviii
Robinson, Sir Thomas, 153, 243, 255, 260, 262
Robyns, Mr., 40
Rockingham, Marquis of, 171, 207
Rushout, Sir John, 73, 91

Index

Rutland, Duke of, 24

S

Sackville, Lord George, xx, 18, 19, 24, 67, 175, 177, 186, 229, 244, 262
Sandwich, John Montagu, Earl of, 117, 125
Sandys, Lord, 207, 217
Sandys, Samuel, 41
Saunders, Captain, 216
Saxe, Marshal, 63, 64
Scarborough, Earl of, 119
Schomberg, Duke, 123
Scott, Mr., 178
Selwyn, John, 59, 72, 108
Seymour, Lady Elizabeth, 5
Shaftesbury, Earl of, 30
Shannon, Viscount, 47
Shaw, Dr., 116
Sheridan, 244
Smithson, Sir Hugh, 5
Sobieski, Princess, 179
Soissons, Fitz-James, Bishop of, 210
Somerset, Algernon, Duke of, 5, 49, 160
Spain, Charles III., King of, 2, 3, 39, 155
Spence, Mr., 58, 60
St. John, Lady, 139
Stair, Lord, 137, 174
Stanhope, Earl, 48, 72, 87
Stanhope, Sir William, 47
Stevens, Mr., 40
Stone, Andrew, 54, 230
Stone, Dr. George, Primate of Ireland, 175
Stormont, Viscount, 180
Strange, Lord, 67, 69, 70, 78, 81, 87, 89, 95, 136, 153
Strange, Sir John, 6
Strawbridge, Mrs., 273
Sunderland, Lord, 48, 103, 144
Sundon, Lord, 13, 22, 272
Sussex, Lord, 59

Sutton, Lord Robert, 24
Sydenham, Mr., 33

T

Talbot, Charles, Lord Chancellor, 40
Temple, Earl, 84, 271
Tessin, Count, 142
Thompson, Dr., 110
Townshend, Charles, 56, 153, 213, 214, 216, 218, 262
Townshend, George, 6, 16, 23, 35, 36, 39, 59, 90
Trefusis, Samuel, Esq., 20
Trentham, Lord, 8, 9, 10, 13, 16, 22, 59, 120, 121, 163
Tweedale, Lord, 172, 174
Tyrawley, Lord, 161
Tyrconnel, Lord, 127
Tyrrel, Sir John, 15, 16

V

Vandeput, Sir George, 8, 10, 19, 125, 185
Vane, Harry, 73, 191, 194, 196, 197, 205, 243
Vernon, Admiral, 18, 62, 136, 227
Villiers, Mr., 279
Vintimille, Madame de, 210
Vyner, Mr., 5

W

Wager, Sir Charles, 13, 22
Waldegrave, Colonel, 117
Waldegrave, James, Earl of, ix, x
Waldegrave, Lady Elizabeth, 152
Walmoden, Baron of, 111
Walpole, Sir Robert, xiii, xvii, xix, 4, 5, 6, 8, 11, 13, 14, 19, 20, 22, 29, 31, 37, 40,

41, 43, 44, 46, 55, 56, 57, 58, 59, 65, 73, 74, 80, 87, 89, 93, 100, 101, 103, 105, 106, 107, 109, 112, 114, 115, 119, 122, 128, 137, 138, 140, 142, 143, 144, 145, 146, 147, 173, 180, 216, 219, 220, 243, 248, 251, 271, 272
Walsingham, Melusina Schulemburgh, Countess of, 32
Warren, Sir Peter, 153, 185
Warton, Dr. Joseph, 272
Washington, Major, 250
Wells, Paul, 110
Wentworth, General, 62
Westmoreland, Earl of, 6
Whitehead, Paul, 125
Willes, Lord Chief Justice, 43, 56
Williams, Sir Charles Hanbury, 13, 59, 127, 128, 142, 274, 278, 280
Willoughby, Lord, 130
Wilmington, Spencer Compton, Earl of, 112
Wilmot, Dr., 44
Winchelsea, Daniel Finch, Earl of, 109
Windham, Sir William, 49, 138
Winnington, Thomas, 109
Winton, Lord, 181

Y

Yarmouth, Amelia Sophia, Countess of, 111
Yonge, Sir William, 13, 14, 18, 19, 20, 30, 33, 66, 69, 72, 88, 89, 95, 153, 159, 161, 214, 230, 272
York, Cardinal of, 179
Yorke, Charles, 78, 81, 91, 215, 218
Yorke, Philip, 71, 100

Z

Zelle, George William, Duke of, 57

Related Nova Publications

Beacon Lights of History. Volume X: European Leaders

Author: John Lord, LLD

Series: Historical Figures

Book Description: *Beacon Lights of History* is a 14-volume set first published in 1902. This collection of John Lord's lectures spans 6,000 years of European and American history. The first 12 volumes are all Lord's work; the 13th was completed from his notes and the 14th is follow-ups by other authors.

Hardcover ISBN: 978-1-53615-242-5
Retail Price: $195

An Introduction to the Industrial and Social History of England

Author: Edward P. Cheyney

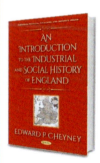

Series: European Political, Economic, and Security Issues

Book Description: This book, originally published in 1901, provides an introduction to the industrial and social history of England from prehistoric times to the early nineteenth century.

Hardcover ISBN: 978-1-53613-684-5
Retail Price: $230

To see complete list of Nova publications, please visit our website at www.novapublishers.com